VILLAGE DEMOCRACY AND RURAL DEVELOPMENT

VILLAGE DEMOCRACY AND RURAL DEVELOPMENT

SUBHASH KANSAL

2008

CYBER TECH PUBLICATIONS
4264/3, Ansari Road, Daryaganj, New Delhi-110002 (India)
Ph.: 011-23244078. Fax: 011-23280028
E-Mail: cyberpublicationsdelhi@yahoo.com

Village Democracy and Rural Development

First Edition 2008

Published by G.S. Rawat

For Cyber Tech Publications

4264/3, Ansari Road, Daryaganj, New Delhi - 110 002

E-mail : cyberpublicationsdelhi@yahoo.com

Phone : 011-23244078,

Fax : 011-23280028

Printed at

Amit Enterprises, Moujpur, Delhi. Ph. - 9810878184

Preface

A democratic policy involves decentralisation or decentralisation of power in a way that the local affairs of the people are managed by means of their positive participation. Known by the popular name of democratic decentralisation, it implies extension of democracy at the grass-roots level in view of the fact that people's participation signifies the constitution of a democratic government not merely at the top but also at the foundation-level of the political system.

Administrative organisations in the modern age is product of certain evolutionary processes. Scholars have examined the subject from various perspectives keeping in view the development.

Every possible care has been exercise to select chapters in accordance with course contents of the universities as well as competitive examinations. Librarians and staff members of various institutions have rendered every possible co-operation and help. We are thankful to them.

My publisher M/s Cyber Tech Publications have always worked hard to assist me in every possible way.

—Editor

Contents

1

Democratic Decentralisation of Regional Administration

Democratic decentralisation is a political ideal and local government is its institutional form of power in a way that the local affairs of the people are managed by means of their positive participation. Known by the popular name of democratic decentralisation, it implies extension of democracy at the grassroots level in view of he fact that people's participation signifies the constitution of a democratic government not merely at the top but also at the foundation-level of the political system. It signifies marked devolution of power from the higher to the lower levels in a way that the units of local government exercise their power with the participation of the people of that area with occasional control and supervision of the provincial and central governments. Thus, Panchayati Raj was introduced in our country in the light of the recommendations of the Balwantray Mehta Committee Report which failed to achieve the desired result. (One of the Directive Principles of State Policy says that the state shall take steps to organise village panchayts and endow them with such powers and authority as may be necessary to enable them to function as units of self-government.)" Hence, the government of Rajiv Gandhi introduced the 64th and the 65th Constitution Amendment Bills in the Lok Sabha in 1989 which, through passed by it, could not be adopted in the Rajya Sabha. The government of P.V. Narasimha Rao took up the issue with the same motive and the two bills moved in the Parliament could be adopted which became the 73rd and the 74th Constitution Amendment Acts of 1992 now placed in Part IX of the Constitution.(The original constitution of India had Par IX relating to the administration of the territories belonging to part D of the first schedule and other territories not specified there. It was deleted by the Seventh Constitution Amendment Act, 1956.)

Regional administration refers to the organisations that function below the state level but above the district. The typical department in the medium and large-sized state divides, for administrative convenience, the entire State into a number of regions (or, divisions) and maintains regional headquarters in each region. Thus, the police department has deputy inspectors-general at regional level. Similarly, the department of irrigation has superintending engineers each of whom is in charge of executive engineers of his region. In some cases the boundary of the region may tally with the Divisional Commissioner's division. But, where workload does not warrant, a region may not be coterminous with the Commissioner's division. Thus, the forest department divides the State into *ranges* which takes into consideration its own peculiar requirements. There are always some departments which are not represented at the regional level.

Whether a department needs an organisational set-up at the regional level or not depends mainly on two factors—size of the State and the workload of the department. The regional officer, in general, supervises and inspects the work of the district functionaries of his department, and coordinates their work at the regional level. He is the latter's boss at the regional level. He is the standard setter, and this role he performs by undertaking frequent visits and inspections, by demanding periodic reports and returns, by issuing necessary instructions and directives, by organising periodic conferences of the district level functionaries of his department etc. He should relieve his head of department of less important work pertaining to the region under his jurisdiction. He would be certainly failing in his duty if he contents to function as a mere link in the hierarchy. Generally speaking, the regional officers perform the following functions: (a) undertaking supervision and coordination of the work of the district level officers of the department; (b) providing technical guidance to the district level officers; (c) keeping themselves in active touch with the functioning of the Panchayati Raj institutions; (d) undertaking inspections and tours to keep themselves in touch with the working of their departments, to identify problems and difficulties experienced in the field, and to help evolve appropriate solutions.

This role of the regional officers needs to be strengthened. In fact, "the responsibility for the achievement of the prescribed targets and making administrative arrangements for supplies should squarely rest with the regional level officers." The most important regional officer is the Divisional Commissioner, who represents the State Government in his region. The institution of Divisional Commissioners exists in all the States except Tamil Nadu, Andhra Pradesh, Kerala and Rajasthan. Rajasthan had abolished this office in 1961, although there is a Divisional Commissioner for the border areas. This institution dates back to the year 1829, when the Government of Lord William Bentick appointed Commissioners of Revenue to supervise the work of collectors, judge-magistrates and district magistrates. Although most of the States, today, have Divisional Commissioners, this office has had a chequered history. In a number of States it has seen a succession of abolitions and revivals, reductions in powers and reinstatements. Madhya Pradesh and (old) Bombay had abolished (Madhya Pradesh in 1948, Bombay in 1950) Divisional Commissionerships but revived these in 1956 and 1958 respectively. U.P. went half way by reducing the number of commissioners, and enlarging their geographic jurisdiction but, soon, the need for maintaining their full strength became compelling when references from the districts to the State headquarters started swelling with no link between the districts and the Government. Rajasthan abolished it in April 1961, apparently to simplify the relationship between the district administration and the State headquarters. It may also be pointed out here that even Tamil Nadu and Andhra Pradesh have at times given serious consideration to the establishment of Divisional Commissioners in their States. As V.K.N. Menon writes, "Divisional Commissioners have been a somewhat controversial matter in India. Their addition as, more or less, a fifth wheel of the administrative coach was one of the early political demands in India and some States have experimented with their abolition in recent years. In some States have experimented with their abolition in recent years. In some States where they were abolished, however, they have been restored and the present tendency seems to be in favour of this institution and even in favour of extending its coordinating and supervisory functions, especially in the context of the development activities at the district level." The Divisional Commissionership came under a cloud immediately after Independence. It was called a costly and unnecessary link between the district and the State Government, a 'post office', 'kings whose subjects are unconscious of their existence', etc. Indicative of the temper of the time was the Report, published in 1948, of the Bombay Administrative Enquiry Committee, set up in 1946. The Committee found little use in this institution and concluded:

"The arguments in favour of the retention of Divisional Commissioners are generally founded on the basis of what they should be rather than on what they are." A couple of years earlier, the Rowlands Committee (Bengal Administration Enquiry Committee) had also favoured the abolition of the post of the Divisional Commissioner on the following grounds.

* The governmental activities in a division have grown too large and too complex to be efficiently looked after by the Divisional Commissioner.
* In terms of the nature and type of work entrusted to the Divisional Commissioner, latter is disproportionately expensive.
* The Commissioner's post has been reduced to the position of a mere post-office. As an intermediate tier between the Government and the district, he only retards the despatch of public business.
* The Commissioner is an experienced and mature officer. His service should be better utilised by the Minister at the headquarters.

The utility of this institution has, however, been gradually realised and, today, most serious administrators appear to be unanimous that there is need for Divisional Commissioners. It is significant that a seasoned administrator like C. Rajagopalachari favoured the institution of Divisional Commissioners in Chennai. There is, thus, a renewed recognition of the general utility of the Divisional Commissioner in the emergent administrative system. It does not, however, mean that he is to be restored to his original position, which is impossible. Both the context in which he has necessarily to operate and the focus of his activities are, today, fundamentally different. Also, he shall have to be content with a somewhat diminished importance of his office. For one thing, the visibility of the Commissioner has been reduced beyond repair. Both the general public and the politicians tend to converge on the state headquarters (not on the Divisional Commissioners), whenever they have any grievance to be addressed or demand to be accepted. Similarly, the State Government, too, finds it more convenient to communicate directly with the district administration in a wide variety of matters. The institution of Divisional Commissioner is generally recommended on the following grounds: (a) Today, the District Collectors are too junior officers, needing guidance and supervision of a seasoned administrator like the Divisional Commissioner. During the British period a member of the I.C.S. was normally appointed a Collector of the district in his twelfth year.

Today a member of the IAS becomes a District Collector after putting in only 5 or 6 years of service. With his insufficient administrative experience a District Collector of today necessarily needs guidance. The Divisional Commissioners, therefore, are a necessary part of the governmental machinery today. "At a time", writes A.D. Gorwala, "when district officials are so often young and inexperienced, there is much to be said for having a body of senior officials who can not only guide them on occasion but be a strong barrier between them and the shocks that come from both above and below.' (b) Divisional Commissioner's elimination would involved the State Governments not only in the loss of expert advice, but in the necessity of direct communication with a large number of heads of Districts and in interference in matters which at present need not come to headquarters at all. "The tradition of official administration in India is against the creation of large central establishments. The inevitable discontinuity in the personnel of the higher posts in the Districts due to emergency changes and other causes—a feature which has increased since the (Montagu Chelmsford) Reforms—may result in there being at a particular juncture a very experienced officer in a group of Districts. Hence the importance of having available the help and advice of the Commissioner." What the Simon Commission had written in 1930 holds good even today.

(c) The Commissioner is a regional coordinator. He, posted at the divisional level, coordinates the work of various departments in his division in a way that no other administrative ingenuity can. The Divisional Commissioners are instruments of decentralised coordination, and their abolition, in the words of the Royal Commission upon Decentralisation (1909), "would inevitably lead to increased centralisation, while a well-devised system of decentralisation must necessarily include the devolution of greater powers to those highly paid officers who are possessed of large experience and ample opportunities for keeping in touch with the people." It was argued in the past that the Divisional Commissioners were obstacles to decentralisation, and that if these are abolished, the Commissioner's power would devolve on the lower authority, *i.e.,* the District Collector's. This is not true. The Commissioner's abolition in some States has resulted in greater centralisation of powers. As A.D. Gorwala writes: "The reality of the Commissioner's power, however, goes not to the Collector but to the higher authority, the Secretariat and the disposal of work, instead of becoming quicker and more thorough, is often rendered slower and more superficial." The Rajasthan Administrative Reforms Committee (1963) pointedly refers to the void created by the abolition of Commissioners in Rajasthan. It wrote: "The activities of different departments of the Government especially those engaged in development programmes, though varying in nature, are interlinked and there are often a number for common problems which need prompt attention and resolution...At the regional level, this coordination was brought about by the Commissioners and with their abolition, a significant vacuum has been created in this respect, which has not yet been effectively filled up... It is only an officer who is intimately aware of the problems of the region and the day-to-day working of different governmental departments at the regional and district levels who can effectively coordinate their working and find agreed solutions to inter-departmental problems."

The Commissioner is the effective agency to supervise and inspect the work of district offices—both police and revenue—to enforce efficiency. In States where commissionership has been abolished, there has occurred a distinct fall in supervision over the district Collectors. In the words of the Rajasthan Administrative Reforms Committee, this state of affairs "is not a very desirable situation and no other agency can fill this role as effectively as Commissioners."

(d) The Commissioner is a necessary intermediate link between the Government and the district administration, shielding one against the other. In the words of an experienced administration, he acts "as a buffer between Government and Administration and eases out the pressures from both sides." This role is all the more necessary in a democratic system like ours.

(e) The Fletcher Committee Report on the Reorganisation of District Administration in the Punjab has supported the institution of Commissioners on a variety of reasons—administrative, political and otherwise. One cannot do better than quote from the Report itself. "Democracy based on universal adult franchise has been launched in a vast and under-developed country, the great majority of whose people are illiterate, and so far inexperienced in corporate organisations, but who are sufficiently awake politically to demand progress, quick results and good administration. In such a context, the inherent and lurking dangers are abuse of authority or incapacity to exercise it properly and effectively, corruption, delays, interference from political parties and personalities, the demoralisation of the permanent services, with resultant inefficiency, indiscipline and corruption, encouragement of opportunistic types of public servant and frustration of those who believe in high ideal and the conscientious discharge of their duties, to mention only the more obvious of these dangers. A sub-divisional officer or Deputy Commissioner, with so much authority and potential for good and evil concentrated in his hands, can, if not controlled, supervised and guided properly, get out of hand, particularly if he is shrewd enough to come to terms with powerful local elements. Such an officer may not have to be unduly concerned with what his immediate superiors think of him. An unscrupulous but shrewd official can, in the present context, by tactful exploitation of local influences, the opportunities afforded by community work and the press for self-publicity, create an entirely false impression of his true worth and neutralise the critical and detached appreciation of his worth and work by his superior officers. Good administration does not lie merely in keeping local influences pleased or in organising community enterprises. Officers in key positions hold many threads in their hands, are responsible for the efficiency and integrity of all those under them, for the collection of revenues, for the welfare of all people, irrespective of their political views or affiliations, and should be judged as integrated wholes—not by politicians and Ministers alone, but also by the well-tried and proved methods of control, supervision and inspections. We must also ensure that a junior and conscientious officer, subject to political pressure or harassed by influential persons, can turn to an authority who is senior and experienced enough to give him the necessary guidance, help and moral support in any righteous stand that this officer may be compelled by circumstances, as exist today, to take. In all good systems of administration, there should be an authority high enough to advise Government in such mattes. Officers in the Secretariat cannot possibly play this role, for they will not, by the nature of their duties, have the necessary knowledge of local conditions or the officer's real worth as a district officer. This is where the Commissioner comes into the pattern of an administration, organised on a sub-divisional and district basis."

Duties of Divisional Commissioners

The Divisional Commissioner is, broadly speaking, the coordinator, at the Divisional level, of all activities connected with general administration including law and order, revenue administration, and development administration. Matters like registration, excise, supply etc. have generally been kept out of this jurisdiction. With such an extensive jurisdiction the Commissioner is a hard worked officer, who needs some relief. Generally speaking, the Divisional Commissioner performs the following functions.

(i) He is head of the revenue administration in his division and hears appeals against the orders of District Collectors.

(ii) He coordinates and supervises the work of all wings of public administration in his division.

(iii) He acts as the trouble shooter; he resolves differences, if any, arising between governmental departments in his division.

(iv) In some States he has been given certain powers in regard to Panchayati Raj bodies.

(v) He has also been assigned a role in municipal administration.

(vi) He exercises general control over all relief operations within his division.

(vii) He examines police administrative reports.

(viii) In Maharashtra and Gujarat where the District Collector has been divested of work in the developmental fields, and the chief executive officers look after these functions, the Divisional Commissioner is the coordinator of work of these two important and co-equal functionaries at the district level.

(ix) In some States (like Maharashtra) he has been charged with O & M responsibilities as well.

(x) He has touring and inspectorial responsibilities.

(xi) He ensures integrity in the officials in his division.

(xii) He also ensures that governmental officials behave properly with the public in keeping with the needs and ideals of democracy.

It may be noted that the Planning Commission had in 1952, recommended, the setting-up of regional officers although it was not too sure of the merits of the institution of Divisional Commissioners in the altered set up. Five years later, it was more specific and forth right in its comments on the utility of the Divisional Commissioner. It wrote: "It was suggested in the First Five Year Plan that with increase in district work and some decline in the quality of district administration there was need for greater inspection, supervision, guidance and training. These could be provided by senior administrative officers in charge of regions or groups of districts. The need for such officers became greater as the volume of business at State headquarters increased, departments and agencies multiplied and at the district level new burdens fell on officers with insufficient experience.

On the whole it may be said that the practice of abolishing posts of regional officers which was gaining ground in many States a few years ago has been discontinued and generally steps have been taken or envisaged for strengthening administration at the regional level." We conclude this chapter with the following observation made by A.D. Gorwala: "The Divisional Commissioners ought to be expediters, coordinators, advisors and supervisors...The usual tenure for a Commissioner ought not to be less than three years. Commissioners should be men of understanding, personality, initiative and courage...They should be sufficiently senior but need not be most senior, for such posts proper choice is very important... The Commissioner's advice must flow both to Government above and the district and sub-divisional officers below. His mind must be wide awake, his study of the important problems in the region, deep. He should be able to instil sufficient confidence in his juniors to enable them to talk to him freely about the difficulties they encounter in their own work.

Perspectives Changes on District Administration

India is a vast country and some areas are not as developed as others. Moreover, the people of different areas have their distinctive social and cultural traits. India is organised administratively into Union, States, districts, sub-divisions, blocks and villages. Of these, the basic territorial unit of public administration is the district. It is the unit of administration for various departments like revenue, police, judiciary, agriculture, animal husbandry, health and medical care, education, industry, public relations, etc. which have their jurisdiction extending over the district.

The districts, therefore, a multifunctional unit of administration. Before Independence, the Indian administrative system was governed by a "ruling bureaucracy" in the sense that the officials combined in themselves a significant measure of political authority with adequate administrative clout. They had unfettered powers and a relatively limited responsibility. The District Collector was the principal functionary, the fulcrum and the pivot of the district administration. He represented the provincial government in its totality. He verily acted as the eyes, ears and arms of the government. Such an overriding role of the Collector was envisaged as early as 1872, exactly a hundred years after the inception of his institution, when Sir George Campbell, the then Lieutenant Governor of Bengal wrote: It is the Lieutenant Governor's wish to render the heads of the districts no longer the drudgery of many departments and masters of none but in fact the general controlling authority over all departments in each district...the real executive Chief and administrator of that tract of country committed to him and supreme over everyone and everything except the proceedings of the Courts of justice.(Bengal Administration Enquiry Committee, Report). With Independence came a sea-change. The old priorities were suddenly gone. The role of the administrative system changed in the context of three major factors, namely democracy, development and decentralisation. The Community Development programme was introduced in the early fifties and the three-tier panchayati raj in the late fiftees and the early sixties. Administration was to carry out the policies and programmes for economic development and social change. This implied transformation not only in the aims of administration but also in its means. This together with a rapidly growing population and its rising expectations changed the entire nature of district administration.

The district administrators were no longer the rulers but the servants of the people. The District Collector is the Chief representative of the government in the district. Rajni Kothari observes: "The office of the Collector in India is in many ways unique and its supposed stature and authority have engendered a sort of institutionalised charisma that is in some ways unparalleled in modern administrative development." His functions can be broadly organised under two heads: regulatory and developmental. Regulatory functions include: maintenance of law and order, collection of revenue, magisterial responsibilities (criminal) and general functions.

District Law and Order

The Constitution has made elaborate and effective arrangements to ensure impartiality and efficiency of the public servants, but some weak points must be mentioned at this state. The District Collector is in charge of law and order which is the basis of civilised life. One effect of complete separation of executive and judiciary, after independence, was to free the police from the control of the executive magistrates. In the new set-up, district magistrates hardly have any control over the police and the Superintendents of Police successfully agitated to abolish the old system of district magistrates initiating their confidential reports. Several Collectors are of the view that the S.P. no longer considers the Collector as his official superior, although the latter as the D.M. is the head of the criminal administration in the district.[3] Whether the primacy of the magistracy over the police should continue or the police be conferred complete organisational, professional and functional autonomy with the S.P. formally made responsible for law and order in the district, has been a subject of debate. In metropolitan cities like Calcutta, Bombay, Madras and Delhi (since 1978) the responsibility for law and order vests with the Police Commissioner, the district magistrate having no say whatever, in his field. The critics of the present relationship argue for an extension of the commissionerate arrangement to other parts of the country. The present practice is that the organisational and professional control of the police upto the district level is exercised by the S.P., above the district level by the D.I.G. of police and the I.G. Nevertheless, subject to certain restrictions, the general functional control over the S.P. is that of the D.M. and in the exercise of this control, the D.M. is guided by the Revenue Divisional Commissioner and by the Government and not by the police hierarchy. Critics of the system observe that the Collector's control over the police is unnecessary as it leads to delays, indecision and inefficiency, for the Collector is often unable to devote adequate time to police matters because of his various other preoccupations. Further, the Collector's exercise of general functional control over the S.P. breeds discontent and confusion as the former is not subject to any control by the Inspector General of Police. Dual control in the administration of law and order is clearly riddled with disadvantage. The report of the study group on Police Administration set up by the Administrative Reforms Commission (1969) questions the rationale of the continuance of the District Magistrate's position as the officer ultimately responsible for the administration of law and order and cautions that dichotomy of responsibility for law and order results in duality of command, which prejudices the efficient performance of the police and, ultimately, the welfare of the people. It underlines the need for accepting the basic principle of sound administrative organisation that authority and responsibility should follow a direct and unbroken line from the apex to the base and that this is nowhere more important than in the administration of law and order.(Anandaswarup Gupta and Venugopal Rao, "Administration of Law and Order: A Trend Report," I.C.S.S.R., *A Survey of Research in Public Administration*) There will have to be some fresh and constructive thinking in regard to the posting of IAS men on the district posts. The trouble is that promotions in the service are so rapid at lower levels that officers often attain super-time scale' even before they attain the age of 40 and no self-respecting supertime scale officer likes to be Collector and District Magistrate – a post generally reserved for senior scale officers. On the other hand, the police officers are unlikely to be reconciled to working under District Magistrates unless mature men who command respect are appointed. The young IAS Collector who is generally years junior in service to the District Superintendent of Police does not command the latter's respect, causing an adverse impact on the district administration as a whole. The need for posting sufficiently senior IAS officers as Collectors of district is obvious. The making of the rank of the D.M. equivalent to that of the Secretary of a Department deserves serious consideration. It is also argued that the district administration is getting diluted not because the Collector is junior to the S.P. but because there has been a tendency over the last few decades to vertically divide the different directorates of the government right down to the grassroots level without any focal point either at the district or the divisional level. In many of the States, the District Collector who presides over the district administration, actually "manages" the officials of different departments over whom he has very little in-built control. B.K. Patnaik feels that no officer, howsoever senior, will be able to deliver the goods. At present the Collector in many States commands the respect of development departments, primarily because he is likely to head those departments in the years to come.

If even this possibility is removed, that will be the end of district administration. On the other hand, it is argued that to advocate a lesser role for the Collector is to belittle the status and prestige of the Collector. The Collector happens to be the fulcrum of the district administration. His unique position as the chief representative of the government in the district demands that he should have full control over the entire administration. This, it is felt, is necessary because while the S.P. looks at the law and order problem from the police angle only, the Collector, who comes into closer contact with various sections of society, looks at it from a broader perspective. In this context, it may be worthwhile to consider the Maharashtra pattern where a senior D.I.G. of Police initiates the confidential character roll of the S.P. and then forwards it to the Collector for his opinion. The Collector is expected to confine his remarks to a general assessment of the S.P.'s work with particular reference to law and order. It may be suggested therefore that as the head of the administration, the Collector should exercise general control over the police administration in the district and as per the recommendations of the Administrative Reforms Commission, except in any emergency, he should not "interfere" with the internal working of the police administration. The other functions of the Collector are revenue, magisterial, general and developmental. He is in charge of fair assessment of revenue and prompt collection of land revenue and other taxes. In revenue and criminal cases, he is District Magistrate both of the first instance and in appeal. Cases regarding land reforms, settlement, consolidation of holdings, weights and measures also come up to him for consideration and disposal.

Further, the Collector is responsible for civil supplies and public distribution and is expected to ensure the rice, wheat, cloth, sugar, kerosine, dal, oil, soap, detergents, match sticks, salt, paper, fuel and other essential commodities should be supplied to the people in adequate quantity, in right quality and in right time. The prices of these commodities should also be within the purchasing power of the common man. The District Collector acts as the returning officer for elections to the Lok Sabha and the State Legislative Assembly and coordinates the electoral work in the district. Moreover, he functions as the District Census Officer and is thus responsible for the conduct of decennial census operations. He appoints enumerators, provides for their training and arranges timely supply of forms, etc. The Collector also maintains liaison with military authorities in his district and looks after the welfare of members of the armed forces, both serving and retired. In addition, he attends to work relating to civil defence managed by Home Guards. Until recently, the Collector had certain responsibilities in regard to local government. In the event of zila parishads, panchayat samitis, panchayats and municipalities being in a state of dissolution, his responsibility about these bodies became direct. The Collector acted as the Executive Officer of the zila parishad. He was expected to make annual inspection of the samities and review their work. The Collector had wide powers of supervision and control over the panchayati raj bodies and was empowered to cancel their resolutions if they constituted a threat to law and order or went beyond their powers. He could give directions to these bodies to perform certain acts. Depending on a particular state legislation, he could order a panchayat samiti to act on behalf of a panchayat, where a panchayat was disabled from functioning. Particularly, in case of a panchayat samiti, the Collector could direct it to execute any work, the immediate performance of which was necessary for the implementation of development plans. The Collector could remove a sarpanch for his failure to convene meetings of a panchayat for three consecutive terms. In times of crisis such as flood, famine, drought, earthquake, fire, epidemic, internal disturbance, war, etc., the Collector can emerge as a natural leader of the district and mobilise men and resources in his area and administer relief measures.

Further, he regulates trade and commerce. He is expected to check blackmarketing, adulteration, hoarding, smuggling and even distress sale of crops. Thus, the District Collector is concerned with almost all areas of regulatory administration affecting citizens in his territory. The Collector is responsible for the direction and execution of developmental plans in the districts. The Balwantray Mehta Committee had recommended : "At the district level, the Collector or the Deputy Commissioner should be the captain of the team of officers of all Development Departments and should be made fully responsible for the necessary co-ordination and co-operation in the preparation and execution of district plans for Community Development." The Kerala Administrative Reorganisation and Economy Committee had observed: "While organisational and professional or technical control over development officers of district rank will be that of departmental superiors, the functional control in non-technical matters will be exercised within certain limits, by the District Collector," The Committee opined that the Collector should be responsible for ensuring that: (a) the development and welfare schemes are such as would meet the needs of the people; (b) whenever necessary, people's co-operation is secured; (c) the time-table for various schemes is adhered to and targets reached in time; (d) there is proper co-ordination and difficulties in the execution of schemes are removed; and that (e) there is no corruption.

Need for Field Visits in fulfilment of such a multiplicity of responsibilities, the District Collector undertakes tours in the district and inspects government offices within his jurisdiction. While on tours, the Collector:

(a) meets the people in their natural surroundings, ascertains their needs and problems and tries to redress their grievances;

(b) listens to people's alternative suggestions for policy formulation and execution;

(c) finds out how development projects are being carried out;

(d) gets an opportunity to assess the work of officials; and

(e) can exhort people to built up their areas through voluntary cooperative community endeavour.

The aphorism that "In Indian public administration tent is mightier than pen" reflects the absolute value of field visits. However, the District Collector's tours have suffered considerably since independence. The visits are increasingly becoming rare occurrences, very much a rapid jeep and dust affair. P.R. Dubhashi observes: A more serious matter for concern is that the district officers instead of moving closer to the people seem to have moved further away. The distance between the people and district administration seems to have increased. In earlier days, intensive tours on horseback used to be undertaken by district officers who camped in villages. Now with mechanical transport at their disposal and constant visits of VIPs from State Headquarters, they return to the district headquarters after flying visits to villages.

The District Officers have started feeling that since they have to attend to any number of meetings of committees where the people's representative are present they need not establish direct personal contact with the people in the villages.

At results of shouldering the Collector with many responsibilities have not been satisfactory always. Too many programmes imposed too swiftly on a semi-prepared administration, with an inadequate socio-political infrastructure, has led to a dilution of both sincerity and effort, on the one hand, and emergence of hypocricy and corruption, on the other, remarks Tushar Kanti Das. He adds that as a result of this, the Community Development programmes could not gather the desired momentum, the co-operative movement failed to get off the ground in most States, the concept of district planning introduced with much fanfare in the early seventies, remained largely a paper exercise and, in many States, eventually degenerated into wishful thinking and a compilation of impossible demands It has been observed that with the shift of emphasis towards development administration, routine work has suffered. The collection of government dues and maintenance of land records has fallen into arrears. Owing to the diminishing importance of regulatory functions and consequently the separation of powers at the field level, the district officer gradually began to lose his earlier grip on law and order. Das asserts:

"Eventually, the Collector could neither attain developmental targets nor maintain his past standards in routine and regulatory functions." It is felt that the "man on the spot" today is a much harassed person. The range and complexity of his functional responsibilities have increased enormously, without any commensurate improvement in the administrative infrastructure. The expectations from him are high while the power and facilities at his disposal have remained totally inadequate. Increasingly, his time is spent as a kind of conciliator, coordinator and moderator over all the existing forces, pressures and activities in his district. In the fifties, it was believed that with a gradual increase in his developmental functions, the regulatory activities of a Collector would tend to decline. This has not come about. Today, in most States, maintenance of law and order is a major assignment which, it is argued, has become even more difficult since the separation of powers. Other regulatory functions relating to exercise, customs, arms control or motor vehicles have growing enormously.

The maintenance of the public distribution system and the supply of essential commodities, welfare programmes specially for the scheduled castes and tribes also demand close attention. Then there are the occasional, but not so infrequent events like elections, natural calamities and communal violence which keep a Collector tied down for weeks together, creating a huge back-log of work. The politics of development has many facets. Because of democracy and adult suffrage, the hitherto deprived classes of the society put pressure on administration to have a greater slice of the economic cake. Besides the pressure of the new rich is there. There are conflicts between the claims of growth and distributive justice. All this puts strain on the law and order machinery. The administration has to be sensitive to these pressures and innovate ways to respond to their challenges. The Collector, it is alleged, gives greater importance to his law and order role than that of his development role.

Apart from the direct responsibilities, a Collector frequently gets involved with the programmes of other departments, like the PWD, irrigation, power, forest, agriculture, health and family welfare. He has to co-ordinate their activities and also help them in sorting out their local problems. This role of the Collector as a co-ordinator is becoming increasingly important as well as difficult. The co-ordination mechanism is weak with the result that the different limbs of district administration do not pull together and indeed often work at cross purposes.

Most of the departments being unwilling to get away from their system of line administration, their district level officers, it is opined, look upon the Collector merely as a first among equals and do not always graciously accept his role as coordinator. There has been a growing tendency on the part of many departmental officers at the district level to look to their own Heads at the State level for guidance rather than to the Collector. The proliferation of agencies and introduction of banking institutions have made things all the more complicated. "In fact, pressures on district administration have increased on all sides and the district officers have started feeling that to survive, they need not only traditional administrative skills but also semi-political manipulative skills," say Dubhashi.

Administrative Reforms

The Collector can be effective through a reduction in his burden. Following the recommendations of the Balwantray Mehta Study Team when the panchayati raj institutions were introduced in the late fiftees and the early sixties, it was envisaged that the Collector would be exempted from the new developmental responsibilities and be asked instead to concentrate only on his traditional revenue and regulatory functions. This idea was endorsed by the administrative Reforms Commission who observed in its report in 1969: No single individual can be expected to take the full load of the regulatory functions as well as of the new functions connected with development. It is therefore necessary to bifurcate the existing responsibilities of the Collector into regulatory and developmental. The Collector will be in charge of the former and the Panchayati Raj institutions of the latter. The States like Maharashtra and Gujarat have made sincere attempts to implement this idea. Both have district level development officers who function almost independently of their respective District Collectors. However, through experience, the States have realised that it is not possible to run two parallel systems of administration in a district and that the development programmes of a district could not really take off without the active participation of the local Collector. Today the Collectors of Maharashtra and Gujarat are again playing a major role in the formulation and implementation of development programmes.

Thus, the artificial dichotomy envisaged between a Collector's developmental activities and his regulatory functions has proved to be an undesirable myth. A Collector cannot be expected to maintain law and order effectively unless he understands the needs and aspirations of the people and can ensure timely formulation and implementation of development programmes meant for them. The Collector's burden can be made lighter by reconstructing the districts into smaller and more compact ones. This is an issue which has yet to receive serious attention. The magnitude of problems in a district is directly related to the size of its population and indeed grows at a faster rate than that of the population. Similarly, it also depends though to a lesser extent, on the geographical area of the district. Since independence, our population has more than doubled but there has only been a marginal increase in the number of districts and that increase too, has not been uniform. While States like U.P., Bihar and Kerala have created a few new districts, there has been hardly any increase in Tamil Nadu, West Bengal or Orissa. The predicament of a present day Collector is not often properly appreciated by others. Tusharkanti Das, a one time Collector in West Bengal writes: "I must confess that I found that task too much of a burden and had a nagging feeling that I did not have as much information, control or supervision over the affairs of the district that a Collector should really have." The Collector is an overworked functionary. Consequently some of his work is apt to remain neglected and some only superficially attended, for omnipotence is apt to breed incompetence, at any rate, in human beings. Paul Appleby had observed: One sits in his office only to hear him receiving along with stream of citizen visitors, telephone calls from all the State Ministries who lay their most pressing problems at the door, he is responsible to everybody for everything, though with varying degree of clarity. No one can hold him responsible for anything in particular and few facilities for checking his performance exist. He struggles valiantly in an outmoded structural situation.The Ashok Mitra Committee on Administrative Reforms set up by the West Bengal Government has suggested: "The optimum size of a district should be determined in terms of a total population size of 15 to 20 lakhs."

In India, there are several districts, which have a population of more than 20 lakhs, while many cover an area exceeding 10,000 sq. kms. This indicates the extent of the problem and the need for an immediate review of the position. Along with the reorganisation of districts, State government should also think in terms of sending more experienced and senior officers to serve as Collectors. Since independence, there has been a steady decline in the average seniority of a Collector. Now, we find experienced and senior officers wasting their time in less important jobs in the Secretariat, while their younger colleagues are being sent to run the districts. Because of the strenuous nature of the job, as John Lall, a former ICS observes: IAS officers try every imaginable dodge to get out of district postings. Life is much more cushy in the Secretariat where the system has seen to it that no one can be held to account. Best of all is Secretariat in New Delhi, and even there the juiciest plums are the economic ministries where patronage is enough to make the brain reel.

In the pre-independence days, and in the early fifties, it was quite common for ICS officers with 15 to 20 years service to serve as Collectors. Today, however a member of the IAS is generally given this posting in his fifth to eighth year of service, which, experts in Public Administration consider to be insufficient preparation for this office. An IAS officer does his brief round in the districts, never to return to field administration unless one becomes a Divisional Commissioner, a post which has been abolished in many States and retained by others only as an appendix of doubtful utility.

The structure of the panchayati raj, according to the provisions of the Seventy-third Constitution Amendment Act is required to be a three-tiered one with elected bodies at the village, block and district levels. While one-third of all the seats are reserved for women, reservations for scheduled Castes and scheduled tribes have been provided in proportion to their population at each level. This Act came into effect on 24 April, 1993 and it was stipulated that all the states (excluding Jammu-Kashmir, Meghalaya, Mizoram, Nagaland and certain Scheduled areas of some other States) should either made new laws of suitably amend their existing laws so as to bring them in conformity with the provisions of this Amendment Act. To facilitate quick action by the States, the Union Ministry of Rural Development had circulated a model bill prepared by the National Institute of Rural Development, Hyderabad, Happily this could be done within a year and 24th April, 1994 became 'a day to remember'. Consequently, elections to the institutions of Panchayati Raj took place within next six months and the State governments set up their Election Commission and Finance commission for the specified purpose. Thus, the task of granting constitutional Status to Panchayati Raj is now accomplished.

Rural development means not only agricultural expansion but the growth of small industry, schools, training centres, improved communications, rural electrification, public health, population control centres and even the stimulation of a rural cultural awakening. By "rural areas" I mean not only the villages and their surrounding farm areas throughout Asia, Africa and Latin America but also the rural towns, ranging from two or three thousand population to many thousands, which serve as marketing centres for the peasants and landless labour of the countryside. By "rural development"

I mean not only agricultural expansion but the growth of small industry, schools, training centres, improved communications, rural electrification, public health, population control centers and even the stimulation of a rural cultural awakening. Although the *Kural* pointed out nearly 2000 years ago that, "The agriculturalist is the lynchpin of the whole social chariot," this truism was largely ignored in practice.

REFERENCES

Report of the (Bombay) *Administrative Enquiry Committee*, Bombay, Government of Bombay, 1948.

Gorwala, A.D.: *Report on Public Administration*, Delhi, Planning Commission, 1951.

Rajni Kothari, *Politics in India* (New Delhi: Orient Longman, 1970).

V. Eswar Anand was told so by several Collectors during his work on a research project on district administration in Orissa. See V. Eswar Anand, "Importance of Being the Collector," The Statesman (Calcutta), 8 November 1984.

Anandaswarup Gupta and Venugopal Rao, "Administration of Law and Order: A Trend Report," I.C.S.S.R., *A Survey of Research in Public Administration*, Vol. II (Bombay: Allied, 1975).

Report of the Indian Statutory Commission, vol. 1—Survey, London, H.M.S.O., 1930.

Report of the Royal Commission upon Decentralisation in India, Cmd. 4360, London, H.M.S.O., 1909.

B.K. Patnaik, "Specialist and Generalist: The Red Tape Binds them All," *The Statesman*, 3 December 1987

Report of the Team for the Study of Community Projects and National Extension Service, Vol. 1 (New Delhi: Committee on Plan Projects, 1957).

Report of the Committee on Reorganisation of the District Administration, Government of Punjab, 1954.

First Five Year Plan, New Delhi, Planning Commission, 1952.

Government of Kerala, *Report of the Administrative Reorganisation and Economy Committee* (Trivandrum, 1967).

P.R. Dubhashi, "Man on the Spot: Failure of District Administration," *The Statesman*, 15 April 1963.

Tusharkanti Das (served as Collector and District Magistrate in West Bengal), "The District Ruler," *The Statesman*, 15 October 1983.

Paul H. Appleby, *Public Administration in India: Report of a Survey* (New Delhi: Publication Division, Government of India

Report of the (Rajasthan) *Administrative Reforms Committee*, Jaipur, Government of Rajasthan, 1963.

2

Village Panchayats and Rural Development

Normal duration of a Panchayat has been fixed at five years from the date of its first meeting. But the State Government shall have the power to dissolve it earlier. If so happens, next elections shall take place within 6 months, provided that where the remainder of the period for which the dissolved Panchayat would have continued is less than six months, it shall not be necessary to hold any election under this clause for constituting it. But a new panchayat constituted upon the dissolution before the expiration of its duration shall continue only for the remainder of the period for which the dissolved Panchayat would have continued, had it not been dissolved. A person shall be disqualified for being a member of the Panchayat if he holds any office of profit under the Central or State government, or is declared by accompanied court to be a man of unsound mind, or is an discharged insolvent, or is not a citizen of India, or is disqualified under any law in force. Any dispute of this kind shall be referred to the governor and his decision shall be final.

The 73rd Constitution Amendment Act inserts Part IX into the constitution. It empowers the State Legislatures to make laws for the organisation of Panchayats at the village level as well as at the higher levels of a district. Such laws shall define the mode of composition, strength of the members including reservation of seats for Scheduled Castes, Scheduled Tribes and other weaker section of the community. The members shall be elected directly by the voters of the territorial constituencies, but the law of the State shall lay down the method of the inclusion of the MPs and M.L.A.s of that area in such bodies and the representation of the chairpersons of such bodies at the intermediate or higher levels of Panchayati Raj in a district. The chairperson of a village panchayat shall be elected directly by he voters of a constituency, but the law of the State Government shall determine the method of the election of the chairpersons of higher units of Panhayati Raj in a district. The law of the State government shall also provide for reservation of seats for Scheduled Castes and Scheduled Tribes in proportion to their population in the State, but 1/3 seats shall be reserved for women under such a category. The reservation system shall come to an end it the provision for such reservations, as given in Article 334 of the constitution, comes to an end.

The State legislature may make laws for the conferment of such powers and authority on these bodies as may be necessary to enable them to function as units of self-government and such a law may contain provision for the devolution of powers and responsibilities upon Panchayats at the appropriate level, subject to such conditions as may be specified thereunder, with respect to: (a) the preparation of the plans for economic development and social justice and (b) the implementation of schemes for economic development and social justice as may be entrusted to them including those in relation to the matters listed in Schedule XI. The State legislatures may also make a law to:

(i) authorise a Panchayat to levy, collect and appropriate such taxes, duties, tolls and fees in accordance with such procedure and subject to such limits; (ii) assign to a Panchayat such taxes, duties, tools and fees levied and collected by the State government for such purposes and subject to such conditions and limits; (iii) provide for making such grants-in-aid to the panchayats from the Consolidated Fund of the estate; and (iv) provide for constitution of such Funds for crediting all moneys received respectively by or on behalf of the panchayats, and also for the withdrawal of such money therefore, as may be specified in the law.

However, the most important feature of this arrangement is

related to financial autonomy granted to such bodies. Within one year of the commencement of this Amendment Act and thereafter at the expiration of every fifth year, the governor shall have the power to set up a Finance Commission to review the financial position of the Panchayats and to make recommendations to the governor as (a) to the principles which shall govern (i) the distribution between the State and the Panchayats of the net proceeds of the taxes, duties, tolls and fees leviable by he State, which may be divided between them under this part and the allocation between the Panchayats of all levels of their respective shares of such proceeds, (ii) the determination of the taxes, duties, tolls and fees which may be assigned to or appropriated by the Panchayats, (iii) the grants-in-aid to the Panchayats from the consolidated Fund of the State; (b) any other matter referred to the Finance commission by the Governor in the interests of sound finance of the Panchayats. The composition, jurisdiction and the procedure of working of the Finance Commission shall be determined by the law of the state. It shall submit its report to the Governor who shall cause it to be laid before the state legislature together with an explanatory memorandum as to the action taken thereof. The State Legislature shall also make law for the maintenance of accounts of these bodies and their auditing. It shall also make laws for the election to such bodies under the superintendence, direction and control of the Chief Electoral Officer of the State. The provisions of this Constitution Amendment Act shall apply to the Union Territories as well with any number of exceptions and modification made by the President of India in it. But these provisions shall not be applicable to the States of Nagaland, Meghalaya, Mizoram, the Hill Areas in the State of Manipur and the Hill areas of the District of Darjeeling in west Bengal. But the Legislatures of these five States may empower the District Councils with such facilities for the sake of decentralisation of power after passing a resolution by absolute majority of the whole House and 2/3 majority of the members, present and voting. The State Legislatures shall also provide by law for the settlement of electoral disputes, but the delimitation of constituencies and the allotment of seats in these bodies shall not be questioned in any court of law. This Act introduces xi Schedule into the Constitution conferring 29 powers on Panchayats as agriculture and agricultural extension, land improvement and soil conservation , minor irrigation and water management, animal husbandry, fisheries, social and farm forestry, minor forest produce, small-scale industries, khadi and cottage industries, rural housing, drinking water, fuel and fodder, roads and other means of communication (like bridges, ferries, waterways etc.), rural electrification, non-conventional energy sources, poverty alleviation programmes, primary and secondary education, technical training and vocational education, adult and non-formal education, libraries, cultural activities, markets and fairs, health and sanitation including primary dispensaries and health centres, family welfare, women and child development, social welfare, of the weaker sections, public distribution system, and maintenance of community assets.

Municipalities

74th Amendment act of Constitution inserts Part IXA so as to define the organisation and working of local self-government in the urban areas known by the name of Nagar Panchayats or municipalities/boards/councils/corporations. The state legislatures shall by law determine the strength of these bodies, the number of sets reserved for Scheduled Castes, Scheduled Tribes and other weaker sections of the community in proportion to their population in the State, including women. These members shall be elected directly by he voters of the territorial constituencies including the chairperson of such bodies. The State Legislatures may be law also provide for the making of committees at the ward level or other levels with in the territorial area of the Municipality including their powers and the election of their chairpersons. The accounts of the Municipal corporations of boards shall be subject to aduditing according to the rules framed by the governor after consulting the Comptroller and Auditor-General of India.

The Comptroller and Auditor-General of India shall cause the accounts of the said Municipal Corporation or board to be audited in such a manner as he may deem fit and the report of the Comptroller and Auditor-General shall be submitted to the Governor of the State who shall cause them to be laid before the Legislature of his State and the Municipal Corporation concerned. The normal tenure of these bodies shall b e five years from the date of their first meeting. In case of body is dissolved earlier, election shall be held within next six months from the date of dissolution. Provided where the remainder of the period for which the dissolved body would have continued is less than six months, it shall not be necessary to hold any election under the clause for constituting it. But such as body constituted upon its dissolution before the expiration of its duration shall continue only for the remainder of the period for which the dissolved body would have continued. A persons shall be disqualified from the membership of this body if he holds any office of profit under the Central or State government, is declared of unsound mind by a competent court, is an undischarged insolvent, is not a citizen of India, or is disqualified under any law in force.

Subject to the provisions of the Constitution, the State Legislatures may be law endow (a) the Municipalities with such powers and authority as may be necessary to enable them to function as institutions of local self-government and such law may contain provisions for the devolution of powers and responsibilities upon Municipalities subject to such conditions as may be specified therein with respect to (i) the preparation of plans for economic development and social justice, (ii) the performance of functions and the implementation of schemes as may be entrusted to them including those in relation to the matters listed in Schedule XII, (b) the committees with such powers and authority as may be necessary to enable them to carry out the responsibilities conferred upon them including those in relation to matters listed in scheduled XII. Besides the State Legislature may be its law (a) authorise a Municipality to levy, collect and appropriate such taxes, duties, tolls and fees in accordance with such procedure and subject to such limits, (b) assign to a Municipality such taxes, duties, tolls and fees levied and collected by the State government for such purposes and subject to such conditions and limits, (c) provide for making such grants-in-aid to the Municipalities from the consolidated Fund of the state, and (d) provide for constitution of such funds for crediting all moneys received respectively by or on behalf of the Municipalities and also for the withdrawal of such money therefore as may be specified in the law.

Rural Development

Rural development means not only agricultural expansion but the growth of small industry, schools, training centres, improved communications, rural electrification, public health, population control centres and even the stimulation of a rural cultural awakening. By "rural areas" I mean not only the villages and their surrounding farm areas throughout Asia, Africa and Latin America but also the rural towns, ranging from two or three thousand population to many thousands, which serve as marketing centres for the peasants and landless labour of the countryside.

By "rural development" I mean not only agricultural expansion but the growth of small industry, schools, training centres, improved communications, rural electrification, public health, population control centers and even the stimulation of a rural cultural awakening. Although the *Kural* pointed out nearly 2000 years ago that, "The agriculturalist is the lynchpin of the whole social chariot," this truism was largely ignored in practice. In Asia and Africa a procession of invaders, emperors, and later colonial powers came and went for centuries with little effect on the rural people most of whom were conscious of their government only when it raised taxes or inducted more young men for military service.

In Latin America the rural areas, too, were largely by-passed by history. Following the struggle of the developing countries for independence after World War II, and the withdrawal of the colonial powers, the primary concern of most of the new leaders was for industrial growth which they accepted as the glamorous symbol of western economic advancement. In this regard India had her full share of urban-oriented skeptics who saw the peasants, in Karl Marx's terms, lost in the "idiocy of rural life," and industrial expansion as the only true measure of progress. More recently the key role of the 80 percent of the people who live in the rural areas of the developing nations has become strikingly apparent. Politicians are beginning to understand that peasants who see no tangible signs of economic progress cannot be expected to identify themselves with their government, and that an orderly political system, therefore, largely depends on what happens in the countryside. Economists increasingly recognise the need to increase the supply and variety of food available for domestic consumption, and, if possible, for export. In many developing countries agriculture is virtually the only existing industry; it must be expanded to the fullest if there is to be any hope for a reasonable rate of capital accumulation. And since half of the gross national product in such nations consists of agricultural products, their output decisively affects the indices of national production on which broader economic judgments are based. Furthermore, rupee for rupee, capital investment in the rural areas will affect more people and accomplish more growth than anywhere else.

A market road or a deeper well provide potentially immediate economic benefits without requiring foreign exchange. The more farsighted also see rural development as an essential prerequisite for industrial growth. If the 80 per cent of the people in a developing nation who live in rural areas lack the purchasing power to buy manufactured goods in increasing amounts—and right now the rural areas in many such countries are not even part of the money economy—the growth of urban industry is bound to be retarded by lack of customers. Moreover, since food constitutes half the weekly budget of an urban worker, the supply of food and the efficiency of its distribution have a direct and major impact on the well-being and political mood of the urban centers.

Finally, sociologists see rural development in its broadest sense as the only democratic means of slowing the movement of ambitious and promising younger people from rural areas to the cities, which in Gandhi's terms drains "the life blood of the villages." This population flow becomes more and more intense as developing nations gather economic momentum and young men, bogged down by the limitations of village life, see the cities as a promised land abounding with employment opportunities and the excitement of modern living. The actual transition to urban life, however, is often an unhappy one. Once the newly arrived peasants have exchanged the comparative security of their villages with their familiar family relationships, rivers and fields, for the harsh life of a crowded city slum, they are likely to experience a sense of personal frustration and insecurity which inevitably expresses itself in political unrest. The only effective way to slow down this movement to the urban centers is to provide increasing economic opportunities in the rural areas in an environment which gives the individual some meaningful personal role to play; he must matter.

Rural development is essential to the orderly political and economic growth of an emerging nation, it is also the most difficult aspect of development. Rural societies are usually dominated by traditional ways of thinking and doing which are not easily changed; because of this, rural improvement is not susceptible to crash programmes which yield immediate, tangible results. The very vastness of an Asian, African or Latin American countyside with its thousands of villages provides in itself a formidable obstacle to dramatic progress. Although a hydroelectric plant can cause an industrial complex to flower virtually overnight, it may be years before the first electric pump appears in a nearby village and an even longer interval before the irrigation water is used with full effectiveness. This brings us again to a point of great importance which I shall take every occasion to stress.

The most difficult aspect of rural development, and at the same time the most significant aspect, is that it deals primarily with PEOPLE, endless numbers of independent hands and minds which cannot be centrally controlled but which are the only significant source of creativity in a developing rural economy. Without the awakening enthusiasm and co-operation of the masses, often buried under centuries of hopeless repression, development is impossible. This underscores one of the five essentials which was discussed in my first lecture: the need for a reasonably equitable and speedy distribution of tangible benefits and the cultivation of a widespread sense of personal participation. Although many economists, with their eyes glued to the movement of the gross national product, overlook this factor, it is of rural people can be engaged in building for the future, no amount of glamorous industry will produce the fundamental economic and social changes which are the proper goal of national development. The primary focus of any rural development programme, therefore, must be to release the enegies of rural majority in their villages and towns. Now let us frankly admit that this challenge is an awesome one for which we have no fully adequate answers. The complexities of tribal loyalties in Africa, caste distinctions in Asia, and ancient values everywhere have little relationship to the priorities of modern planners.

They create obstacles to change which should never be underestimated. Nevertheless, certain positive steps are obvious. For instance, with sensitive leadership the peasant's efficiency as a producer can be raised through education, extension work and demonstration projects. His requirements as a consumer can be increased through exposure to new products. Finally, his position as a citizen can gradually be enhanced, for it is an article of faith in a democracy that the participation of the citizens is a prerequisite for effective and responsible government and that such participation directs the energies of the state into the most desirable channels.

The objective of all these approaches is to enable the cultivator slowly but steadily to develop his own capacity for growth and increasingly to use those abilities effectively for his own benefit and the benefit of his family and community.

The emphasis, however, must be on the delicate process of opening people's minds to new possibilities; efforts at arbitrary control will almost certainly fail—as the Chinese have discovered. In this context it may be worthwhile briefly to consider why communist efforts in rural development have failed in China and lagged in Russia. Marx's primary concern was for the urban "proletariat"; he devoted relatively few paragraphs to rural problems. The *Communist Manifesto* of 1848 limited its policy for the tens of millions of impoverished and exploited peasants o Europe to the following rather casual recommendation: "The establishment of industrial armies, especially for agriculture, combination of agriculture with manufacturing industries, a gradual abolition of the distinction between town and country by a more equable distribution of the population over the country." In short, Marx saw the peasant simply as another industrial worker in a particularly low state of development. As an economic historian with a tidy concept of both past and future, Marx considered the peasant an intruder and something of an annoyance.

It was part of Lenin's genius that he understood this weakness of Marxist theory and, therefore, sensed the decisive importance of the Russian peasant to the success of the Bolshevik Revolution. Only when he proclaimed on November 7, 1917, that all Russian land belonged to those who tilled it, did Lenin feel confident that the revolution had in fact become "irrevocable." The peasants, he knew, would defend their newly acquired land to the bitter end against any effort to restore the status quo.

From 1918 until 1928 the Russian peasant was relatively free and in most cases possessed his own land. By 1930, however, Stalin abruptly reverted to the old industry-oriented revolutionary dogma. Sensing that thirty million Russian peasant families, most of them with their individual plot of land, offered a formidable political barrier to the creation of a communist state, he embarked on a savage effort to force them into huge collective farms. According to Stalin's own admission to Winston Churchill, some ten million peasants died in the process.

In this massive reorganisation of Russia's rural life, Stalin was favoured in several respects by the make-up of Russian agriculture. Food production per capita was high and population per square mile, relatively low. Before World War I, Czarist Russia had exported as much as ten million tons of grain annually. Although this built-in food surplus provided a sizeable cushion against lagging production. The Stalinist collectivisation programme brought the Soviet Union to the brink of poitical and economic disaster. In China the situation developed along somewhat similar lines but under even less advantageous conditions.

As we shall see when we contrast the Chinese and Indian experiences China now faces a grave national crisis. Although Soviet and Chinese Communist agriculture has failed in different degrees and in different ways, the basic reasons are similar. Both countries ignored the need for a reasonable balance between economic and social growth; instead of providing meaningful incentives, they depended on a maze of controls which drained the vitality of the cultivators and offered them no real hope of improving their condition, no matter how hard they might work. The significance of incentives for peasant families was impressed upon me some months ago by Prince Sihanouk of Cambodia. When I asked him why most Cambodian farmers with their rich soil and bountiful rainfall produced only one crop of rice annually, he answered, "Because we do not produce enough bicycles." In the absence of an appealing assortment of consumer goods to improve his living standards, why indeed should a Cambodian peasant with ample food for his family work the extra three or four months in the fields necessary to produce a second crop? In the United States, the nine percent of our population engaged in farming produce more than twice as much grain as we can consume.

Each year we ship nearly two crores tons of wheat abroad, nearly one-fourth of which comes to India. There are several reasons for this extra-ordinary agricultural productivity. For instance, Americans have always been willing to get their hands dirty experimenting with new techniques for improving their output. Furthermore, the government has always played a vital role in assisting the farmer. But above all, the great majority of American farmers have had the incentive which comes from owning their own land. Low interest loans for implements and fertilisers are readily available.

Each farm family has real and tangible reasons for improving its operations and thereby raising its own living standards. Our first steps to provide a favourable framework for increased agricultural production were taken more than a century ago. In 1862 our Homestead Act offered what was then considered a "family-sized farm" of 160 acres free to any American or foreigner who would till it. The Morrill Act of the same year gave each of our state governments vast tracts of public land, the income of which was used to establish our so-called "land grant colleges" for research and training in agricultural sciences.

In 1887 the Hatch Act provided additional federal funds to the states for research and experimentation in agriculture. The fruits of this extensive government-supported research were carried to our millions of farmers through a comprehensive farm to farm, rural extension service which operated through the land-grant universities and which continues to function today. Since the Second World War the federal government has also provided generous agricultural price supports and crop insurance to guarantee our rural population a steady income. As a result the hardy, independent farmer of American folklore not only exists in modern times, he flourishes.

This is largely because his government has helped him to develop improved techniques within a framework of personal economic security and at the same time has respected his independence and initiative. An indication of the nostalgic feeling we Americans have for our rural tradition is the lengths to which most candidates for public office will go to identify themselves with the agricultural community. A political leader fortunate enough actually to have been born on a farm never ceases to remind the voters of this fact.

The America rural experience is challenging and instructive but, in my opinion, the developing nations of Asia, Africa and Latin America have most to learn from a study of Japan. Japan was the first Asian country to transform a tradition-bound agricultural economy based on subsistence farming and hierarchical social relationships into a dynamic, contributing element of a modern economic system. This effort goes back many years.

When the Meiji emperors regained power in 1868, a major effort was made by the Imperial Government to stimulate agricultural production as part of a national effort to arouse the slumbering Japanese society. In order to unify the economic life of the country internal tariffs were eliminated. A tax was imposed on the feudal landholders, part of the proceeds of which were used for the establishment of educational, extension and see improvement services which directly benefited the rural economy. Local banks began to offer credit to landowners at what were then considered low rates of interest. Warehouses were built to store products for which there was no immediate market. Agricultural prices were more or less established. Although those steps helped to increase Japanese agricultural output to an average of 2.3 per cent a year, the tenant farmers still remained grossly under privileged with most of the benefits accruing to the large landowners. Independent farmers were increasingly burdened by debt and exploitation and more and more of them drifted into the status of tenants.

By the 1930s half of the land of Japan was tenant-cultivated, with land rentals averaging more than half of the crop. In the bad crop year this meant that the tenant farmer was bound to fall into debt, on which he paid usurious interest rates either directly to the landlord or to the local bank which the landlord often controlled. This tied him tighter and tighter to the land which he tilled but tighter and tighter to the land which he tilled but did not possess. The landlord paid only the modest land tax. The tenant paid for the fertiliser, buildings, implements, seed and various dues. Even in a good year this left him a net share of not more than 25 to 30 percent of the crop. Thus, the politically explosive gap in the Japanese countryside between the few thousand "haves" and the millions of "have nots" grew dangerously. While the real gains of the early Meiji period were not wholly lost, by the late 1930s they were largely emasculated by the injustices of the near-feudalistic land tenure system. As incentives declined, production showed down.

In poor years the cities suffered food shortages. Even in more favourable years, agriculture had become a depressed area of the economy which no longer contributed to Japan's industrial growth. Shortly before the war the Japanese Imperial Government attempted to stop this drift. Legislation was passed which forced landlords to renew leases with their tenants except in cases of proven "bad conduct." An effort was also made to fix the value of land at sixteen times the annual rent and to provide easier credit so that the farmers could purchase their land in twenty-five annual installments. But an effective revolution in Japanese agriculture did not come until after the war. In 1946 the Japanese Government, on recommendation from General MacArthur's Allied Military Government, embarked on the world's most sweeping land reform. Its purpose, in the language of the legislation, was to "insure that those who till the land of Japan shall henceforth have an equal opportunity to enjoy the fruits of their labour."

Seven and one half acres became the upper limit on all land holdings, except in a relatively small number of cases—largely orchards—where the owner could himself care for a larger area. All land in excess of this amount was bought by the government with bonds and within two years distributed to the farmers. As a result 94 percent of all Japanese farmers now own and cultivate their own land; the average holding is two acres. The social, economic and political effects of this rural revolution were dramatic. Suddenly the emancipated Japanese farmer realised that for the first time in his life, or his father's or grandfather's lives, he, a peasant, really counted: At last he had some rights of his own; most important of all, he had land of his own. As a result for the first time he had self-respect, hope and, consequently, the will to better himself, hope and, consequently, the will to better himself, his family and his community.

With assistance from the government, he promptly set up credit co-operatives to provide readily available credit at low rates. He also established marketing co-operatives which now assure him an average return of nearly sixty percent of the retail price of his produce in the city markets. The existing extension service was improved and expanded to familiarise him with the newest techniques. As a result of this many-sided development effort, the per acre yields in both rice and wheat on the average Japanese farm are now among the highest in the world; a full fifty percent above the pre-war level. The cultivator's return from his labour has increased proportionately.

The impact of this comprehensive development effort on rural life in Japan has been dramatic. Villages which until twenty years ago had been virtually unchanged for a thousand years are now electrically lighted. Many Japanese farmers' wives now do their laundry in electric machines. Nearly one half of all rural homes sprout television aerials while thousands of farmers take their wives shopping on motorcycles.

Significantly, one of the causes of the rural prosperity in Japan, and a major by-product of it as well, is the large number of prosperous small factories now sprinkled through the countryside.

Although sufficiently modern and mechanised to compete effectively in an industrial economy, they are specially suited to the available part-time labour and to the special commercial needs of rural areas. Three out of four Japanese farmers now add to their agricultural earnings through part-time and seasonal jobs in small fish-processing plants, canning factories, agricultural implement manufacturing concerns and scores of other industries and service organisations.

In the immediate postwar period, the extraordinarily efficient cultivation of Japan's small farms which had been sparked by the land reform was carried on largely by each family's own hand labour. Because of the care with which each plant is tended, it is more accurately described as "gardening" than as farming. Now as more part-time jobs become available, many Japanese farmers are purchasing small-scale farm implements to free more of their time for work in the small factories and service organisations which are springing up everywhere. The decline in agricultural production which might otherwise occur as a result of mechanisation has been made up by increased use of fertiliser and innovations in cultivation.

Because the new industries are rooted in the countryside, the traumatic social cost of uprooting millions of peasants for work in the cities which so deeply concerned Gandhi has largely been avoided. Although the Japanese rural revolution is dramatic and instructive, it is a mistake to assume that it will easily be duplicated elsewhere. Japanese farmers already had advanced techniques at their command. Thousands were familiar with the use of fertilisers and irrigation and needed only the all-important incentive provided by the ownership of their own land to increase their investment and production. Furthermore, they were literate, and this was probably the greatest single legacy of the Meiji emperors. Nine out of ten recipients of land in the great reform of 1946 could read the legislation which granted it.

Since everyone was aware of his new legal rights, the reform could be carried out quickly and fully. Many leaders of Asia, Africa and Latin America who despair over the political obstacles to an effective land reform also stress that the Japanese land reform was vigorously backed by the United States Military Government which at that time held the ultimate political power. They remind us that in our modern era only two democratic countries, Czechoslovakia in 1926 and Mexico in the mid-1930s, were able to distribute farm land widely to all cultivators through the vote of democratic parliaments. Although this is sobering testimony to the political power of the traditional social structure and the landlord opposition in predominantly agricultural countries, it does not follow that competent democratic governments genuinely dedicated to the welfare of their people cannot win the political support necessary for these essential reforms.

I began this discussion with a principle in which I deeply believe: Successful rural development can be achieved only by liberating the energies of the people. In the light of the Japanese experience, let us now consider how this principle may be applicable here. In dealing specifically with India's development I am treading difficult ground. The subject itself is complex and open to many differing interpretations, and as a foreigner I necessarily speak with some hesitation.

However, the fact that I have had a unique opportunity to observe India's economy over a period of many years encourages me to offer my views. Although the problems of India's rural areas are still appalling, a substantial beginning has been made in meeting them. The community development programme was conceived in 1952 as a modest effort to show villagers how to help themselves in a way that would liberate their energies, make them active participants in their own development, and show them that their government was concerned about their future. This concept of local co-operation and self-help has been given an important boost by the recent establishment of the Panchayati Raj, the purpose of which is, as the Prime Minister has emphasised, to give "the millions of our people the chance to share responsibility, do good work, and grow in the process." As we have seen, nothing can be more important in a developing country than the creation of this sense of responsibility.

If the Panchayati Raj is well organised and vigorously supported,

I believe that it has a significant contribution to make to rerual development in India. Another important objective of the original community development programme was to promote integrated growth by improving educational, health and sanitation facilities, and roads and communications while placing special emphasis on agricultural production. It was felt that an interdependent programme of this kind would give the villager a feeling of his own worth and that the values fostered would encourage him to work for the improvement every aspect of his daily life. These new values with the help of land reform, better seeds and improved techniques, were expected to improve his agricultural output.

Because of budget limitations, because of the newness of the approach, because of the obstacles which the tradition-ridden guardians of the status quo always strive to place in the path of change, and because of the massive administrative task of organising such a complex effort in 5,00,000 villages, progress thus far has failed to meet the excessively optimistic standards of the programme's proponents. Under the circumstances it is not surprising that a debate should develop between those who might be described as "community firsters" who believe in the balanced development of the whole rural community and the "agriculture firsters" who think primarily in terms of increased agricultural output. In my opinion those who favour integrated development have the best of this argument. Experience in every developing country has demonstrated that the sustained increase of agricultural output simply cannot occur in a social and political vacuum.

It must be at one and the same time a product and a cause of a general betterment in the life of the farmer. In this context let us consider what is clearly the most formidable question of all – land reform. The Congress Party has been traditionally aware of the importance of individual ownership as a basis for community development. In 1935 a party resolution adopted in Allahabad correctly stated that "there is only one fundamental method of improving village life, namely the introduction of a system of peasant proprietorship under which the tiller of the soil is himself the owner of it and pays revenue directly to the government without the intervention of any zamindar or taluqdar."

In the first years after independence there was considerable progress towards this objective. The zamindars, some of whom controlled thousands of acres, were eliminated, in several states ceilings were placed on land holdings with additional ceilings on land rentals and tenure of rented land was made somewhat more secure. However, the most difficult part of the task lies ahead. The zamindars were a small minority and the fact that their privileged status was created under the British made them an easy political target. Even with their removal from the scene and some additional curbs on large holdings, ten percent of India's cultivators still own more than fifty percent of the land, while one percent of them own nearly one-fifth.

Here the debate tin regard to India's rural development takes on a new dimension. Some agricultural authorities accept the existing pattern of land ownership as reasonably satisfactory and argue that the process of land redistribution has gone far enough. By and large, they assert, it is the larger landowner—the man who still controls 50 to 250 acres—who has the education, the skills, and the personal incentives which enable him to understand and accept new techniques and rapidly to expand his production.

According to advocates of this theory, the primary task is to identify a single cultivator in each village with the necessary qualities and then train him in modern farming techniques. He then may be expected rapidly to pass on his superior knowledge to his neighbours and thereby unlock the door to vastly greater agricultural output for the entire nation. Although this trickle-down concept of rural improvement may seem appealing at first glance, I submit that it ignores the fundamental principles of rural development. The reasons for my doubts may best be explained by a conversation which I had recently with just such a "door opener" in a village in South India. This cultivator was greatly pleased with the increased yields per acre which he had achieved with the help of new techniques sponsored by the Village Level Worker. As the conversation continued, however, it became evident that his personal success was unlikely to have much effect on his fellow villagers.

When I asked him how many acres he owned and how he farmed them, he told me that he controlled 150 acres and that his land was farmed not by tenants but by "servants." Since only thirty-seven families lived in his village I found myself wondering how many of them worked as his "servants," and how many had any land of their own. I also wondered how much good his increased yields were doing the other villagers, how much more they were able to buy and contribute to the economy, how much incentive they had to work the extra hours which are essential to increases in their own production.

Most important of all, I wondered how much personal dignity among the villagers generally would be developed under his guidance. As I looked at the subservient, insecure attitudes of those standing nearby, I knew there could not be very much. Although the larger and often more productive farmers in Asia, Africa and Latin America undoubtedly have a role to play as leaders and initiators, there is, I believe, a strict limit to what can be accomplished under their sponsorship. Rural people the world over want land of their own and the fertiliser, better seeds, and credit required to till it more effectively. There are no shortcuts, in my opinion, to the rural democracy which offers the only assurance of orderly political growth in the developing countries.

Yet, as important as I believe it to be, individual and tenure is only one aspect of the problem. Although it provided the essential stimulus for the rural boom in Japan, it was particularly potent there, as we have seen, because the education, modern techniques, fertiliser and credit and marketing facilities were available to allow and encourage the farmer's new initiative literally to bear fruit. In Mexico, where these additional features were absent, a sweeping land reform in the 1930's following years of bloody fighting, resulted in lower outputs and increased peasant frustration. In the last few years India has made impressive progress in experimentation with fertilisers, seed improvement, livestock improvement and pest control. As I visit India's rural installations and talk to India's agricultural scientists, I am impressed with the strong foundation of agricultural research that already exists in India.

The fruits of this research may be made available to the farmer through the Village Level Workers on a mass scale, through printed material for the farmers who can read, and through film strips, radio, and perhaps even village puppet shows for the many who can't. Such information can also be distributed through sales programmes and demonstrations by public and private fertiliser and seed firms. In the United States these have been among the most effective vehicles for communicating improved techniques to the farmers. The Indian cultivator must also have the credit facilities necessary to avail himself of advanced techniques. More efficient marketing mechanisms are needed to ensure him a worthwhile return on his salable produce. This suggests marketing co-operatives as in Japan with more easily accessible marketing centres in the rural areas themselves.

Finally, I believe that consideration should be given to realistic price support on essential crops with a two or three year guarantee to enable the cultivators to plan their production with assurance of a fair income. Although expenditures for food comprise half of the budget of Indian urban workers, little more than one third of the prices charged in the markets for food grains goes to the cultivator. The rest, as in most developing nations, is absorbed by a maze of middlemen and speculators.

With well organised and financed marketing co-operatives this gap can gradually be reduced; indeed, experience has demonstrated that retail prices of the consumers can be lowered while the income of the cultivators is being increased. India can also benefit from Japan's success in creating local industries as a source of supplementary rural income, as employment for surplus agricultural labour, and as a market for farm products. Gandhi himself foresaw this need for small-scale industries when he remarked that while khadi was the "image" of Swadeshi—self sufficiency in the rural areas—it was not the only kind of industry appropriate to rural needs. Recently I read with interest of the small scale Panchayat industries, using modern skills and equipment, which are now being enthusiastically revived in Orissa. Although these industries are government-financed, they are run by the local

Panchayats. The six official objectives of these particular enterprises are worth quoting, because they also constitute a concise summary of the role of Japanese rural industries: "(a) to improve local skills and to introduce new skills; (b) to diversify the occupational pattern and help in reducing unemployment and under-employment; (c) to meet the requirements of the consumers in regard to building materials to provide better housing facilities; (d) to provide servicing and repair facilities for agricultural machinery and implements used in the Panchayat blocks; (e) to process agricultural produce to ensure better cash returns to the producers; and (6) to provide a growing source of income to the Panchayat Samities without straining the taxable capacity of the people."

The small industries in the Orissa experiment include tile factories, saw mills, a cold storage plant, and others, each directly relevant to the needs of the local population and appropriate to the existing level of skills. Here we see the Gandhian ideal of Swadeshi interpreted in modern terms. The enthusiasm of the Gram Panchayats in Orissa for these industries as well as the Japanese experience suggests that such Panchayat industries can and will make a major contribution to rural development all over India. The success of American mass market experiments in Latin America also illustrates the possibilities of marketing the products of local and urban manufacture in the rural area.

In several countries Sears Roebuck of Chicago, after studies of local needs, available skills and potential production facilities, opened large local stores and proceeded to stock them with locally produced products. Craftsmen with the necessary facility and energy were given intensive technical training mass production plus loans to purchase the necessary equipment. The result was the creation of hundreds of local producers and a rapidly increasing output of appealing, moderately priced consumer goods which in some instances are now peddled through the villages in marketing trucks. I see no reason why a similar producer-to-market-to-consumer system cannot be set up under both co-operative and private management throughout rural India.

At the risk of entering a particularly controversial area, I suggest that until local industries are created in adequate number to provide more employment for rural labour, agricultural mechanisation except in some exceptional situations will prove to be uneconomical.

Procedures of Officer Oriented System

Worse than this, there have been, as Sir Richard Tottenham had pointed out in 1946, few officers of the right kind and too many clerks of the wrong kind. The officers constitute what may be called the decision-making level, while the staff is the 'noting level.' The present manner of functioning in the Secretariat—Central as well as State—may be briefly described to drive home the deficiencies and shortcomings of the existing arrangement. A recipt is first handled by the dealing clerks and assistants who examine it in the light of existing rules, orders and precedents, and note upon it, suggesting proposals for disposal. The case is put up to the Section Officer who scrutinises these notes and even suggests the line on which proposals for disposal should be made.

The Section Officer, then, puts up the case to the next higher level, *i.e.,* Under Secretary or Assistant Secretary. It then, progresses step by step the entire hierarchy of Deputy Secretary, Joint Secretary (if there is one) and Secretary. As a direct result of this system, there are prolific notings on files and, secondly, a file is made to pass through a large number of hierarchical levels for a final decision. This entails three serious drawbacks. First, persons write who have no business to write; secondly, inordinate delay occurs before a decision is taken; and thirdly, in the maze of diverse notings, the original purpose outlined in the case tends to get overlooked and even obscured. The remedy lies in cutting down unnecessary noting on the files, and in minimising the number of hierarchical levels through which a file is made to pass before a decision on the issue under consideration is taken. This is to be secured by establishing officer-oriented system of staffing which implies a pattern of staffing where the bulk of the work is done by officers, with the office (*i.e.,* the clerical staff) providing the minimal assistance in respect of purely routine procedural matters like indexing, filing etc.

Major factors which have led to an intensification of the demand for officer-oriented system are following:

(a) This is the pattern which is in vogue in the progressive countries of the world.

(b) Pakistan introduced this pattern—known as Section Officers' Scheme[1]—in 1959, which had led to the elimination of much red tape such as routine notings on files and submission of drafts by Clerks and Assistants, and shelving of responsibility. Pakistan's switch-over to officer-oriented pattern has acted as a proof of its feasibility in India as well.

(c) The exasperation, even humiliation felt by the Heads of Departments with the prevailing system under which their well-considered proposals are subjected to the scrutiny of clerks and assistants in the Secretariat.

(d) Work of the Government has become complex, requiring specialised and more thorough handling thus, beyond the comprehension of clerk and assistants. It has become essential, therefore, that an officer's mind is brought to bear on a problem from the beginning.

(e) A marked deterioration in the quality of noting at lower levels which in many cases today are not fit to handle important cases and, have, consequently, no contribution to make beyond paraphrasing the proposal or raising some insipid queries, thereby causing avoidable delay in the disposal of cases.

(f) Increasing politicisation of the civil services at the lower levels, manifesting itself into frequent recourse to pendown strike, mass leave public demonstration, general strike, etc. As a result of this the Government has been forced to feel it not safe to place much reliance on the personnel at the office level.

(g) The apparent efficiency of business and commercial undertakings which have the officer-oriented system of functioning.

The officer-oriented system is known by a variety of names in the country. Until some years ago, this was known as the "Whitehall System"—being in vogue in Whitehall, the head-quarters of the British Government. In Rajasthan it is known as "Cell System". The Punjab Administrative Reforms Commission (1966) coined the name "action-oriented system" for it. The Administrative Reforms Commission has called it as 'desk-officer system'. It is known as 'Attache System' in the Ministry of External Affairs, and as 'Attach System' in the Ministry of Defence.

The most widely used nomenclature, however, is the *officer-oriented pattern*. The officer-oriented system is one in which the initial consideration of a proposal is at the hands of an officer rather than of 'office', *i.e.*, clerks and assistants. The diarist in the section puts up a paper immediately to the officer concerned. The latter issues appropriate direction, and the reference clerk/stenographer who is attached to him puts up he relevant file to him, after docketing and referencing. The first noting respect of the paper is, as a rule, done by the officer himself and in case the paper is such as can be disposed of at his level, he, of course, dictates the reply. The cases, final disposal of which is not within his competence, are to be put up to the appropriate officer. The general principles underlining the officer-oriented system are the following: (i) It seeks to do away with routine notings and drafting by clerks and assistants. That is to say, it replaces the system of dealing by clerks and assistants by a system of dealing by officers. (ii) Clerical assistance is not entirely dispensed with; it is, however, provided for purely routine duties like receipt, despatch, docketing, referencing, maintenance of files and typing. (iii) It eliminates the multiplicity of hierarchical levels through which a paper has to pass before final disposal and thus materially shortens the procedural course of disposal. Ideally, the officer who initially handles the paper should also be empowered to take decision in cases of appropriate categories at his own level. At any rate, however, there should not be more than three levels of consideration. (iv) It facilitates fixing of definite responsibility for delay in the disposal of cases with the officers as well as the office.

The officer-oriented system Historically, the concept of officer-oriented system is not new in India. As early as 1944, Sir E.C. Coates noted that the administrative machine in the Central Secretariat had broken down and cried for reorganisation and reinforcement so as to cope effectively with the emergent administrative tasks. "It is evident," he remarked in a paper submitted to the then Finance Member and, through him to the Governor-General, "That the institution of "office" must be abolished." To carryout a detailed examination of the question of replacing "office" by officer, a Committee of Secretaries was set up in the same year (1944) under the chairmanship of Sir E. Conran-Smith. This committee was in full agreement with the views of Coates and observed: "The general lay-out of the new type of office would be the requisite number of, say five or six, class I officers headed by an Assistant Secretary in the Home Service and not to the Assistant Secretary in this country. They would deal with the vast majority of cases themselves and would carry on negotiations with opposite numbers in other departments in order to obtain the information necessary for a decision.

Important questions of policy would be referred by the Assistant Secretary to the Deputy Secretary in charge of a group of sections and by him, if necessary, to the Secretary who would cease to be a febrile file number, and become, as he is at home, a sort of elder statesman." The concept, however, was shelved in the face of sustained opposition by a section of secretaries. Two years later (in 1946) the Interim Government appointed The Machinery of Government Committee headed by Sir Eric Coates. This Committee, finding that the nature and complexity of the business of Government was beyond the capacity of assistants and clerks, recommended replacement of the office by officers: "The days when the business of the Central Government largely consisted of the application of precedents or in running the country on a core and maintenance basis are over. New problems and new activities have crowded in on the Centre in recent years, new policies are constantly having to be formulated, and fresh ground has constantly to be broken. The nature and volume of the work now confronting government require much specialised and more thorough handling. This cannot be achieved by a system of non-gazetted assistants nothing to a few overstrained officers. The work is of a nature which can only be performed by officers who know their subjects inside out, and who can hold their own in departmental, and if need be, in international discussions." The Committee recommended that case-noting assistants and superintendents should be replaced by officers of new service.

The concept was examined, in 1952, by R.A. Gopalaswami in his—what has now become a classic report—The Machinery of Government-Improvement of Efficiency. Gopalaswami set his face against its adoption in India on the ground that a larger number of officers were to be employed under this system and, since the manpower resources of the country were severely limited, this would verily amount to a competition with the other executive and administrative services both under the Central and State Governments. He also felt that having recruited competent officers it would have been neither possible nor even desirable to restrict their promotion prospects but by doing so, the system of exchange of officers with the States and the benefits that the tenure system confers would have been lost. He summed up: "In the circumstances, the considered conclusion that was arrived at was that the Whitehall System, as a whole, was not suited to the conditions prevailing in India."

In 1954 Asok Chanda, in his *Notes on Changes* necessary in the system of Budgetary and Financial Control and in other matters to eliminate delays in execution of projects recommended the officer-oriented system for adoption in India. He conceded the utility of examination of a case being entrusted to clerical personnel particularly where decisions must necessarily be based on a variety of rules and regulations or follow precedents but, all the same, felt that the scope for this kind of examination was extremely limited in a different type of cases and the latter type tended to increase significantly in the present context. He concluded: "Precedents and continuity are not so important today as they were in the past, nor should a reform, if desirable, be rejected on the score of difficulty in getting trained personnel...For a time both the new and old systems will run in parallel. This would introduce complications and might prove initially more expensive. Ultimately, however, there will be economy in manpower and, therefore, in expenditure. Even assuming that a certain increase in the total expenditure is involved there is no doubt that the system, to the extent that it induces speed in the transaction of Government business, will be worthwhile." As a complementary to the officer-oriented system he recommended strict observance of two conventions: Firstly, cases should be directed to the appropriate level in the hierarchy, thus making it not necessary for a case to run the usual course through the entire hierarchy. Secondly, the senior officer must give clear and specific directions about the manner in which a case should be disposed of instead of remaining content with merely passing it on to a subordinate officer to be dealt with at his (subordinate's) discretion.

Although Asok Chanda had submitted these proposals in 1954, no action on them been taken. In the meantime, there continued a steady proliferation of personnel at the clerical level, creating in its wake demand for additional office and residential accommodation. Surprising though it may appear, the Central Cabinet while considering in 1964 the demand for additional office space and housing saw in the officer-oriented system the seed of a permanent remedy. It decided to depart from the prevailing pyramidal structure to make for greater speed and efficiency in work. A committee of secretaries was instantly constituted to examine the existing staffing pattern and to recommend appropriate changes. The committee pointed out in 1964: (a) Large number of personnel at the clerical level act as a drag on administration, and the main objective must be to effect substantial reductions at this level. (b) One of the reasons for excessive numbers at the clerical level is the existing procedure which itself requires every paper, normally, to be first noting upon in the "office". Therefore, the introduction of a system of first noting at officer level should be seriously considered, so that it would automatically lead to a reduction in the number of clerks. (c)Clerks will still be necessary for purely routine duties like diarising dispatch work and typing. (d) The total elimination of office noting, without an examination of how the volume of work could be reduced, might require too large a contingent of officers and may lead to wasteful results.

In 1965 another committee called, Committee of Officers on the Reorganisation of the Structure of the Ministry of Works and Housing[2] went into this problem in all its ramifications. The Pink Report offers a brilliant exposition of the office-oriented system, enunciating as it does the following five general principles: (1) Office staff should be cut down to the minimum. Clerical staff should be necessary only for routine duties. (2) As far as possible, an 'officer oriented' system should be introduced, in which the initial consideration of a paper should be at the hands of an officer rather than of 'office'. The aim thus should be the elimination of office noting wherever possible. The distinguishing feature about the officer who does initial handling should be that he is empowered to dispose of cases of appropriate categories at his own level. (3) The number of levels of consideration should be reduced. Within a Joint Secretary's charge, there should not ordinarily be more than three levels of consideration upto and including that of the Joint Secretary. (4) There should be no stinting in the matter of providing stenographic assistance at all 'consideration' levels. (5) There cannot be a uniform prescription for the staffing pattern of the divisions for each division a tailor-made pattern should be devised taking account of the workload, handling procedures and other circumstances obtaining there.

The pattern for a division handling the work coming from an Attached Office would, for instance, be different from that of a division handling original work. Enough has been said about the history of officer-oriented system in the Central Government. One should now scan the development at the State level. This concept has not been a stranger to many States. Indeed, the Secretariat manual of Uttar Pradesh first compiled during the British period, prescribes the initial handling of a case by the officer himself. It lays down:

"(a) On receipt of dak from the department the officer should pass suitable orders on each reference in one or the other of the following ways according to the matter of each receipt:

(i) Prepare a reply (with fair and office copies) and send it to the department concerned for issue;

(ii) Submit it, with his own note, for higher orders without calling for an officer note;

(iii) Give instructions to office to prepare a note for a draft on the lines briefly indicated by him on the receipt itself; and

(iv) Ask office to examine the proposal.

(b) In regard to remainders the officer should, as far as possible, ask his stenographer to obtain the relevant file from the department concerned and then see for himself how the matter stands.

(c) In some cases officers should themselves note instead of asking office to submit a note. They can of course take the assistance of office in collecting information or putting up references.

(d) On return of file from Minister the officer concerned should, as a general rule, himself dictate to his stenographer the draft of the order to be issued and return the file to office with the fair copy duly signed by him"

In 1958 A.D. Gorwala recommended the adoption of officer-oriented system in his report on Mysore Administration submitted to the Government of that State. He felt that the assistant merely summarised a paper which was obviously unnecessary and, what is more, in doing so, he only impeded the disposal of the file by holding it up for several days. He, therefore, recommended that noting on the file must begin at the Under Secretary's level, relevant papers being just collected and put up by three or four clerks attached to him—there being no place for assistant and superintendent.

The Rajasthan Administrative Reforms Committee recommended this system for Rajasthan in its report submitted in 1963. It recommended that apart from establishment and accounts work, the initial examination of a paper in the Secretariat must be done by an officer who should be provided adequate clerical support for maintaining records and files, linking papers with the relevant files, and assisting the officer in consulting laws, rules, orders and precedents relevant to the issues involved in the case. The officer would himself take decision in the case and then inform all concerned if the matter fell within his jurisdiction; otherwise he would submit the papers to the Secretary concerned. The committee also laid emphasis on the fulfilment of certain basis requirements. First, the officer must definitely be 'of above average ability and should posses initiative', and continue in his post for at least three years. Secondly, adequate arrangement should be made to ensure that wher any member of the staff is absent, a substitute is readily made available.[3]

The Administrative Reforms Committee appointed by Andhra Pradesh, has emphasised the adoption of this system in its report submitted in 1965. The committee took pains to point out: "We are convinced that examination of a case at lower levels is not only not necessary but also often results in inadequate and superficial scrutiny. Sometimes trivial points, precedents and other digressions result in so confusing the real issue that the wood may be missed for the tree. We, therefore, strongly feel that examination of cases in the Secretariat should be done only at or above the level of Assistant Secretaries. So long as the staff at lower levels, such as Assistants, Section Officer, etc., are available, the tendency will continue to allow them to initiate the noting. Therefore, we recommend that in the Secretariat there would be no sections at all on the pattern existing now in many of the departments and the Assistant Secretary should form the base. Of course, each officer in the Secretariat including the assistant Secretary should have a stenographer and one or two Assistants merely to put up files without noting and to prepare other purely clerical work."[4]

A brilliant exposition of this system, and fervent support for it, has been made by the Administrative Reorganisation Committee appointed in 1962 by the Government of Maharashtra. Impressed with the serious shortcomings of the existing pattern it posed a question to itself: was there any essential quality of governmental work that required the conventional pattern? In its interim report submitted in 1965 it wrote: "In this country such a pattern of working, which involves a large clerical strength, seems to be peculiar to Government offices...It is true that Government is bound by certain obligations; obligations arising out a legal requirements, the need for uniformity of treatment, for adherence to declared policies and so on, which do not severely fetter the operations of organisation outside Government. These obligations necessitate a certain amount of preliminary study on a number of cases, so that previous decisions relevant to them can be referred to and taken into account in the disposal of the cases in hand. The committee is of the view that these considerations do not necessarily imply the kind of structure not prevalent in Government if these requirements can be met otherwise."[5] The Committee has clearly spelled out its concepts of oriented system. It observed: "The obvious course is bring about an arrangement whereby work is handled at a sufficient level of competence at the very first stage of its entry into the organisation. This can be achieved by replacing the clerical branches by units consisting of a section officer, a stenographer, an assistant and a clerk. Section officers would receive communications, dispose of simple matters and note on important matters for submission to superior officers. The assistant would directly work under the section officer's guidance to assist him with simple cases. There would be only one note by the section officer, on the basis of which the case would either be disposed of or submitted higher. The clerk would assist in filing and tracing files, etc. In addition, there would be a common typing pool and other house-keeping staff to attend to the registration of in-coming mail, the issue of letters, the preparation of pay rolls, cash work, record keeping etc."[6]

The Punjab Administrative Reforms Commission has lent its support to this system which it has chosen to call 'action-oriented system although there seems to pervade some vagueness in its thinking. According to the commission the lowest decision-making level would be that of the Assistant Secretary, Under Secretary or, in some cases, the Section Officer who are to dispose of all routine matters without any reference to the higher authority. The clerical staff would substantially disppear and whatever remains would be utilised for linking of previous papers, putting up relevant references to rules and regulations and recording of papers finally disposed of. The commission warned: "There should be no noting by an assistant."

Officer-oriented system in practice

A departure from the conventional secretariat staffing and working pattern was made for the first time in 1946 when a limited experiment was carried out in Finance Ministry by the appointment of finance officers who themselves initiated examination of a case without any noting by assistants. Although the scheme of finance officers was short-lived, the question of launching a new scheme was raised again after a few years on account of an undiminished decline in the quality of work.

Pilot section scheme

Accordingly, in 1956 a new experiment was launched by the introduction of what is known as the pilot section scheme. Broadly speaking, the pilot section consisted of three upper division clerks and three lower division clerks, one or two of whom were to be stenotypists. Not in was initiated in every case by the Section Officer who exercised some responsibility at his own level and even disposed of simple cases finally. Level-jumping[7] was also introduced in an appropriate manner. The scheme was introduced in most of the Ministries and the sections brought under it totalled 95. An evaluation of this scheme was undertaken in 1957-58 by the O & M officers of the Ministries. The general conclusion emerging from the evaluation was that the quality of work done had shown perceptible improvement and that the results were generally satisfactory, particularly where the personnel had been selected with care; results, however, were not quite satisfactory in some sections in which the nature of work was not suitable for this experiment or in which the volume of work registered an abnormal increase. The evaluation team, however, felt that it was too early to a final decision on the utility of the scheme and that a detailed review should be conducted later after the scheme has had a fair trial. It was decided, therefore, to extent the period of the experiment till February 1959. In the meantime the evaluation report was circulated among the Ministries and the latter were again asked in September 1958 to send their comments. Most Ministries perceived a distinct improvement in Pilot Sections but some of them found the scheme not suited to them.

This review by the Ministries was followed by sample studies of eleven sections in six selected Ministries/departments. These sample studies revealed that there had been uniform and considerable improvement in the quality of work done and that disposal also was speedier.

A fresh lease of life was given to the experiment and towards the end of 1959 a study group was set up to review the working of the entire O & M drive including the Pilot section scheme. The views of this study group were:

1. Compared with the conventional sections, the pilot sections showed better quality of performance and greater speed.
2. As Section Officers were freed from routine coordination and supervision of assistants' work and had more time for original thinking and creative work, the system proved a suitable field for the conscious development of Section Officers for exercise of greater responsibility at the next higher level.
3. The pilot section scheme could not be considered suitable for every type of work. It was most suited for work which was not routinised or which involved difficulties, issues or problems of a wide variety or which related to the execution of projects requiring prompt and efficient attention or for work of a specialised nature requiring deliberate and thorough attention by experienced staff in the very first stage of examination.

The study group accordingly recommended that the pilot type of section should be accepted as recognised structural unit for suitable kind of work.

An important drawback discerned by the study group was the absence of reserve assistants for filling up the gap when one of the three Section Officers abstained. The study group suggested that the staff composition of the new type section could be suitably modified and that, depending upon the nature and volume of work, the number of Section Officers could vary from two to four and that each section could be given one or two assistants. It also recommended that upper division clerks should be replaced by stenotypists.

The Director of O & M in his report on the working of the O & M Organisation (1956-59) stated that his views on the subject generally coincided with those of the study group. He felt, nevertheless, that the differences of opinion observed in the replies of various Ministries underlined the need for having more than one pattern of staffing in the Secretariat. The approach of the study group, he felt, permitted a flexible approach on the question and he recommended its adoption. He, however, suggested that while existing pilot sections should be continued, no additions must be made without consulting the O & M Division, as it would be wasteful to have it with the usual complement of three Section Officers for work which could be done as well by lower grades of staff. Accordingly, the pilot section scheme was permitted to continue for one more year, *i.e.,* upto February 1960—the final decision to be taken only after the recommendations of the Pay Commission on the merger of the two grades of Section Officers were available.

The two grades of Section Officer (Rs. 275-500 and Rs. 530-800) were merged on the recommendation of the Section Pay Commission into one grade of Rs. 350-900, raising thereby the average cost of the pilot section. The new Director of O & M who was also the head of the Special Re-organisation Unit (now called Staff Inspection Unit) in the Ministry of Finance, had a sample study conducted of two pilot sections in the Ministry of Commerce and Industry, mainly with a view to assessing whether the nature of work was suitable for pilot sections. This disclosed that in these sections high-cost personnel had been employed to deal with work which could be dealt with by low-cost personnel. This finding made it necessary to have all pilot sections evaluated. Accordingly, liaison officers belonging to the O & M Division and the S.I.U. were appointed to liaise with the Ministries; and the general criterion laid down by the director of O & M was that sections generating more than thirty percent receipts of a routine character should not be considered fit for the pilot section scheme and should, therefore, be 'depilotised'. Studies were completed in thirty-two sections out of sixty-four. On the criterion given by the Director, agreement was ultimately reached between the liaison officers and the Ministries to depilotise 18 sections. It is significant that no view on he actual performance of these sections was sought for or given. Despite the criterion given by the Director of O & M, the Ministries urged the continuance of fourteen pilot sections. The liaison officers, however, recommended the continuance of only four of these and even these four were discontinued as general orders were immediately issued abolishing all pilot sections. As a result, studies in the remaining thirty-two sections were not completed. The Director of O & M advanced the following reasons for the discontinuance of the pilot section scheme:

(i) *Nature of work:* The proportion of receipts considered suitable for initial action at the section officer's level did not generally exceed thirty-five per cent, the lowest being as low as one percent.

(ii) *Quality of disposal*: The contribution made by the Section officers was also not found to be beyond the capacity of an average assistant.

(iii) *Level of disposal*: The Section Officers were also not in a position to dispose of finally a large part of really important receipts, the percentage of such disposal being relatively high only where purely routine papers formed a substantial part of the intake.

(iv) *Speed of disposal*: As in the case of the two sections in the Ministry of Commerce & Industry, the apparent speed of disposal noticeable in the sections was attributable to the comparatively high percentage of routine items of work (*e.g.*, 'acknowledgements,' forwarding of papers, inviting comments; furnishing routine factual data).

(v) *Employment of personnel of higher grade than warranted by the nature of work*: As a corollary to the finding that routine items formed a major portion of the work in these sections, employment of Section Officers for their initial handling meant the utilisation of costlier personnel for work of low intrinsic value. In particular, it has been calculated that in the officer of the Chief Labour Commissioner, at least sixty percent of the time of Section Officers was being spent on items which could be handled by even and upper division clerk at any rate not by a grade higher than assistants.

(vi) One of the reasons that partly led to the introduction of the scheme, namely, the dearth of efficient assistants, has also since ceased to exist in that direct recruitment to the grade was resumed in 1955 and a large number of such directly recruited assistants were working in all the Ministries.

It must, however, be pointed out that the paper submitted by the Director of O & M to the Committee on Administration suggesting abolition of the pilot section scheme did not give a truly complete picture. Out of the twenty-nine Ministries/departments, eighteen clearly felt that the Pilot Section Scheme had led to an obvious improvement both in the quality of work done and in the speed of its disposal; two Ministries argued that while speed had not improved perceptibly, the quality of noting had definitely improved; two Ministries observed that while the quality of work had remained the same, speed had improved considerably; and only seven Ministries/departments thought that the experiment on the whole had not been successful. This general opinion of the Ministries on the working of the scheme was not placed before the Committee on Administration, and this view does show that in a very large number of sections the scheme was a pronounced success. The apparent reasons given for the abolition of the pilot sections also need to be re-examined. The criterion adopted that a section having more than thirty percent routine receipts including subsidiary receipts should be 'depilotised,' was arbitrary, to say the least. Quite clearly, practically every section generates more than thirty per cent routine receipts. Besides, it tended to be forgotten that even in a conventional section a routine receipt was first seen at the dak stage by a Section Officer and after noting by the assistant was again seen by him, so that some part of his time and energy even in a conventional section was necessarily given to routine receipts. Again, the observation made on the quality of disposal was in conflict with the views of the Ministries generally, or even with the findings, of the sample surveys conducted earlier. Increased speed in disposal was noticed but was ascribed to the comparatively high percentage of routine work. Is not increased speed desirable even in routine items of work? Moreover, increased speed was not necessarily confined to sections having a comparatively high percentage of routine work; the percentage of incoming receipts disposed of routine work; the percentage of incoming receipts disposed of within a fortnight was perceptibly higher in two-thirds of the pilot sections than in the conventional sections. While by themselves these findings may not be conclusive enough, they acquire significance when read with the views of the Ministries. Again, the comparative average cost of a pilot section was surely higher than the conventional section, but there was scope for economy without jeopardizing the efficiency and existence of the system.

It is significant to note that the Ministry of Defence strongly resisted the decision of the Committee on Administration and obtained the latter's concurrence to the continuance or creation of eight pilot sections in the Ministry of Defence. The Defence Ministry has modified its pilot sections slightly in that its pilot section consists of three section officers assisted by three stenotypists, one assistant for co-ordination and management of records and to serve as leave reserve and one lower division clerk. The pilot section in the Defence Ministry costs a little less than the normal pilot section.

Besides the pilot section other attempts have also been made at introduction the officer-oriented system. Thus, for instance, the Ministry of External affairs and the Department of Tourism have tried systems suitable for their organisations. The Ministry of External Affairs has the *Attache System*. In the pattern evolved by it, in each normal division having about 5,000 annual receipts the Deputy Secretary is assisted by three officers of the rank of Under Secretary or Attache, (an Aattache is a Section Officer who gets a special pay of Rs. 75-100). The number of officers increases if receipts exceed 5,000. All work is handled initially at the level of

Under Secretary or Attache, except for some very confidential or very complicated work, which is handled initially at higher levels. The Under Secretary or the Attache has a stenographer and is also helped by an assistant who does miscellaneous work, e.g., preparation of statements, referencing of files, etc. Each division has a divisional registry, which is under a registrar of the rank of a Section Officer and is assisted by an assistant archivist of the rank of an assistant and three lower division clerks who attend to diarising, typing, despatch to the central registry and other routine work. A divisional registry normally handles 15,000 receipts per annum. Under the instructions, level-jumping is also practised. The reorganised pattern was introduced in March 1962 in the Ministry of External Affairs and has now been extended to all its divisions.

Officer-Oriented System in the Ministry of Works, Housing and Supply

At the request of the then Ministry of Works, Housing and Urban Development, a comprehensive study of the structure and procedures of the works division of the Ministry dealing with all works relating to attached office of the Central Public Works Department (C.P.W.D.), was made by the Department of Administrative Reforms. This study disclosed that a significant volume of work handled in the Works Division in the Ministry was unnecessary and sometimes of petty nature. It was also clear that the decision-making process could be simplified and secretariat work could be reduced if the Ministry receives and processes the case in the file of the C.P.W.D. itself. The remaining work originating in the Secretariat itself could be more conveniently handled at not more than 3 levels, *viz.,* Joint Secretaries, Deputy Secretaries or Section Officers; no case from the C.P.W.D. being examined or noted upon at clerical level. The first examination will be either at Section Officer's or Under Secretary's level.

The method of working and the structure of the Works Division were consequently re-organised according to an officer-oriented system in 1965. Two schematic charts, one showing the position before and the other after re-organisation, are also enclosed to describe the 'pre' and 'after' positions.

The salient features of the scheme of re-organisation are:

(i) Enhanced delegation of powers on the chief engineer of C.P.W.D.;

(ii) Introduction of a single file system eliminating the maintenance of duplicate files in the recipient office and duplicate consideration at clerical level in the Secretariat, and consequent reduction of staff, mainly assistants;

(iii) Introduction of a standardised, subject-wise coded file index for the entire rage of cases dealt with in the division facilitating the storage and retrieval of files;

(iv) Reduction in levels of consideration from five to three;

(v) Provision of a full-time stenographer steno-typist for each Under Secretary or Section Officer, who besides furnishing complete stenographic assistance carries out the following duties:

(a) opening of files with the help of file index and under the guidance of officers,

(b) maintenance of current files and intervals movement diary and collection of relevant papers,

(c) routine liaison work;

(vi) A registry for the division as a whole to handle work relating to receipt, despatch, typing, maintenance of non-current files, etc.

The Section Officers' Scheme has been introduced in the Pakistan Central Secretariat since October 1959. According to the scheme each secretariat branch has been reconstituted into 2 sections, each under the charge of a Section Officer. The Section Officer combines the duties previously performed by the branch officer, the Superintendent and the dealing Assistant. The formula of conversion has not been applied too rigidly and in certain instances the work has been so redistributed as to formulate 3 sections out of 2 branches or even one section out of one branch. The Section Officers are of the rank of Under/Assistant Secretary and are assisted by one Assistant and one Stenotypist each. The Assistant is responsible for: (a) putting up the case, properly referenced and flagged, to the Section Officer; (b) keeping notes of important orders and decisions; and (c) any other clerical duties assigned to him (he is not supposed to note on cases or to put up drafts.) About 6-8 Section Officers have been placed under the control of one Deputy Secretary but this formula too has not been very rigidly applied.

The initial method of recruitment of Section Officers has been as follows:

(1) All Assistant Secretaries and Under Secretaries have been redesignated as Section Officers. Some Section Officers have been selected from amongst the Class I officers employed in the Central Secretariat, its Attached Departments and Subordinate Offices.

(2) Selection for the remaining posts have been made by the Central Selection Board, subject to the approval of the Federal Public Service Commission from amongst:

(i) Superintendents of the Central Secretariat; (ii) Assistants-in-charge; (iii) Assistants.

Section Officers thus selected have been placed on a common seniority roster drawn up for the Secretariat as a whole.

The following types of branches have been excluded from the operation of the scheme: (i) Receipt and Issue Branches; (ii) Cash and Account Branches; (iii) Branches dealing with statistics.

The scheme was announced on 5 August 1959 and was implemented on 1 October 1959.

The officer-oriented pattern has, thus, been in operation in a number of organisations at present. It is also in vogue in selected sections of the Secretariats of some of the States such as Uttar Pradesh, Gujarat, Tamil Nadu and Rajasthan. Four major advantages are attributed to it. First, it quickens the disposal of cases. Secondly, it ensures decisions by officers. Thirdly, it leads to reduction in the levels of consideration. Fourthly, it results in economy both in administrative expenditure and personnel. The present author had carried out studies of the functioning of this system in a few organisations, the general findings of which may be broadly summarised below:

1. The cases under the officer-oriented pattern were dealt with more expeditiously than under the conventional one. Saving in time was to the tune of about hundred per cent.
2. The pay-bill of the organisation went higher than under the conventional system.
3. A paper took less time to reach the officer.
4. There was no delay at the level of the diarist.
5. The reference clerk whose work under the officer-oriented pattern is confined to merely putting up the paper after docketing and referencing was found to put up short notes, of course, in routine matters.
6. Files were not arranged scientifically with the consequence that the reference clerk had to spend considerable time in tracing out their relevant papers. New files were indiscriminately opened by the reference clerk without seeking or getting any guidance from the officer.
7. Norms of work laid own for different functionaries under the officer-oriented pattern could in no case be complied with. The prescribed norms, it appeared, were not very realistically developed, warranting upward revision.
8. Transfers of officers took place with disturbing rapidity causing dislocation of work. As the new officer naturally took time to familiarise himself with all the current files, this had an adverse effect on the quality and speed of work.
9. There was an adequate provision for leave reserve staff.
10. Cases in which compliance or reply was delayed by a sister organisation, there was no systematic follow up under the officer-oriented system.
11. The powers of officers under the officer-oriented pattern were not enhanced since the inauguration of this pattern.

The above analysis shows that a careful planning must precede the adoption of officer-oriented system. In other words, certain basic conditions must be fulfilled before this system can be really effective. To these we now turn our attention.

1. Delegation form the Finance Ministry to the administrative Ministries and from the latter to Attached and Subordinate Offices should be made to such a degree that only the really unavoidable functions and powers are retained in the Ministries.
2. For such work as much continue to come to the Ministry even after delegations, there should be no need for examination at the office level. This can be best done by having what has now come to be known as the 'single file system'. The single file system provides not only for substitution of letters by files but also means elimination of duplicate files in the recipient office and of duplicate consideration at the office level.
3. Stage is then, set for office-oriented system at the Secretariat level in which 'office' staff should largely disappear.
4. It must be clearly borne in mind that the officer-oriented pattern is suitable to handle work which is non-routine in character, or which involves difficulties, issues and problems of a wide variety, or which requires prompt action or is of a specialised or technical nature requiring attention by experienced officers. It is not suitable for sections such as those dealing with work involving routine checks. The conventional pattern is appropriate and adequate in such sections.
5. The officer under the officer-oriented system must be of a sufficiently high caliber to be able to process the cases independently and should have the capacity to taking quick and correct decisions.
6. Frequent transfers of personnel must be resisted with all might. The continuity of officers for at least three years is among the basic necessities of this pattern.
7. There should be adequate leave reserve staff to keep the administrative wheel moving when someone goes on tour or leave. As a stenographer is vital to the working of the officer-oriented system, there should preferably be a poor

of stenographers to serve as 'leave reserves'. Also, there should be 'link officers'. This means that when an officer is absent for short periods, automatically his link officer would look after all urgent and important matters pertaining to the former's work.

8. There should be an adequate number of stenographers to be attached to the officers, without which, the officer-oriented pattern can not prove successful. To quote from the Pink Report, "there should be no stinting in the matter of providing stenographic assistance at all 'consideration' levels."
9. There should be a scientific indexing system for files so that these may be traced out easily, and, also, quickly. Also, files and other tools of office should be kept as near the officer as possible.
10. Training programmes should be simultaneously launched to impart training to the staff declared surplus under the officer-oriented pattern, in new skills such as stenography, accountancy etc. Also, attractive terms should be offered to the personnel at the office level, to induce them to leave government. Even then, there may remain a sizeable number of surplus personnel who shall have to be retrenched.

Mention may in the end be made of three principal drawbacks which are inherent in the pattern itself. First, the 'memory' function which an office today performs gets lost under the officer-oriented patterns. For this memory function the office essentially depends upon the assistants and clerks who normally remain in the section for a much longer period than the officer. In the officer-oriented pattern there will be only one assistant or clerk in a section, who is to act as the organisation memory. The memory function would be lost if this person, for any reason, leaves the section. This shortcoming, however, can be overcome by installing an improved file-indexing system. Secondly, it is pointed out that the office has been the training ground for future administrators which is completely overlooked under the officer-oriented pattern. Denied the privilege of dealing with cases and noting on these, the assistant, under the new pattern, would learn little, and when promoted in course of time to the position of an officer, would display little skill in handling the cases. And, lastly, unlike the conventional system, the officer-oriented one cannot 'hide' an incompetent officer.

Desk-officer system

In 1973 the Central Government announced the introduction of the desk-officer system in its Ministries and departments and thus changed the procedure of work. This move was understandably motivated by a desire to speed up decision-making and reduce expenditure. The desk-officer system has been adopted for that wing of a department which has a high degree of homogeneity of functions, and whose sizeable amount of work relates to policy-making and planning. A 'desk' is the basic unit of work, manned by two functionaries—Under Secretary and Section Officer, or Section Officer and assistant—so as to ensure that the work assigned to it does not suffer on account of the temporary absence of any single desk officer. In simple cases the desk officer (who may be an Under Secretary, or a Section Officer, or even an assistant, depending upon the nature of work handled) would either himself dispose of the matter or straightaway submit draft replies to the head for signature. In other words, any examination of a matter by clerical levels has been done away with. The success of the desk-officer system depends upon proper selection of personnel to man the desk, sufficient delegation of powers to them, adequate provision of stenographic and clerical assistance, and, above-all, an efficient system of storage and retrieval of information.

Pandit Jawaharlal Nehru had defined "level jumping' thus: "When work is organized in hierarchical system, the tendency is for papers to pass through all levels before a final decision is reached. The popular expression "level jumping implies that such authorities in the hierarchy as do not contribute to decision-making should be eliminated."

Critical Appreciation

Within one year of the commencement of this act and thereafter at the expiration of every fifth year, the Governor shall set up a Finance Commission to review the financial position of these bodies and to make recommendations as to (a) the principles which should govern (i) the distribution between the State and the Municipalities of the net proceeds of the taxes, duties, tolls and fees leviable by the States, which may be divided between them under this part and the allocation between the Municipalities at all levels of their respective shares of such proceeds, (ii) the determination of the taxes, duties, tolls and fees which may be assigned or appropriated by the Municipalities, (iii) the grants-in-aid to the Municipalities from the Consolidates Fund of the State, (b) any other matter referred to the Finance Commission by eh Governor in the interests of sound finance of these bodies. Moreover, the State Legislatures shall be law define the composition, strength and procedure of working of the Finance Commission. It shall submit its report to the governor who shall cause it to be laid before the State Legislature with an explanatory memorandum as to the action taken thereon.

The State Legislatures hall have the power to make law relating to elections to these bodies under the superintendence, direction and control of the chief electoral officer of the State. The provisions of this Act shall apply to all Union Territories and the President of India shall have the power to make necessary alternations or modifications in their application. But the validity of any law relating to the delimitation of constituencies or the allotment of seats shall not be questioned in any court. The State Legislatures shall make law for the settlement of election disputes. The Provision of this Act shall not apply to the existing municipalities, but the State Legislatures shall have the power to dissolve them before the expiration of their term and to implement the provisions of this Constitution Amendment Act. The provisions of this Act (the 74th Constitution Amendment act of 1992) shall not apply to Scheduled Areas and Tribal Areas, though the Parliament shall have the power to apply them to such areas with some exceptions and modifications. It inserts Schedule XII into the Constitution which assigns 18 powers to municipalities as urban or town planning, regulation of land use and building construction, planning for economic and social development, roads and bridges, water supply for domestic and commercial purposes, public health and sanitation including conservancy and solid waste management, fire service, urban forestry and promotion of ecological aspects, safeguarding the interests of weaker sections of society including physically handicapped and mentally retarded, slum improvement and upgradation, urban poverty alleviation, urban recreational facilities, promotion of cultural and educational activities, burial and cremation grounds, cattle pounds and prevention of cruelty to animals, and vital statistics including registration of births and deaths.

The structure of the Panchayati Raj, according to the provisions of the Seventy-third Constitution Amendment Act is required to be a three-tiered one with elected bodies at the village, block and district levels. While one-third of all the seats are reserved for women, reservations for Scheduled Castes and Scheduled Tribes have been provided in proportion to their population at each level. This Act came into effect on 24 April, 1993 and it was stipulated that all the States (excluding Jammu-Kashmir, Meghalaya, Mizoram, Nagaland and certain Scheduled Areas of some other states) should either make new laws of suitably amend their existing laws so as to bring them in conformity with the provisions of this Amendment Act. To facilitate quick action by the States, the Union Ministry of Rural Development had circulated a model bill prepared by the National Institute of Rural Development, Hyderabad. Happily this could be done within a year and 24th April, 1994 became a day to remember'. Consequently, elections to the institutions of Panchayati Raj took place within next six months and the State governments set up their Election Commission and Finance Commission for the specified purposes.

Thus, the task of granting constitutional status to panchayati Raj is now accomplished. No doubt, the provision of Part IX and Part IXA have their own significance in the sphere of democratic decentralisation in our country. For the first item, the units of local self-government in the rural and urban areas have been accorded a constitutional status. Now their existence is not dependent on the whims and caprices of the rulers of the States. Obviously, it would strengthen democracy at the grass-roots level. And yet a critic may throw light on certain weak points. It may be feared that the innocent people living in the rural and urban areas would suffer from the hazards of struggle for power in which violence would have its own part in vitiating the peaceful atmosphere of the rural and underdeveloped areas of country. It may also be feared that these institutions of local self-government would be grabbed by crafty and mischievous politicians who would abuse their powers recklessly by committing acts of impropriety like misappropriation of public funds. The judiciary would not appreciate the provision that any law made by a State Legislature for the delimitation of territorial constituencies or the allotment of sets in the rural and urban bodies shall remain immune from its scrutiny. The who arrangement looks like a distortion of the dream of gram swaraj as seen by Mahatma Gandhi and his followers of the Bhoodan movement like Acharya Vinoba Bhave and others. Real swaraj would prevail if it moves from the bottom to the top. But in this case it has been imposed from the top on the bottom, The politicians occupying high offices at the Centre have made arrangement for the recruitment of leaders of their choice at the base who would throw leaders of their choice at the regional or provincial levels so as to secure their position at the top. Nothing but politicisation at each level would be the net result of all this arrangement. The people would have to suffer the consequences of this hasty and ill-conceived mechanism. As former Presiden of India R. Venkataraman, in the course of his suggestions for the restructuring ofIndian polity, has observed: Modern democracy is based on the rule by majority which means that 51 per cent can rule to the exclusion of 49 per cent. Ancient Indian tradition has been different. The pachayats were not run by the majority to the exclusion of minority. The elders were chosen for their honesty, inegrity, fainrness and good reputation by Gram Sabas. In some cases, as in the chola period, the acceptable names were put into a pot and lots dran. There was consensus and consent. The councils of the rulers consisted of saints, sages and scholars, but decisions were not taken on the basis of majority of those members.

REFERENCES

1 Since the report of this committee has a pink cover, it is proposed to refer to this report as the Pink Report.

2 *Report of the Administrative Reforms Committee*, Jaipur, Government of Rajasthan, 1963, paras 3-15, 7-3, 15-10.

3 *Report of the Administrative Reforms Committee Hyderabad*. Government of Andhra Pradesh, 1965, para 24.

4 *Interim Report on the Working of the Sachivalaya*, 1965, para 22.

3

Central Participation in Integration and Development

Nationalism is generally defined as "a state of mind in which the supreme loyalty of the individual is due tothe nation-state." As such, it implies "identification of the sate or national with the people or at least the desirability of determining the extent of the state according tothe ethnoraphic principles." It also signifies a common political consciousness or partriotism which the people of a dependent country share among themselves for the purpose of winning self-rule. In other words, it represents the consciousness of a society at an advanced stage of material development; it is also implies and integrated political system on the country-wise basis. A study of nationalism in relation to India shows that she acquired this conspicuousness with the growth of her society on modern lines and with the unity of her political and economic life achieved as an indirect consequence of foreign rule in the nineteenth century. The increasing resentment against the British colonial rule sharpened this consciousness and gave birth to the nationalist agitation that had its triumphing August 1947.

The peculiar situation and conditions in .India that its many-sided ill-effects have grown to dangerous levels. Also, the public administrative system is being so misused and abused that its ability to maintain administrative stability has been seriously weakened. This paper suggests sensible and feasible alternative models for PEM in order to avert the inevitable disastrous consequences of allowing the present trends to continue. India has certainly made remarkable progress on the technological and industrial fronts.

It is one of the few countries to harness atomic energy and to enter the space arena. India manufactures most of the production machinery and produces consumer goods it needs. It has achieved self-reliance in many sectors. More significantly, India has been able to retain democratic polity. Most developing countries have gone in for authoritarian regimes of one kind or other. It is doubtful whether this frail PEM framework will endure for long. But these achievements, significant as they are, are offset by miserable failures in vital sectors—political, economic and social Notably, two-thirds of India's population of 960 million are still illiterate.

In another decade, the majority of the worlds illiterate will be in India. Women's literacy in the Hindi belt is less than ten percent, which is, by any reckoning, a great failure. One third—almost 300 million-are below the so-called poverty line. It has not been possible to provide even rudimentary facilities, such as water, sanitation, health care, housing and schooling to millions living under sub-human conditions in urban and rural areas. Population control has fallen well below the targets fixed; so much so, India's population may exceed that of China in less than 20 years. Forest cover has been dwindling fast. Rivers are being polluted by effluents from industries and sewage from towns. Crime and violence have increased manifold. Corruption and nepotism are rampant. Moral values have deteriorated. The list seems endless. India cannot solve these problems unless the present PEM is changed drastically.

Transport power and communication – so vital to the economy – have fallen far short of the country's requirements. Due to neglect for many years, infrastructure has been lagging far behind industry. While India boasts of her expertise in planning, regional and sectoral distortions continue, the capital out-put ratio, which ought to have come down in the seven five year plans, has actually gone up. This means colossal waste of investments made and low utilisation of assets created. The most explosive situation is on the political and communal fronts. Centrifugal forces have been unleashed by the ramifications of the political process. Secessionists movements in Punjab. J & K and Assam have evoked a measure of popular support and assumed fighting strength. Innocent lives are being lost daily in Punjab.

People have become insensitive to violence and large scale killings. It is quite possible that similar violent separatist movements may arise in other parts of the country, when conditions become ripe. Using her military, security and police forces, India may be able to contain terrorist activities and retain national unity and integrity. But the emotional unity of the people is waning fast. Linguistic and other parochial forces are assuming monstrous proportions. Communal and caste feelings have hardened.

Conflicts and confrontations have become a feature of daily life. Who, or what, is responsible for this chaos? It is the contention of this paper that the culprit is not the individual politician, but the wrong PEM India adopted after independence. Even well meaning and capable leaders are compelled to succumb to the compulsions of the wrong PEM, such as the need for collecting huge funds for elections, manipulating institutions, corruption, etc.

Indian intellectuals and media bitterly criticise individual leaders as mavericks seeking power. Proposals for drastic changes in the PEM hardly get any attention. An open democratic society ought to have fora and institutions for bringing about orderly changes. Unfortunately, in India, the popular proven method of changing leaders and policies is violent and blood-stained. Starting with the agitation for linguistic States in Andhra, all along the past 40 years, and recently, in the Mandal and Mandir—Masjid controversy, and the Tamil – Kannada dispute over Cauvery, the standard weapons have been street violence, destruction of public property, looting, arson and *bandh*. Impact of these abnormal methods on people and their faith in democracy is totally lost sight of Ministers lead demonstrations. A Chief Minister lay down in front of the Secretariat. A great protagonist of democracy declared that, "Democracy is the worst form of government, till somebody discovers something worse."

It is murder of democracy when ruling party in Government

declares State *bandh*. It is a strange spectacle that State governments themselves are organising bandhs, as a protest against Central government actions. Since Independence, the Centre has dismissed State governments more than 90 times. Let it not be forgotten that the lead for this misuse of constitutional provision was given in 1959 by Nehru as PM and Indira Gandhi as Congress President by organising agitation and dismissing the Communist government in Kerala. Motive for the violation of the spirit of the constitution has been partisan political gain. Even the sad situation in Punjab can be traced to the nurturing of Bhindranwale for parisan political gain. Invariably, most agitations, manoeuvres for political one-upmanship, demands for more wages, etc. are generally settled by violence.

Economic Performance

This is natural because India used to repay loans regularly, whereas the loans to South American and African countries had to be written off. The World Bank and the IMF regularly praise India's achievements in economic development. India has been a dependable borrower till the 80s. But during the last 10 years, our credibility rating in international circles has come down. In order to avert a collapse of the fiscal system, liberalisation was launched by the Narasimha Rao Government. The Finance and Commerce Ministers introduced far-reaching changes. But earlier we refused to learn from the excellent experience of other countries in Asia. On a global basis, we are at the bottom of 100 odd developing countries in terms of per capita income. It is argued that the per capita income is not the correct indicator of development.

But our rating in terms of Quality of Living Index is equally appalling; and the inequity that exists in our society is glaring. Since India boasts of her achievement in food production, it will be revealing to compare it with that of China. As against India's 175 m.t. of food-grain production over an area of 150 m.ha., China produces 350 m.t. in an area of 100 m.ha. This means that their productivity is 3.5 tonnes per hectare, while India's is a mere 1.2 tonnes. A Chinese eats 350 kg. per year, and an Indian 200 kgs. China's output is equitably distributed, while India's skewed. India subsidises inputs—fertilizer, water, power, credit etc., to the tune of Rs. 15,000 crores per year, which shows the hidden subsidy and low productivity. In major sectors, China produces three to five times that of India (India's output is given in brackets) – Steel 45 m.t. (10), Coal 1000 m.t. (200) and Petroleum 110 m.t. (30). In the social sphere, Chinese are far better off in sanitation, health care, education etc.

India's present policies do not even claim theoretical solutions – not to talk of practical – to problems of housing, slums handicapped (30m), poverty, illiteracy, etc. South Korea had the same per capita income as India (60) in 1960. Today her per capita income is ten times that of India. While Korea competes with Japan and exports cars to the USA, our cars are not purchased by even our neighbour Nepal. (Maruti exports are a welcome change). ASEAN countries show a far better performance than India. We might like to note the perceptive comments of a public administrator of Malayasia to a visitor from India: "We Malays are dull witted; so we find simple solutions to our problems, however complex. You Indians are unusually brilliant; so you evolve complicated solutions even to simple problems." How true! The productive apparatus is strangled in a web of bewildering rules and controls evolved by the bureaucracy to harrass people in the name of socialism. Outside the planned economies, India has an all pervasive government, which blocks the initiative of people. The politician – civil servant combines have become demi-gods, to whom citizens are compelled to go as supplicants for favours, licenses, permits, etc.

The present government is cutting out a few; but the residue is still strong enough to permit change for the better. Corruption has assumed monstrous proportions. Half of the political news in newspapers is about corruption and scandals. The public are aghast that the amount involved runs into crores of rupees. Political executives and those who handle government functions in economic development got opportunities for amassing fabulous fortunes out of business deals and dispensing licences and quotas. Once such opportunities are reduced or plugged, the amount of corruption would be reduced. We do not know any other way of governing the country except through the democratic framework. If such corruption continues, the faith of the people in democracy may wane and India also may succumb to an authoritarian regime. What is submitted here is that the government should hand over most of the economic development functions to the private sector and also reduce the government control over industries by removing rules and regulations, permits and quotas etc. Much more than corruption, the PEM is doing a great damage to the innumerable organisations and institutions by interfering with appointments, promotions, transfers, resource allocation etc. Society can progress only through organisations – economic, social, educational etc. The political executives and civil servants are directly interfering with autonomous institutions to such an extent that the morale of the organisations and institutions has come down drastically. Several public sector undertakings and nationalised banks have become sick primarily on account of their unit level failure on the one side and external interference on the other. Many public units do not even have a Chief Executive.

Many Chief Executives are being treated like clerks—dismissed or replaced, apparently with no rhyme or reason. During the last few years, the situation has become grave with mounting public debt, depleted foreign exchange reserves, huge debt servicing, high inflation, colossal public expenditure, poor return from public sector investments, corruption and wastage in public systems, increasing sickness in banking and industry, etc. The PEM chariot is the same dilapidated one; so are the ill-trained horses – unenthusiastic employees. Merely changing the drivers can only produce marginal impact. The above remarks are sure to hurt our ego. But the intention is only to plead for changes in PEM which would suit India's peculiar situation. Criticism is more out of anguish. This dangerous trend can be reversed by a more appropriate PEM, which is implementable even under the present desperate conditions.

Basic Weaknesses

India copied Britain's parliamentary democracy system, using the Government of India Act of 1935 as the model. This is understandable since Indians had exposure to and experience only in that model. But Britain is a monosociety, with one single language and religion and an advanced industrial society. But India is a plural society, divided hopelessly into castes, religions, languages, ethnicity, etc. Loyalty to these subgroups is deep rooted and highly emotive. Taking advantage of the affiliation to one's own group, and prejudice to other groups, politicians have been pampering and exploiting the electorate. In the process, these divisive forces have become powerful and have developed a vested interest in perpetuating these divisions. Loyalty of the nation has been subordinated to loyalty to group; caste rigidities have hardened; linguistic passions have been so roused that minority groups feel alienated. The Shiva Sena movement against South Indians is still fresh in the memory. Such movements are being fostered in metropolitan cities, to which people from all over India flock for jobs or business. Choosing the party candidates is a difficult task, since many interests have to be satisfied. The moment candidates are chosen for the party tickets, rivalries come into the open. The disappointed aspirants from separate groups in order to topple the ones which got in. In order to satisfy many disgruntled elements, most are given either ministerial berths or positions of power in public corporations and bodies.

Politics have become a lucrative profession with high risk and stakes; and many winners (and even lowers in collusion) make fortunes, which are used largely for fighting elections, purchasing loyal followers, etc. To add to the complication, linguistic States were formed with the justification that it was to satisfy people's aspirations. Many knowledgeable citizens feel that this was an unfortunate step, which may ultimately lead to the Balkanisation of India. Language is the most potent divisive factor. Advanced nations of Europe and Tribals all over the world are divided on language. In spite of the strong appeal of Islam, Pakistan broke up on the language issue. Sri Lanka is in civil war over Tamil—Sinhala language tussle. Tamil Nadu feels for the Tamils for Sri Lanka, while it is not an emotive factor in the North. Even Canada has a language-based tension.

But it is conceded that Arab Moslem States are quarrelling.

though they speak the same language. So too the Spanish speaking South American Christian nations. But Europe has shown the strong appeal of language. The Soviet Union and Yugoslavia have broken up on language, reinforced with ethnicity. This should be a warning to India. Seventy years of regimentation could not hold them together. But in India, language passion has been inflamed to an extent that minority language groups in metro cities and industrial complexes are feeling insecure and alienated.

The "sons of the soil" theory has been given informal legitimacy in order to restrict "outsiders" from other States, seeking jobs, Strangely, this pernicious idea was blessed by the National Integration Council in 1969. Thus, though the Constitution gives freedom to Indians to seek jobs and settle down in any part of India, all kinds of obstacles are put up to prevent outsiders from coming to their States.

Central Participation in Development

But the problem got compounded by the active participation of the State in economic development and the central allocation of development resources to the constituent States of the Indian Union. In Britain, the Government's direct involvement in economic development is minimal, except for broad policies, regulations and control. In India, the centre is intensely and extensively involved in a variety of ways – as facilitator and supporter, lender and insurer, entrepreneur and manager, etc. – besides the traditional governmental role of a regulator. In a situation of industrial backwardness, the role of the public sector was inevitable. Even South Korea has a sizeable public sector.

Though India pretends to be a socialistic State—the proof being the creation of a monolithic public sector – there are capitalistic nations in Europe with a large share of public sector as a proportion of the Gross National Product. Also, the public undertakings could have been an excellent instrument for national integration. But in practice, linguistic and caste prejudices are producing conflicts, eroding emotional integration. Also, the dismal performance of public sector has become a drain on the nation's resources. Many units are making colossal losses. The overall earning is only a meagre two percent rate of return on an investment of 1,00,000 crores of rupees. If the investment in the national monoplies, such as railways, road transport, power, telephone, irrigation schemes, etc. is added, government investment may be closer to Rs. 200,000 crores. All these are over-manned with indifferent employees, who are overpaid with total security of service. The point at issue is not the inefficiency and under – utilisation of public sector. The crucial decisions on these investments and their management are taken by political executives on a partisan basis. States compete for Central undertakings to be located in their States.

However well meaning a Minister may be, he cannot ignore pressures from his Party and the electorate he represents. Instead of correcting regional imbalances—which was one of the main objects of public sector—the situation has become worse. States, which have larger number of MPs and some heavy-weight politicians, get a larger share of public undertakings and institutions. In the Chandrashekhar Cabinet, there was only one South Indian (he cannot be blamed since South Indians did not join his group) in the Cabinet. The same thing had happened when Janata was in power earlier. Such anomalies would not matter in Britain, since Government is not dispensing resources and patronage. But in India, political executives use their enormous powers and the opportunities for favoring their home States as well as their followers. There is clamour for entering politics in order to grab power somehow which will enable them to make fabulous fortunes later by manipulating public funds. Nursing the constituency in Britain does not cause any damage to the nation's unity or economic progress. If industrial undertakings are to be attracted to a region, the local government has to offer to the private sector favourable terms and essential infrastructure.

But in India, public undertakings are located in backward areas with poor transport and communications. Consequently, the protect cost with budgetted estimate for Rs. 100 crores swells to Rs. 500 crores, simply for the infrastructure. Even that is understandable for dragging regions from backwardness to modernity.

But in India, the objective is to provide employment somehow, at a heavy cost to the nation. Thus we have a strange spectacle of employing five times the staff required, compared to manning in other countries in identical situations and using the same technology. The trade unions, which are powerful, cannot be displeased. South Korea is able to produce five times, with half the manpower. The losers are the non-organised labour (200 m) and the nation. Those who object to retrenchment ought to note that there is grave injustice to the unemployed and the underemployed, when only the organised sector is pampered and protected.

Non-organised Sector

Indian work force is about 280 million. High wages and low workload and over manning are typical in the organised sector, which may form about 20 percent of the total. Thus, over 220 m in the non-organised sector—putting in hard work – receive earnings as low as 10 percent of their counterparts in the protected and pampered organised sector. Even respected labour leaders, who ought to have helped the non-organised sector, are constantly pushing up the wages in the organised sector. To the vast millions seeking a living wage, their advice is to draw inspiration from their brethren. Muscle power is in the organised sector—consisting of regular employees and those assembled on payment for rallies and demonstrations. Politicians favour this organised sector, as it provides ready manpower who are vocal and can agitate during office time, with no risk of losing jobs.

In some metro cities, they are contemplating State legislation to earmark bulk of the employment to the locals. There is rationale for giving State Government jobs to locals. But Central resources belong to the whole nation. The foreign exchange, earned by Keralites, working in the Gulf, are utilised for putting up industries elsewhere. Bank deposits of backward regions go to developed States. Under-developed areas provide raw materials and ready markets to the industrially advanced countries. What Britain did to India is being copied by the forward regions. And they are not prepared to share the gains with all Indians.

Though politically divided, European nations have come together economically through the EEC. But India is already a single nation, whose natural resources, processing factories, talent, money, and finally markets, are scattered all over the country. Optimisation would have been possible in the public sector, taking into account all these factors. But PEM succumbs to political and partisan compulsions, thereby destroying the unifying forces.

Hyderabad and Bangalore together have more central undertakings and institutions than all the other cities put together. The resources for these undertakings have come from all over India. States which do not get Central undertaking naturally are jealous. Every State is lobbying. MPs put pressure on the Central government for helping their States. They threaten to withdraw their support to PM, if a particular industrial unit is not given to their State. Location decisions of every undertaking become a political game with techno-economic considerations given low weightage. In the final analysis, Nation's interests are sacrificed; disintegration is encouraged by the imperatives of the PEM. Strangely, those States and cities, which benefitted most from development, are shouting that injustice has been done to them.

The State winning the battle considers these units as their own. A reasonable share of jobs is denied to the non-locals, which generates separatist feelings and unleashes centrifugal forces. Agitations to keep out non-locals assume many forms, often violent. The Centre is blamed for all problems, which is slowly losing its moral strength and political power, as it is perceived to be partisan. Even when the Centre takes rational decisions, politicians attribute motives, which are echoed in the media. The Central Government has no effective means to justify their decisions.

Industrial Infrastructure

The Central investible resources should be shifted from industrial ventures to infrastructure facilities like power, transport and communications – which have been denied adequate funds all these 51 years. The Indian Railways network of 62,000 kms is a magnificent system left behind by the British. India has hardly added 9,000 kms in 40 years, to the 53,000 kms in 1950. Half the tracks and rolling stock are over-aged, but cannot be replaced for want of funds. When Europe is operating with trains of 300 km per hour, India calls her trains to 60 kms of average speed as 'super fast.' Five million people are waiting for telephone connections. There is power shortage in many States. Power losses are 20 percent. Water supply and drainage systems are collapsing. State governments are throwing away good money in State road transport undertakings. Why should government continue to lose? They are obviously in the wrong business.

But in the existing PEM, political leaders would not agree, since their empires would shrink. Further, their socialistic souls would weep since private sector is considered as an exploiter in India. And labour unions would certainly oppose privatisation. Though their slogan is "Socialists are selling away assets to private tycoons," their hidden objective is to protect secured jobs and income for nominal work. When privatised, the politicians and union leaders cannot squander public money. Strangely, the print media—owned by private sector – is against the private sector. Intellectuals are invariably on the Left, come what may. The public seen to have no decisive voice in a democracy, unless they organise and agitate. The silent majority would rather suffer than get into trouble by going in the streets.

Reforming the System: Proposals for Reorganisation

Is there a solution – feasible and acceptable – under the prevailing constraints? It seems "Yes". The main problem is lack of political leadership and will. Public opinion may help to persuade the polity to face the reality before it is too late.

The major reforms proposed are:

(a) Changes in the political model.

(b) Reorganisation of the States into smaller units.

(c) Decentralisation of powers by the Centre to the States.

(d) Centre to concentrate on governance and infrastructure—power, transport, communication, primary health care and education, help to the poor.

(e) Privatisation of non-essential sectors and partnership between the government and the private sector in economic and social sectors.

Most of these reforms can be carried out without any change in the Constitution. Only the electoral reform proposed would need amendments to the Constitution.

Electoral System

The present "single member, simple majority" system should be replaced by multiple (say three to five) member constituency, the aggregate of which (for each political party will form a *list*. It is easier to choose three candidates (by each party leadership) for the party ticket for each constituency, instead of one as at present. Most of the interest groups – caste, religion, language, charisma money, etc. – can be accommodated in the all India *list*, and sometimes in individual constituency itself, since usually there are only three serious candidates competing for the party ticket in each constituency. Most of the ills and their ramifications, now taking place immediately after the party ticket allocation is announced, can be eliminated in the proposed system.

At present, aspirants, who are denied party ticket, gang up against the political party and also later work against the candidate chosen (at the time of election). When three (or even five) serious candidates are accommodated in the *list*, such party squabbles can be pre-empted. The political parties should ensure that all interests are represented in the *list* at the constituency, State, or national level. In the list for Lok Sabha, each political party will have ample elbow room to give representation for all interest groups. The electorate can judge the political parties by the weightage they give to all interests—an index of the fairness of the political party. Illiterates (who actually vote in large numbers) would still look for the symbol only. The educated and discriminating voters now keep away, since they find that all political parties are partisan, and there is nothing to choose amongst them. The *list* will be welcomed by the them.

At present, when the political party has put up a candidate of one caste group, other dominant caste groups keep away. In Karnataka,

Vokkaligas and Lingayats have been pitted against each other in every election. In Kerala, Christians, Muslims, upper caste and backward class Hindus are the major communal/caste groups. When the candidate is from one of these groups, others keep away or work against. The merit of the candidate evokes low priority. Such situations prevail all over India – Kamma vs. Reddy, Yadav vs. Rajput, and so on. The electorate itself gets split on the lines of such interest groups. When the candidate is chosen by the political party at the headquarters in Delhi, the State Chief of the political party non-cooperates, and vice versa. In order to get a party ticket, candidates give huge sums of money to the political party. The candidate has to collect large amounts from businessmen in order to fight the election and so gets indebted to them, who have to be compensated later. During his tenure in power, he has to favour them with quotas and permits. Liquor lobbies pull the strings in the States; and big business at the Centre. In fact, country liquor barons are upholding the State level democracy by financing the candidates and the political parties. Big business and foreign collaboration deals provide funds for the Centre.

Money power has become the predominant factor in the election process. Future law makers break laws and moral codes in order to get elected. The egalitarian values, which were visible in the political scene in the fifties, have slowly, vanished. In the eighties, open pursuit of power and naked self-interest became the primary motivation for entering politics and seeking office. Decent and competent citizens keep out of the dirty game, as they perceive it. Politics has been vulgarised and criminalised in certain States. People's faith in democracy in waning, and orderly progress becomes difficult. Professional politicians have made the political process a big business, with high stakes where fortunes can be made quickly.

Some of these ills will be reduced in the system proposed. While canvassing, he candidates cannot ask for their 'caste' votes. All the three candidates can jointly canvass. In Kerala, a Hindu-Muslim-Christian combination will be seeking votes; and so divisive factors will not be exploited. Minorities and professionals can be included in the *list*. At present, they can never get elected unless they belong to a cadre party like CPM, which gives less emphasis to partisan considerations. Individualism is sub-ordinated to group interests, which would promote national integration. The next important measure is to replace the "simple majority" by proportional representation" to the political parties based on the percentage of votes polled.

The number of legislators each political party can send to the Parliament or Assembly will be in proportion to the percentage of votes polled. This reform will remove the present absurdity, where a political party polling 35 percent of total votes polled (usually 50 percent of the total electorate) *i.e.*, 17.5 percent of electorate, gets 80 percent of the seats in the Parliament/Assembly. A political party polling 25 percent of votes cast gets no seat. This means that the political party in power gets disproportionate representation, which will be eliminated in the proposed system. All India political parties are really no longer national now, Regional political parties are claiming to be all India. It is amusing that a regional political party like All India Anna DMK claims to be national political party, by adding. "All-India" as prefix! These anomalies will be removed. Professionals can be inducted through the list, and they can be sent to the legislatures. At present, bulk of MPs and MLAs have no understanding of the complex process of development, and they become chief executives of large economic and social understandings. Professionals can provide an element of expertise. The main problem will be "whom to choose" from the list for sending to the Parliament. Here also money and other lobbies may come in. But the damage will be less. There can be provisions to recall MPs, to be substituted by others in the *list*. This provision will act as a deterrent to non-performance or partisanship in the legislature. At present, several MPs hardly open their mouth in the Lok Sabha and Rajya Sabha.

The Prime Minister

The Constituent Assembly came to the conclusion that the British system of government would be more suitable for our county in view of our familiarity with it. But one may feel surprise at the fact that while our constitution has detailed provisions about many things, the principles of the cabinet system of government have been in exhaustively specified in articles 74, 75 and 78. It may be pointed out here that the Constitution uses the term 'Council of Ministers). The word Cabinet has bene used in the 44th Constitution Amendment Act, 1978. It means a body consisting of the Prime Minister and Ministers of the Cabinet rank according to Article 352 (3)

In the Parliament, two alternatives are possible. The present system can continue, where the majority political party can form the government alone, or in coalition with like-minded political parties; or, the substance of the Presidential system can be obtained by the Parliament electing the Prime Minister who can form the government from all political parties, drawing from the *lists* or restricting to the members of the Parliament. This means that India will have a national Cabinet, and the Prime Minister will be a national figure. At present, he is a mere party leader. The practice of the opposition opposing, just for the sake of it, will no longer be effective. In the present system, different political parties are in power in the States. When the PM visits the States, he is perceived as of the Opposition, and not the PM of the nation. How can Central Ministers favour a State ruled by the Opposition. How can Central Minister enjoy the confidence of State Chief Ministers and Ministers? The problem is because the Central government is looked upon as a dispenser of resources. If it were only 'governing,' with no role in economic issues, he could act in national interest.

We may compare our situation with that prevailing in U.S. and Western Europe; and we can appreciate the absurdity and dangers of our system. The next major reform is to re-organise the State system/which can be done by the Centre without any change in the Constitution. The following structure is proposed: (i) Ten city provinces to be formed, composed of metro cities and their adjoining areas to form a population of about 10 million. (ii) Rest of India to be divided into 60 Uni-lingual provinces, by splitting the existing States. (iii) The present tiny states—Manipur, Goa, Pondichery, Tripura etc., to remain; so also, the Union Territories.

In such a set-up, the city provinces will be Delhi, Calcutta, Bombay, Madras, Hyderabad, Bangalore, Lucknow-Kanpur, Ahmedabad-Baroda and two industrial conglomerations. To these will be added the adjoining environmental satellite towns, which will make the total population between five and ten millions. Provinces will be unilingual, while City Provinces will be cosmopolitan. A number of new cities will become Capitals of Provinces—Mysore, Nagpur, Indore, Ranchi, Allahabad, Coimbatore, Vizag, Jamnagar, Nasik, Jodhpur, etc. The present exodus to metro cities will be reduced. State capitals will be closer to the people.

Eighty nations in the world have less than three million people. But many districts in India have three million people. What is being done by a Cabinet and a Secretariat in New Zealand and Denmark is being handled by an IAS officer – typically 30 years old. He functions as magistrate and development manager as well as maintains law and order. The concept and practice are patently absurb and unworkable. The State of Uttar Pradesh with 120 million people, is larger than 150 nations, and ranks as the sixth most populous administrative entity–after China, U.S.A. USSR (Russia), Japan and Indonesia. Administrative costs for legislatures and secretariats may go up. But the economic and other gains will be enormous.

The principle of linguism as the determining criterion for a State will be retained. The dominant population will be Maharashtriyans in Bombay. Tamils in Madras, Bengalis in Calcutta, Andhras in Hyderabad, Kannadigas in Bangalore – and so on. These are the treasures of the wh ole nation, where investment and talents, technical manpowers, etc. of the whole country have helped to nourish them. These should be centers for national integration. Minorities should feel at home there. Their prosperity depends on raw materials and markets outside the cities, and therefore, people from allover India should receive the same consideration. At present, these are the areas where parochial forces are born, raised and trained. The crux of the problem is that the bulk of the Central Government's allocation of development resources to the States and location of public undertakings are on a discretionary basis.

One major purpose of such Central control is to correct the existing regional imbalances and disparities amongst the States, which have resulted from many years of lopsided development and neglect of certain regions.

However, the States perceive these Central decisions as politically motivated -- often partisan, in favour of States ruled by the party in power at the Centre or to win votes in opposition ruled States, and finally not based on merits of each case. Agitations are launched by States for a larger share of resources as well as Central undertakings and institutions. Most of these agitations are mounted on a linguistic platform. Language is an emotive factor which arouses the passions of people. Rationality and the need for a national view are sets aside for promoting linguistic interests. Even in the case of rational decisions, parochial groups can easily sway the sentiments of masses by appealing to linguistic and caste loyalties. Print media give them a ready channel for the propagation of vested interests. The silent majority stands by, aghast and helpless. Inherent inertia paralyses non-organised people from initiating action.

In the proposed set-up, the disputes will be confined to the small affected provinces only. They will not take an inter-linguistic pattern of rivalry, influencing and prejudicing the minds of the masses over the entire linguistic State. The Centre can successfully intervene as the smaller provinces will not defy the centre as they depend on Central help for resources. At present, Centre has become a helpless witness to inter-State conflicts. Inter-group rivalries are taking advantage of the dispute for gaining their self-interests.

Inter-State cooperation is essential in areas such as irrigation, power, transport and communication. The Telugu-Ganga Project and the National Power Grid are classical examples for inter-State cooperation. But such disputes are adversely affecting the unity of the country. Each State is adhering to inflexible positions that appeal to popular sentiments in the States. In the proposed set-up, the problem will be narrowed and localised. Leaders can take bold decisions in the national interest without succumbing to the pressure tactics of vested interests. The Telugu-Ganga may get completed, as a result of the recent agreement.

Though federal in spirit, our Constitution is unitary in practice. Unlike in the U.S., the Central Government, is actively participating in country-wide economic and social development in all sectors, scattered from all over India. A participant cannot easily be an arbiter too. In recent months, opposition parties, ruling in some States, are treating the Centre as an adversary. Abuses and accusations are hurled at each other without restraint, which are slowly eroding people's faith in the system. A feeling of separateness is spreading affecting the integrity of the country. Armed terrorism in Punjab, Assam and Kashmir can perhaps be contained by military. But if such movements sprout and grow to similar proportions in Bengal, Tamil Nadu and Andhra, it may be difficult to control. Law and order is a State subject. When States themselves organise *bandhs* and agitations, the Centre faces awkward situations.

The problem can be rendered manageable with smaller provinces. Smaller provinces can be easily controlled and disciplined. Further, other provinces, belonging to the same language group, will help the centre to reduce confrontations and parochial forces. It may be recalled that the original Congress Party lost Tamil Nadu, largely on the language issue; and Andhra on the self-respect episode. Centre baiting, focussed on personalities and programmes, has become a routing phenomenon. Can we assume that all these vituperations, projected and amplified in the media, will not have any adverse effect? We are literally playing with fire, which may assume a raging ferocity and spread beyond the control of the Government. The trends is towards regionalism—DMK, AI-ADMK, TDP, AGP, NC, etc. have set this trend. The Centre then should decentralise certain powers, and play the role of an arbitrator between provinces, rather than be a party to disputes.

Smaller provinces will facilitate decentralisation without the risk of the State running amuck with parochialism. Since the Centre is in charge of development, States are resorting to populist measures, such as writing off loans and giving doles and subsidies, thus emptying the treasury. Purchase of votes, by hook or crook, is accepted since States have no role in policy making. When provinces get development functions and authority, they need not resort to populist extravagance in order to prove their bonafides to the electorate. But decentralisation is not possible now, nor desirable, since States may not then care for the Centre thereafter. Bigger States may bully and blackmail smaller ones, particularly in inter-State affairs. When agitations take violent forms of unmanageable proportions, governments invariably buckle under pressure. In the past, when all the States were ruled by the Congress, it was relatively easy to suppress or pacify agitators. In the next few years, nothing is certain about the character of the political parties and who would rule the States and the Centre.

The National Development Council which implicity approved what the Congress Working Committee decided during the first two decades) is now a forum for confrontation between the party at the Centre and the opposition parties ruling the States. Most empires collapsed due to centralization of power and taking on responsibilities beyond their management capacity. World's top 100 companies (with revenues more than our Central government) have devised organizational structures based on federalism and decentralization. This concept can be adopted in India only if the states are made small, and Centre shares responsibility and power with the provinces.

Finally, development will be fast, as in the case of Punjab and Haryana, which made rapid progress due to their small size U.P., Bihar and M.P. continue to be backward in every sphere because of their huge size. In addition, all districts should be made smaller—say of half to one million people, which means about 1000 districts in the country. Blocks also should be smaller. In this reorganization, considerations such as natural boundaries resource endowments, homogeneity of population etc. should be taken into account. The British Divisions are of the ideal size for States. More CMs will be required, which would be welcomed by the many aspirants. In the states, jockeying for CM's post (and dismissal too) are regular events. Some of it will subside. CMs of small provinces can be controlled in the interests of national unity. But the Centre should shed its load of development and govern the country, instead of frittering away its energy in managing hotels and making watches, however lucrative they may be. There may be equally important aspects, which ought to receive attention.

However, does not mean that in our political set up the Parliament has become either like an orgamental institution or virtually redundant. It is true that the members of both the Houses have lost their autonomy in the name of discipline in the rank of the party and they have to vote in the House according to the whip issued by the party leaders so as to avoid the penalty of defection amounting to the loss of their membership of the house, it should not be lost sight of that the deliberations of the parliament have their own impact on the administration to stick to the right side or to face a situation of exit.

Today, in India there are signs of welcome changes. The government has taken a number of steps for the welfare of the people. It includes providing basic amenities like after supply, electricity, building of roads, hospitals, dispensaries, schools and centres for adult literacy. Even in rural India, many villages have electricity, drinking water, roads, health centres and schools. The living standard of the people has been improving. The literacy standard has been improving every year. The percentage of school going children in 6-14 ages group has been increased. Besides, the government has launched various adult education programmes to tackle the problem of adult illiteracy such as national Adult Education Programme (NAEP) and National Literacy Mission (NLM). As per 2001 census, the literacy rate of our country has reached to 65.38 per cent. India has also taken steps to alleviate rural poverty through the centrally funded schemes. The social welfare schemes are aimed at improving the condition of the poor people. The schemes included mid-day meal scheme for primary school students for poor families, a rural group life insurance scheme, where the government would provide half the premium and the construction of dwelling units.

There are a number of special prgrammes like swarnjayanti gram Swarozgar Yojana, Indira Awaas Yojana and Jaahar gram Samridhi Yojana. At present our country is undergoing a spectacular change. The modern age, with its satellite and information technology has greatly influenced the quality of human life. The covergence of computer and communication has brought about enormous opportunities as well as changes. Computer has made in roads into rural India and computer assisted education has had its impact upon the children in the state.

4

Perspective Development of Democratic Panchayati Raj in India

Every constitution is a living instrument. As such, it grows with the passage of time. Old provisions are either deleted or amended so as to meet the new conditions and requirements. In course of time it changes so much so that if the founding fathers were brought back to life by any source of alchemy, they would probably not be able to recognise their own creation. Thus, a constitution becomes both a make and a growth. In this connection, we may refer to major constitutional amendments, important decrees of the executive, principal legislative enactment, leading judicial pronouncements, and usages and conventions which form the unwritten part of the fundamental law of the land. Democratic decentralisation is a concept which associates people with local administration through popularly elected bodies.

It recognises the right of the people to take initiative and to execute policy decisions in an autonomous way. It is, therefore, both an end and a means. It is a political ideal and local self government is the applied form of this political ideal.The debate on the local self government in India centres round on whether it should be perceived as an institution of democracy or as an instrument for implementing development programmes through people's participation or both. The colonial rulers had raised the issue particularly after the Sepoy Mutiny which had caused tremendous strain on the exchequer. Added to it was the problem of increasing struggle against the colonial rulers. India under Curzon began to realise the need for channelising the energies of a more articulate section of the population. Although it was Andrew Laing who was the first to emphasise that the Indians were capable of administering their own local affairs themselves, the founding father of the Indian Local self government was Ripon. He was deeply influenced by the British liberal ideas. He felt that the system of local self government was necessary to train the people in the art of governance, to enable them to learn from experience and to open up avenues for political participation of the elected people. Although the colonial rulers had floated this idea for the purpose of maintaining and sustaining the colonial rule, we find in Ripon a concern for development of local self government as an institution of democracy. In fact inspite of his ambivalence he appeared to have been influenced by the institutionist and instrumentalist perspective of local self government.

Indian Constitution

In the first place, we may refer to major amendments of the Constitution which have, to a great extent, changed the form of the original Constitution as inaugurated in 1950. But the draft constitution had made no reference to it. During the days of the nationalist struggle the leaders had promised to the people a vibrant system of local self government after India became independent. It generated a lot of heat in the Constituent Assembly. And, finally, the issue was resolved through an amendment motion moved by K. Santhanan. Thus same article 40 requiring the states to organise village panchayats and endow them with such powers and authority as may be necessary to enable them to function as units of self government became an important provision of the constitution. Evidently, the architects of the constitution had conceptualised panchayats as units of self government, as institutions of democratic governance in rural India. The other places where we find mention of the local government for procedural reasons are the seventh schedule of the constitution where in the state governments have been given powers to legislate on local self government and article 171 which describes the arrangement for the formation of the legislative council. It is provided that at least one third of the members of the legislative council will be elected by municipalities, district boards or by other self governing bodies. But it is purely a lip service because the article 40 forms part of the directive principles of the constitution which are unenforceable through courts of law. Secondly, the pattern of centre-state relations designed by the framers of the constitution has a very strong pro-centre bias. There is no list in the constitution for the local government. In fact, they had opted for a kind of a unitary system with some federal features. Hence the idea of panchayats as units of self government in the countryside conceived by the architects of the constitution did not commensurate with their conceptualisation of distribution of powers, functions and resources between the centre and the states in the constitution.

Thus the idea of panchayats as units of self government in the villages has a congenital defect. The idea however remained dormant for some time because the country opted for state-sponsored rural development through the community development programme in rural India. As expected it failed to unleash popular initiative. This was the background against which the Balvantray Mehta Committee recommended the introduction of three tiered panchayati raj in the countryside. It was responsible, among other things, for the examination of the question of reorganisation of district administration "so that democratic bodies should take over the entire general administration and development of the districts or sub divisions perhaps, other than such functions as law and order, administration of justice and certain functions pertaining to revenue administration." It was therefore beyond the terms of reference of the Balvantray Mehta Committee to look into the question of panchayats as full-fledged units of village self-government. The Committee, however, called for creation of a single representative and vigorous democratic institution to take charge of all aspects of development work. It was argued that such a body had to be elective, comprehensive in its duties and functions, equipped with necessary machinery and in possession of adequate resources. The committee pleaded for a three-tiered structure of panchayati raj, the lowest one being at the block level—an attempt to take the government closer to the people. In the ultimate analysis it must be an instrument of local people's will in regard to local development. Clearly, the committee was haunted by the idea of local development through local participation and recommended people's body at the block level. Some sort of ambivalence was evident in the approach of the Balvantray Mehta Report. In fact it was influenced more by the instrumentalist than by the institutionist perspectives on local government. It talked in terms of institution building through election to facilitate development work. One may argue that this may be attributed to their assessment that the community development programmes had failed because the people could not be mobilised. People's bodies were absent at the villages. Significantly, because of its being guided by the Gandhian and Sarvodaya philosophy the Committee did not plead for participation of political parties in the democratic process. In a parliamentary democracy party is the life blood.

Secondly, the committee had not cared to go into the question of the objective conditions for the growth of village people's participation. Interestingly, it did not examine the concept of panchayats as units of self government, although article 40 of the constitution had clearly mentioned it. The next Committee which delved deeply into question of the panchayati raj in the country was the Asoka Mehta Committee (1977). The committee was required to take stock of the state of panchayati raj in the country and to suggest measures for revamping the system. The committee claimed that it looked at panchayats as both an end and a means. As an end it is an inevitable extension of democracy and as a means it would be responsible for discharging obligations entrusted to it by the national and state governments. Although there was concern for panchayats as grassroots democratic bodies in the Asoka Mehta Committee Report as is evident in its emphasis on participation of political parties and holding of elections at regular intervals, it has gone in for a two-tiered panchayati raj structure. It was argued that the institutional design was made after taking into account the functional necessity of on-going developmental thrusts. The committee considered district as the first point of decentralisation which assures technical expertise of a high order for development. It was further argued that higher level leadership could emerge at the district level. It therefore stood for doing away with elective, participative organisation at the village level. It talked in terms of panchayats as extension of democracy but opted for two tiered panchayati raj structure. What mattered most was the question of development, but not of democracy.

Clearly, the Mehta Committee thought of panchayats primarily as instruments of rural development. In his dissenting note E.M.S. Namboodiripad said "I am afraid that the ghost of the earlier idea that Panchayati Raj Institutions should be completely divorced from all regulatory functions, it haunting my colleagues." He refused to accept panchayat institutions as anything other than integral parts of country's administration with no difference between developmental and regulatory functions. The Mehta Committee however pleaded for constitutional amendment for making panchayats a part of the constitution and called for the reduction of state control over these bodies. Besides it stood against supersession of panchayat bodies on partisan grounds, and if the same ever takes place, there should be election within six months. The same approach was echoed in the G.V.K. Rao Committee Report (1985). The Committee envisaged restoration of the original concept of integrated development at the block level through the directly elected body like the panchayat *samiti* to be responsible for planning and implementation of development schemes under the guidance of the Zilla Parishad. Although the committee felt that there should also be *gram sabha* at the village level, its emphasis was on panchayats as instruments of development. It called for decentralisation of development functions.

The L.M. Singhvi Committee perceived panchayats as units of self government. It was pointed out that panchayats had to be organised as a part of the process of democratic decentralisation for building up institutional edifice, not as a gift of devolutionary process. It recommended for constitutionalisation of panchayats and looked at these bodies as vehicles of homogenisation, secularisation and socialisation of national goals.

But the committee did not turn its eyes to the reality—to the objective conditions in terms of constitutional allocation of resources, powers and functions in the constitution between the centre and the state, the power structure in the countryside, although it attempted to identify the factors contributing to the decline of panchayati raj in our country. There was therefore contradiction in the approach of the Singhvi committee to the Panchayats.

The judiciary also participated in the debate on the status of panchayati raj in the constitution. The decisions of the judiciary in two recent cases are worth mentioning. The Allahabad High Court in *Anugrahanarayan Vs UP Government Case* (1992) argued that local self government formed part of the basic structure of the constitution. The parliamentary democratic edifice of the country rests on the local self government. The parliament and the state legislature have therefore no right to pass any act which seeks to damage the democratic character of the local self government.

Constitutional Amendment

A historical survey of our freedom strugge bears testimony to the fact that the demand that India's political destiny shoudl be determined by the Indians themselves had been put forward by Mahatma Gandhi as early as in 1922 when he said: "Swaraj will not be a free gift of the British Parliament. It will be a declration of India's full self-expression. that is will be expressed through an Act of Parliament is true, but it will be merely a courteous ratification of the declared wish of the people of India even as it was in the case of Union of South Africa." The demand for the setting up of a constituent assembly in very clear terms, however, assumed a shape of its own after th efailrue of the Indian Statutory (Simon) Commission (1928-29) and the three Roudn table Conference held at London (1930, 1931, 1932) that led Jawaharlal Nehru to say n early 1934: "Politically and nationally, if it is granted, as it must be that the people of India are to be the sole ariters of Indi's fate and must, therefore, have full freedom to draw up their Constitution, it follows that this can alone be done by means of a Constituent Assembly elected on the widest franchise.

Parliament appeared on the scene when Rajiv Gandhi approached the parliament with the 64th Constitution amendment bill in 1989. The bill evoked countrywide protests and was subsequently withdrawn. The V.P. Singh government also tabled a bill on this issue. This bill was largely modified after carefully considering the points of contention raised by the opposition parties during the regime of Rajiv Gandhi. But the government was shortlived. The latest in this series is the Seventy Second Constitution Amendment bill 1992 turned into the Seventy third Constitution Amendment Act, 1993. The constitution (73rd Amendment) Act defines panchayats to mean institutions of self government. The state legislatures are required by law to endow such powers and authority as may be necessary to enable them to function as institutions of self government. Such law may contain provisions for the devolution of powers and responsibilities upon panchayats at the appropriate level with respect to: (a) the preparation of plans for economic development and social justice, and (b) the implementation of schemes for economic development and social justice as may be entrusted to them including those in relation to the matters included in the Eleventh Schedule.

The Act enjoins the state legislature to bestow such powers and authority as may be necessary to enable the panchayats as institutions of self government. How is it possible? There is no third list in the Constitution. Clearly, the Act conceives panchayat bodies not only as the units of self government but also as instruments of rural development and planning. In fact there is no contradiction between them. It has been proved by many studies that people's participation is a *sine qua* non for rural development. Panchayat bodies are supposed to ensure people's participation and thus rural development through panchayats means rural development through people's participation. The point is: What is the class background of the panchayat leaders?

Interestingly, the idea of panchayats as mooted by E.M.S. Namboodiripad n his dissenting note appended to the Asoka Mehta Committee Report has been half-heartedly accepted through the amendment of the constitution. Nor was there any commitment by the ruling party on the floor of parliament that this was the beginning of a process. The kind of confusion created by the architects of the constitution seems to have been persisting unabated.

One therefore should not unnecessarily be enthusiastic about the amendment. Secondly, the amendment is not an end itself, but a means to an end, the end being the development of panchayats as institutions of democracy and instruments of development. The amendment will certainly go a long way by providing for reservation of seats for women, Scheduled Castes and Scheduled Tribes. It will put a stop to the partisan use of panchayats by the state governments as they would be compelled to hold elections to panchayat bodies at regular intervals and will not be able to postpone elections to panchayat bodies even after the dates of elections are announced or to supersede the elected bodies for years. But the fact remains that the institutions of panchayati raj have not grown in our country not simply because of the fact that elections were not held at regular intervals. Nirmal Mukherjee had identified four threats to panchayati raj namely, the central government and state level politicians, the bureaucracy and the rural power structure. To my mind threats come from the nature of the economy, society, polity and the constitution of India.

Languishing Panchayats

The Panchayats in our country have passed through two phases, the first phase ending with the submission of the Asoka Mehta Committee Report and the second phase beginning with rise of the second generation political panchayats in line with the Asoka Mehta Committee Report. As things stood before the Asoka Mehta Committee submitted its report the panchayats had only some formal existence in some parts of the country. They were devoid of real content. Elections were not held. They had neither any effective powers or resources. They were captured by the landed rich and high caste people. They languished in almost all parts of the country due to absolute lack of political attention to them for a number of reasons. In fact rural development administration became so bureaucratised that community which was central to it, was pushed to the periphery. In the second phase in the history of panchayati raj in our country the status where the institutions of political panchayats emerged with some promise are West Bengal, Karnataka, Andhra Pradesh and Kerala. But as we find today the experiments did not survive changes in the government at the state level. And expect in Kerala and West Bengal leadership of the panchayat bodies remained in the hands of the landed gentry. The Karnataka and Kerala legislation had devolved a lot of powers on the panchayati raj bodies. The leadership however remained in the hands of the high caste people. But the Karnataka Panchayati Raj Act of 1983 has recently been replaced by the Karnataka Panchayati Raj Act, 1993. The earlier Act was based on three principles of democracy:

1. Sovereignty vests ultimately with the people who elect the government;
2. the elected representatives are accountable to the people; and
3. that no outside functionary, elected or otherwise, has any authority in the areas assigned by the constitution or statutes in force to the local government.

The new Act reportedly aiming at fulfilling the objectives of the constitutional amendment tightens the control of the bureaucracy over the panchayat bodies and reduces, for example, people's control over the bureaucracy. The chief secretary of the zilla parishad has now been made accountable to the state government, rather than to the zilla parishad. It seeks to reinstate the MLA at the taluka level and gives him greater authority over the village panchayats. It reduces the importance of the Zilla Parishad's *abhyakshya* as he would no longer be the head of the panchayat. The chief executive officer shall not implement any resolution of the Zilla parishad which is, in his opinion, inconsistent with the Act. He will refer such matters to the government. He thus becomes a resident exerciser of veto' to use L.C. Jain's words. Earlier the *adhyakshyas* had power to initiate confidential reports against the Chief Secretary (now chief executive officer). The *adhyakshyas* sit in the district planning committees as ordinary members, while the CEO is the secretary to the committee. The divisional commissioner has been given powers to inspect and supervise the offices of the panchayats. The government has been given sweeping powers for suspension of the resolution on the basis of the report of the CEO, to make model legislations and bye-laws on any matter and to direct the panchayats to accept them.

Interestingly, the same has reportedly been the situation in Bihar which has brought a bill in the legislature called the Bihar which has brought a bill in the legislature called the Bihar Panchayati Raj Bill 1993. Although the avowed objective of the bill is to strengthen the system of democratic decentralisation in the state in line with the constitutional amendment, the bill in effect turns panchayati raj into official raj. It empowers, for example, the government to take any steps for the removal of hindrance in the way of the execution of the provisions of the bill. It also provides for the removal of the heads of the panchayats and panchayat samities by the government on ground listed therein.

The Kerala District Administration Act, 1979 providing for a two-tier system of democratic decentralisation and direct election of all the members of the district council devolved on the local Government subjects. The structure was strengthened by providing staff support and making the district collector the *ex-officio* secretary of the zilla parishad. All this was done at the time of the Nayanar government. The election results indicated the rise of the poor in the executive structure of the council as the study done by Institute of Social Science brought out. But things changed after the installation of the Karunakaran ministry. It resorted to dual membership of the MLAs and MPs, took away the staff placed at the disposal of the district council, modified the list of subjects assigned to the district council.

West Bengal is the only state where panchayats have been functioning effectively. Elections have been held regularly. There has been emergence of the poor in the leadership structure. Panchayats have played their roles effectively in implementing rural development programmes, in responding to natural calamities like floods, in handling communal challenge etc.

Thus ultimately, it is the political will and the class character of the ruling party or parties at the state level which determines the fate of the panchayati raj both as institutions of democracy and as instruments of rural development. But the point is, have the panchayats in West Bengal been really able to emerge as effective units of self government? The answer is certainly not positive. The point has been raised by the Mukerjee-Bandyopadaya Report. It is now an open secret that panchayats in West Bengal have not been able to make good headway in respect of resource mobilisation which could have given them some amount of autonomy in the implementation of rural development programmes formulated by them. Increasing dependence on central funds seems to have created a dependency syndrom in panchayats. It cannot be doubted that the West Bengal Panchayat Act lagged behind the earlier panchayat act of Karnataka in terms of devolution of powers and functions on the panchayat bodies and reduction of bureaucratic control.

But the more fundamental question is: is there really much scope left for the development of panchayats as real units of self government without other necessary changes in the constitution? Panchayati raj bodies in our country were brought into being with a congenital defect and confused perspective.

It cannot be denied that a weak state government cannot deliver a healthy panchayat body. This calls for restructuring of the centre-state relations. The issue was feebly raised by the Asoka Mehta Committee also. To quote, "while we are not competent to say what should be the pattern of distribution of powers between the Centre and the states, our recommendation of the transfer of a substantial quantum of powers from the state government to the local bodies has implications for the existing scheme of distribution of power." It was carefully sidetracked by the Sarkaria Commission (1988). If we have to translate the ideal of panchayati raj as developed through the Seventy Third Amendment Act, 1993, it is time to accept the concept of a federation with strong centre and strong states. The idea was mooted by the government of West Bengal in its memorandum on centre-State relations in 1977.

The 73rd amendment act requires the state to form panchayati raj finance commission and empowers the state legislatures to enact laws authorising panchayats to levy, collect and appropriate some taxes, duties and tolls. It assigns to panchayats some taxes, duties, tolls levied and collected to the states. But the states' financial health is very weak. The Task Force on Panchayats consisting of eminent intellectuals like Ch. Hanumantha Rao, L.C. Jain has also raised the issue. At present, almost all the rural development programmes are sponsored by the centre. The states have to accept because the latter has financial clout. This approach cannot help grow panchayats as units of self government.

The political environment of the country has for long been a standing threat to the development of panchayati raj system. Centralisation has been a dominant theme in Indian Politics since the colonial days. The loss of the Congress hegemony has given a blow to this feature but not a deadly blow. The attitude of the Indian ruling classes has not changed considerably. It has been reported that the central finance ministry in charge of examining the proposals of the Sarkaria Commission on financial matters has refused to talk to the chief ministers on this issue. From the experience of the Western countries we know that a democratic system functions somewhat effectively where there is some degree of consensus in the society on major social and political and economic issues. Democracy operates through persuasion and persuasion can be an effective instrument when differences are not irreconcilable. In our country there is still a lack of consensus on major socio-economic issues facing the country.

West Bengal Experiment

Panchayati raj institutions operate in the socio-economic environment of the countryside which is hierarchical and insensitive to change. The success of the panchayats in West Bengal is largely attributed to the changes in the rural power structure brought about by the government through land reforms and the irresistible political will of the state government. The former has made it possible for the poor to make their presence felt in the panchayat bodies and the latter acted as locomotives of panchayats.

Tasks Ahead

We have found from experience that socio-economic changes brought about by land reforms do not *ipso facto* bring about a change in the value system. Panchayati raj calls for new values, new awareness, new orientations which cannot be created overnight without a sort of cultural revolution in the countryside. The literacy campaigns hold a great promise for this purpose. The leaders are required to commit themselves to democratic values. By democratic values, I mean values of sharing power within the institution and a realisation on the part of the leaders that the people are the real sovereigns in a democratic system and they have to be taken into confidence while dealing with all major issues. People have to be made to feel that democracy is an ongoing process and a way of life. It does not stop at participation in elections. The impact of long colonial rule and subsequent domination of the countryside by the landed gentry cannot be eliminated in a couple of years. The process of creation of new values required for the growth of panchayati raj system started after 1978, it has to be carried forward, otherwise it might be difficult to reap the good harvest after some time. It may be recalled that the slogan of the Left Front in the first panchayat elections was: destroy the centre of vested interests and curb the power of the bureaucracy. In the second elections the slogan became: expand democracy at the grassroots. The third elections were fought on the slogan of the consolidation of democracy in the countryside. Legislative changes have been made to establish frequent and regular interaction with the sovereign. But those who are familiar with the field situation, would agree that much ice is still to melt in this regard. The recent amendment providing for delegation of responsibility by the *pradhans* among the members are expected to bring in collective leadership at the institutional level.

Although panchayats in West Bengal have gone a long way in mobilising the poor on many socio-economic issues, it is true that they have not been able to set new examples in the country by taking new initiatives in matters of resource mobilisation, mobilisation of the poor, for example, for cooperative movement for making them feel that the institutions are theirs and they have to contribute to their growth. Local development through locally raised resources by panchayats will encourage people's initiative and participation not only at the stage of implementation of the programmes but also at the stage of maintenance of assets. There is no doubt that successful realisation of the objectives enshrined in the Seventy Third Constitutional Amendment is not possible without further constitutional amendment. But this is a long-drawn process. Given the class character of the Indian state it is too much to expect that it will be done tomorrow. Hence it is high time to use the present panchayats not only for the purpose of political education of the masses but also for the work of local development through mobilisation of local resources and generation of new awareness required for the growth of more democratic functioning of the panchayat bodies. It should not be forgotten that the assets created by the people through their own efforts, initiative and contribution are likely to evoke spontaneous initiative from the people when the question of maintenance occurs. Panchayats should motivate the people for the purpose of protection and maintenance of public properties created out of huge investment of public funds in the locality over the last few years.

Role of Government

The government has also much to do in terms of restructuring legislation for facilitating the emergence of initiative from below and reduction of control from the top over the panchayat bodies. In fact, the Left Front Government started with a piece of legislation which was based on the philosophy of panchayats as agents of rural development. Over the last few years there have been many amendments to accommodate the Left Front government's approach to panchayats, the latest being some sort of comprehensive amendment in 1992. But the basic structure still remains to be seriously attacked. The Left Front government certainly believed in panchayats as units of self government, otherwise it would not have voted for the 73rd Amendment. The Hedge government in Karnataka came out with a better piece of legislation. The old Bengal Municipal Act has just been thoroughly restructured.

Panchayati Raj and the Asoka Mehta Committee

Panchayati Raj was introduced in the country with great fanfare. Rajasthan and Andhra Pradesh were the first States to adopt the panchayati form of rural local government, the year being 1959. They were joined by other States in course of time.

Panchayati Raj in India has come to be associated with three broad images. It is viewed as an instrument for the realisation of the ends of community development. Equally if not more importantly, it is perceived as an organ of the State Government to execute the community development programme and such other schemes as the latter may entrust to it. There is also the local government approach to panchayati raj according to which it is in the first place—and ultimate analysis—an extension and embodiment of democracy at the village level. In contrast to the first approach which looks at panchayati raj as but an instrumental value, the second belief makes panchayati raj as in itself a purpose, an end, a value. Panchayati raj is also a cardinal part of Sarvodaya; and especially Jayaprakash Narayan looks at it, not as a unit of the existing social system but basically as the harbinger of a new order of the society which is to be ushered into existence through this institution. Panchayati raj has thus found itself subject to a variety of interpretations, perceptions, even pulls. To the State Government as well as to the bureaucracy, it has an agency role, and its relevance essentially lies in terms of the community development programme. To the politician particularly of the grassroot level, it is, first and foremost, local self-government and thus consciously modelled after the western-type democracy. Finally, to Sarvodaya it is a bulwark of a new social order to replace the present exploitative system.

The multiplicity of images did not pose a problem at the beginning. Rather, all shades of thought assured, even extended, support to panchayati raj institutions. It was only after some interval that differing perceptions came in conflict with each other. Since the mid-sixties, panchayati raj has been in particularly low profile. As a form of local government, it has fallen out of favour everywhere, even in Maharashtra and Gujarat where it has been relatively more successful. Increasingly, its justification is sought purely in terms of an agency to augment agricultural production.

The ascendancy of this view may be accounted for by four major factors. The new national and state level political leadership which emerged around 1966 had much thinner links with the ideals of Mahatma Gandhi and thus much weaker ideological commitment to panchayati raj. As such, the emergent national political leadership was visibly cool, even indifferent towards panchayati raj, and the state level leadership was more inclined to treat the panchayati raj leadership as its competitor and rival and even a potential threat to its own position and standing. Obviously, panchayati raj institutions began to be kept in a state of impoverishment. Secondly, the mounting food shortage of this period and the crop failures of 1966-67 led to a reshuffling of priorities in the community development programme itself, resulting in an overriding emphasis on agricultural production. In the process, a comprehensive concept of rural development got reduced to a mere project for agricultural production. Thirdly, the trend of the Indian political system has been markedly centralist since the mid-sixties but the pace towards centralisation of power got considerably accelerated from 1971. Under the contemporary political leadership, the State Governments were being made subservient to the Central Government. This is not exactly the climate under which panchayati raj can grow and flourish. Fourthly, the technology discovered at this time served only to reinforce the already powerful centralist pressures, in the process relegating panchayati raj to a lower, even unimportant status. New varieties of wheat were discovered, making what has come to be called the 'green revolution' possible in many parts of the country. From new on, a distinct technological orientation began to be given to agriculture, inducing the Central Government to make direct inroads into this sphere of activity to the detriment of both the State and local Governments. Backed by the new technology, the Central Government began to develop its own independent administrative hierarchies to carry out the special programmes, and in the process the panchayati raj institutions were systematically bypassed. Mention must here be made of special resource development programmes designed for either definite 'target' groups such as Small Farmers' Development Agency (SFDA), Tribal Development Agency (TDA) and Marginal Farmers and Agricultural Labourers Development Agency (MFAL), or area development such as Command Area Development, Drought Prone Areas Programme, Hill Area Development. All these programmes are financed and operated by the Central Government and they have no relationship, whatever, with the panchayati raj institutions. The present practice is to use the bureaucracy for the transfer of technology in rural development and to keep out popular institutions. Nor has the bureaucracy been kindly disposed towards panchayati raj which has provided for the primacy of the grassroot politician in the ordering of affairs has thus come to be viewed as some kind of a thorn in the local level administrative flesh.

As a cumulative result of all these forces, panchayati raj, today, is but a dull echo of its former self. ".... The activities of panchayati raj institutions were meager, their resource base weak and the overall attention given to them niggardly. The functioning of the panchayati raj system thus became discouraging. As if this was not, some of the State Governments would postpone the holding of elections or supersede some of the important tiers of panchayati raj institutions for one reason or the other...In the ultimate analysis, all this led to a weakening of political support to panchayati raj institutions and of administrative will to work through them." Indeed, it may not be very inappropriate to say that India is on way to have a strong rural administration but not rural government.

It was in this overall context that the Central Government appointed, in December 1977, the Committee on Panchayati Raj Institutions to suggest measures to strengthen the Panchayati Raj institutions and made Asoka Mehta as its Chairman. The Committee submitted its report in August 1978 making 132 recommendations.

The Asoka Mehta Committee's principal thesis is the functional necessity for decentralisation of administration. Where millions of people are involved and where the lot of the poor is sought to be improved through a very large number of micro-projects, decentralised administration is an unavoidable necessity. At the same time, in order to remain continually sensitive to popular will and aspirations it requires democratic supervision. This is how the Committee enunciates what it calls a 'new approach' towards panchayati raj. This is: "The formulation of structure, functions and the utilisation of financial, administrative and human resources of panchayati raj institutions should, in our opinion, be determined on the emerging functional necessity of management of rural development." This is an unduly narrow concept of panchayati raj as visualised by the Committee. It gives one a feeling that panchayati raj is no better than an administrative contrivance whose justification lies only in terms of rural development. It would have been more sensible if it is regarded, like its counterparts at the state and central levels, as a system of government having a measure of autonomy in the matter of its functioning and existing in its own right. Sovereignty inheres in the people, and it is from the people that governments, irrespective of their level or ideologies, derive their legitimacy and authority. This implies that a level of government created in the country owes allegiance to the people, and not to each other.

The most momentous recommendation of the Asoka Mehta Committee is for the creation of a two-tiered system of panchayati raj in the place of the present three-tiered one as recommended by the Balvantray Mehta Report. It regards the revenue district as the first point of decentralisation below the state level which assures the technical expertise of a high order required for rural development. It argued "... The technical assistance and organisation of a high order is necessary to sustain the momentum. While the State Government has the requisite competence in this regard, the work is even now being decentralised at the district level. When a process of administrative decentralisation is already taking place, analysis of the changes, and of the ensuing development emphasis point to the need for democratic management of rural development below the state level so that the entire programme can be effectively implemented, coordinated and supervised. The inescapable compulsion is that the first point of decentralization should be at the district level. District heads of sufficient competence are already stationed here. Their capabilities are also being upgraded both in industry and agriculture sectors. A group of subject matter specialists in agriculture is being stationed at the district headquarters. The District Industries Centre will have a component of experts with different specialisations; a district planning unit has been separately suggested with technical expertise in several fields. The district is also traditionally a unit of administration to which will are acclimatised. Further, it is the key planning unit for evolving the overall strategies, resource allocation including credit and the delineation of the different types of projects. Further, experience shows that higher level leadership also can emerge at this level. The establishment of a strong panchayat tier at the district level appears to respond both to organisational needs within the district and the demands of emerging linkages with the State." In short, the zila parishad should be the executive body—as in Maharashtra and Gujarat.

Below the zila parishad is to be a mandal panchayat which is to be constituted by grouping a number of villages and having a population of 15,000 to 20,000. A mandal panchayat would ordinarily cover the central village and the hinterland villages linked with the former and would be the point of decentralisation below the district level. The Committee wrote: "While our preference is for two tiers –a district-level zila parishad and mandal panchayat—we are conscious of the fact that two other tiers are already in existence and it may take time for the suggested institutional design to take shape and become fully operational. The block-level panchayat samitis, where they exist now, would be converted into non-statutory executive committees of zila parishads and when the mandal panchayats become active, most of their functions would be taken up by the mandal panchayats."

The Committee has made specific recommendations about the composition of the various tiers of panchayati raj. The zila parishad is to consist of six types of members—members elected from suitably demarcated electoral wards (or constituencies), presidents of the panchayat samitis (till they continue), nominees of bigger municipalities as well as of the district cooperative federation, two women (who have secured the highest number of votes in the zila parishad election; in the case of no women contesting election, they are to be coopted), and two coopted members—one having special interest in rural development and the other drawn from the local teaching profession. Seats for scheduled castes and scheduled tribes are to be reserved on the basis of their population. The Chairman of the zila parishad is to be elected by the members from amongst themselves. This body would have a number of its standing committees through which it would function.

The mandal panchayat is to consist of 15 members directly elected on village-cum-population basis, representatives of farmers' service societies and two women. Seats for scheduled castes and scheduled tribes are to be reserved on the basis of their population. Its president is to be elected by the directly elected members from amongst themselves.

It may thus be seen that three features characterise the Asoka Mehta Committee recommendations regarding the composition of the panchayati raj bodies. First, the elected element in each tier is to constitute the majority and thus to pre-ponderate over the others. Secondly, seats in each tier have been sets aside for scheduled castes and scheduled tribes, the basis of reservation being their population. Thirdly, the Members of Parliament and Members of Legislative Assembly coming from the locality do not have any formal association with these bodies; they are only to be the *ex-officio* members of the zila parishad's committee dealing with planning. One may also note that the term of office of each tier has been uniformly fixed at 4 years.

That the zila parishad should be the level of democratic decentralisation which is to be entrusted with functions of an executive nature is a pattern already in operation in Gujarat and Maharashtra. But the suggestion for the creation of mandal panchayats (which are to be the implementing bodies) covering a population of 15,000 to 20,000 is a new and novel one. The Asoka Mehta Committee adduced technological and administrative arguments in support of its recommendation for mandal panchayats. According to it, a mandal panchayat would alone be able to ensure a balance between technological requirements and possibilities of popular participation in decision making. The size of the proposed lower tier should be such as to make projects and schemes economically viable. Besides, there are many programmes which need a larger unit than the present block to handle them. In short, mandal panchayat would ideally bring about symbiosis between development and democracy. Thus ran the argument.

The Committee's recommendation favouring a two-tier form of panchayati raj does not appear to have been soundly conceived. It does not recognise the need for an elective participative organism at the level of the village; it is content with mere village committees. Such a view makes the village too conspicuous by its absence in the Mehta scheme of reorganisation. Moreover, it is not very easy to snatch away what has already become part of the apparatus of local level governance. People may not take kindly to the process of dismantling of village panchayats. Besides, political institutions do not operate in a vacuum, and by overlooking the village, which is an organic entity, the Asoka Mehta Committee runs the risk of suggesting precisely such a kind of remedy. It may perhaps do us good to recognise the full organic personality of the village and build the decentralised structure upon it.

This apart, the Committee has to clear some other doubts as well. By not recognising the block as a separate and distinct entity it is apparently in conflict with the recently published Dantwala Report on Block-level Planning, and this has got to be resolved. Most importantly, the present structure of panchayati raj was designed in the early sixties, and it necessarily takes time for such a structure to grow roots and enter into the minds of the rural people. Rural people have their own psyche; they are rather slow in accepting innovations but having accepted, gravely sceptical about proposals for their abrupt abandonment. It is only recently that the panchayati raj glossary has gained their understanding and even acceptance; words like 'block', 'panchayat samiti', 'gram panchayat, etc., have now become household expressions in rural India. One would like to be convinced more than the Committee has done in its report about the distinct superiority of the proposed scheme. Perhaps, the weaknesses of the panchayati raj system are rather inaccurately ascribed to the structure alone. The fact is that it has not been given a really fair trial—and a sympathetic analysis. It appears that the proposed two tier system of panchayati raj and the exact location of the tiers are the structural manifestations of an over-sensitivity on the part of the Committee to technology and a studied under-appreciation of democracy at the grassroots.

The Asoka Mehta Committee wants the panchayati raj institutions to have 'compulsory powers of taxation', to mobilise the necessary resources on their own, thereby reducing their dependence on devolution of funds from the State Government. As we know from experience this is easier said than done: the Centre, too, exhorts the State Governments to display vigor in the matter of taxation but without visible effect on the latter. It is utterly necessary that panchayati raj overcomes its shyness in levying taxes. The Committee has hinted at areas such as profession tax, entertainment tax, house tax and special taxes on lands and buildings which can augment the financial resources of these bodies. There is also a problem here; at certain levels of income these are the zones of the State Governments while at a lower level there is not enough income left for these local level bodies to levy taxes on.

A central feature of the local government in India is the lack of its inherent power of taxation as the Constitution of India does not specify any taxes for its exclusive use. This has occasioned a demand that local government in India be given a separate list of taxes, and that, in order to ensure definite and elastic sources of revenue, the Constitution needs to be suitably amended to include, on the lines of the union and the state lists, a list of local taxes also. It is to be remembered that the Government of India Act, 1919, which remained in operation for 16 years from 1921 to 1937, reserved eleven taxes for the exclusive use of the local government. The Asoka Mehta Committee examined the larger question of according a constitutional base to panchayati raj and wanted the Central Government to give 'careful consideration' to the proposal. One wishes that the Committee had lent a more positive support to the plea for making panchayati raj a part of the organic law of the land, for a constitutional base is apt to impart both sanctity and stature to the grassroot government.

A remarkable feature of the Mehta Report is its recommendation favouring 'open participation' of political parties in panchayati raj affairs. This marks a departure from the hitherto followed policy under which political parties abide by a gentleman's agreement not to contest elections to the panchayati raj institutions. The reality, however, is otherwise. It may be mentioned that West Bengal and Jammu-Kashmir have held panchayat elections on party basis. In many States, where partyless polls are claimed, the political parties have been upto their necks in the fray. The fact is that the party less polls acquire in practice the same competitive character, except, of course, for the labels. The recommendation that political parties be allowed to contest the panchayat elections is thus pragmatic as well as desirable. Not only are the political parties the main channels of mass involvement in current issues including local ones, but they also become accountable when they are openly involved in the panchayati raj institutions. The view that political parties are a species of impurity from which the rural local government in India needs to be shielded, failing which the rural life would get polluted, carries little meaning. They are an essential ingredient of the democratic process. But the political parties must re-orient themselves and learn a new style of functioning at the local level. Otherwise, their entry may convulse the rural society into perpetual turmoil and strife, and thus would prove to be full of dysfunctionalities. As viasualised by the Committee, the panchayati raj elections are to be based on political parties with reserved constituencies for scheduled castes and scheduled tribes and a minimum of two reserved for women.

The Committee has also expressed its views on administration of election to the panchayati raj bodies. According to it, the election will be conducted by the chief electoral officer of the State in consultation withthe Chief Election Commissioner. This may well be a step towards centralisation, and may indeed be not very necessary either. At present, the secretariat department in the

State being in charge of panchayati raj institutions is in charge of conducting elections through the District Collectors.The statute lays down detailed rules for the purpose and its procedures are fairly-standardised.

The Committee has also made some very interesting recommendations favouring the creation of certain monitoring forums to safeguard and promote the interests of the vulnerable social and economic groups that is, scheduled castes and scheduled tribes in the villages. It suggests a regular social audit by a district level agency as well as by a committee of legislators, to check whether funds allocated for these groups are actually spent on them. This is a wholesome recommendation. An absence of such bodies in the present structure has made it easy for smart operators to monopolise the benefits at the expense of those they profess to serve. The Committee has also proposed a social justice committee in each zila parishad to ensure that panchayati raj bodies function so as to show keen interests in the welfare of these groups. These bodies proposed by the Committee have great potential, provided their members are carefully selected and they are truly representative of the diverse interests in the locality. Further, the state legislatures will have a committee on panchayati raj with adequate representation for scheduled castes and tribes and this body will attend to the needs of the weaker sections. The Committee has suggested that each State in India should have a Minister for panchayati raj who, among others, would take care of elections to panchayat institutions and review their work. What is more, the State Governments should arrange for periodic evaluation of these self-governing bodies by independent agencies.

An important recommendation of the Committee is that the State Government must not supersede the panchayati raj institutions on partisan grounds and, further, if the super session of a body becomes necessary, there should be an election within six months. This is a salutary recommendation. It should be remembered that the local government is as much representative of its areas as the latter is of the State as a whole. Having been elected by the freely expressed will of the people, a local government ought to run its full course set out in the governing statute itself. Punitive actions like suspension and dissolution of local governmental institutions may be invoked only when absolutely necessary, and even in such cases it would be a good practice if the State Government puts itself under an obligation to seek its legislature's endorsement of such a measure. Supersession and dissolution of the grassroot government must not occur except with the approval of the state legislature, and what is more, there must be a fresh election within six months.

It is to the Balvantray Mehta Committee that the present pattern of panchayati raj owes its parentage. It is given to the Asoka Mehta Committee to take a close look at this institution with a view to revitalising it. Between the two Mehtas lie two decades of the functioning of this grassroot government. Both are easily the two landmarks in the history of local government in India though each has its distinctive conceptual framework of analysis and examination. In certain aspects the second Mehta builds upon the first, but in many others seeks a deliberate departure from his predecessor. While the first Mehta made the block as the level of decentralisation and thus the corner-stone of panchayati raj structure, the second one treats the district level zila parishad as the lynchpin of the new proposed pattern. The block is a standardised unit being a product of thinking in the developmental context. The same may not perhaps be claimed in favour of the districts.

The District is a very important unit of the administration in India. There are nearly 500 districts in our country. Administration performs three important functions in a district. They are (i) Maintenance of law and order (ii) Maintenance of land records and revenue collection, and (iii) delivery of development schemes and benefits to the people. The district is a large unit, therefore for administrative convenience, each district is divided into subdivisions under the supervision of the district Collector and the Sub-Divisional Officer. The subdivision is divided into Tehsils and each of them is headed by a Tehsildar who is responsible for the maintenance of land records and land revenue. The Block

Development Officer takes care of development schemes and the Deputy Superintendent of Police is for the law and order. The head of the District Administration is called the District Collector. The collector , as the head of the District Administration, occupies a unique position. In some States he is known as Ziladhikari, Ziladhish or Zila Magistrate or Deputy Commissioner. He is an important officer from the Indian Administrative service. The District administrative Officer is responsible to coordinate all the activities of different departments being the principal agent of the estate Government, and the District Development Officer is responsible to get prepared the district plans.

NOTES AND REFERENCE

1. *Report of Committee on Panchayati Raj Institutions*, New Delhi, Ministry of Agriculture and Irrigation, Government of India, 1978, p. 6.
2. For details of the debate, see, Association of Voluntary Agencies for Rural Development, *Panchayati Raj As the Basis of Indian Polity* (New Delhi, 1962).
3. *Report of the Team for the Study of Community Projects and National Extension Service* (New Delhi: Planning Commission, Delhi, Vol. 4, 1957), p. 1.
4. *Report of the Committee on Panchayati Raj Institutions* (New Delhi: Ministry of Agriculture and Irrigation, Department of Rural Development, 1978), p. 38.
5. See extracts of the L.M. Singhvi Committee Report (1986) in *Kurukshetra*, February, 1986, p. 44.
6. Cited by Budhadev Ghosh, "Bhartiya Sanbidhana Sthaniya Sarkarer Bhumika" in *Panchayati Raj* (in Bengali) (Calcutta : Dept. of Panchayats, Government of West Bengal).
7. Nirmal Mukarji, "Panchayat Governments" *Seminar*, August 1989.
8. L.C. Jain, *Grass Without Roots* (New Delhi: Sage India, 1986).
9. Amal Ray and J. Kumpatla, "Zilla Parishad Presidents in Karnataka. Their Social Background and Implications for Development," *Economic and Political Weekly*, 17-24, October, 1987.

10.K.S. Krishnaswami, "Karnataka's New State Backwards" *Economic and Political Weekly*, 1 May, 1993.

11. L.C. Jain, "Panchayat Act Clerical in Outlook" *Deccan Harald*, 2 August, 1993.

12. *The Statesman*, Calcutta, 17 August, 1993.

14. N. Mukarji and D. Bandyopadhaya, "*New Horizons in West Bengal Panchayats—A Report for the Government of West Bengal* (Mimeo) 1993.

5

Rural Development and the Role of Civil Servants

Since India is a federation, the civil servants are recruited at two levels: The members of the civil service at the centre are recruited by the central government with the help of a body known as Union Public Service Commission. Those at the State level are recruited by the state governments with the assistance of their respective State Public Service Commissions. Although the members of the Indian Administrative Service and Indian Police Service are recruited by the Central Government, they are placed under both central and state governments.

It has rightly been described as one other salient features of the Indian Constitution that it incorporates chapters on some such subjects which ought to have been covered by the process of ordinary legislation or administrative action or both. Part XIV titled 'Services under the Union and the States' is a case in point. What had an impact of its own on the minds of the Makers was to have independent, impartial and efficient public services in the country going to adopt a constitution irrevocably added to the ideals of a democratic, secular and social welfare state after overthrowing the vestiges of a long colonial rule that had converted the top administrative class into a 'new caste' of autocrats ruling over the destiny of the teeming millions of India.

The earlier years of my career when some talk had already started about the relevance of a civil service which the country had inherited from a colonial power to the new dimensions of governance. Doubts were being expressed whether the civil service would be able to meet the challenges of a developing country and a Welfare State. Whether the civil services will be able to adjust to their new roles and discard the old mantle of a basically regulatory body. Though the controversy has not completely died down I am glad the civil services have not only survived all these years but have also risen upto the demands placed on them and by and large have performed well. We have all adapted to the new requirements and acquired necessary skills for handling new problems and new situations. I think this has been possible largely because there were some basic fundamental attributes which the civil service had acquired which facilitated acquisition of new qualities required with changing times. Though the expectations from a civil service may have undergone a change, the relative importance of different aspects of work may have changed, a totally new type of jobs may have been required to be performed, certain minimum set of qualities expected in a civil servant have remained unchanged and I would think will remain unchanged irrespective of the job one is performing or the organisation or the government one is serving. It is some of these basic tenets of civil service which I would like to discuss with you today. Whatever part we may have to play in the country's development and progress these essentials will form the foundations of the civil service and if the foundation is firm, the civil service would be able to stand firm and discharge its duties and functions admirably.

And if these basics are shaky, the extent of trust reposed to it so far will go down. When we talk of a civil service we talk of an efficient civil service. The word 'efficient' is not used but implied. The first and the foremost requirement is therefore efficiency. All members of the civil service have to be individually efficient and the department or the organisation of which they are part should be efficient as a whole. If in an organisation the individuals are competent, the changes are that the organisation would also be efficient. But if the individuals are inefficient, the organisation they serve cannot be expected to be efficient. I am talking about efficiency because I notice this aspect being relegated from its pre-eminent position which it should occupy in a civil service to a position of less importance. What exactly is meant by efficiency is also sometimes not clearly understood. I do not want to enter into an academic discussion on what is efficiency or what is lack of it but I do want to dwell a little on this purely from a practical point of view. Broadly speaking, what an administrator does can be divided into two parts. One what he does himself and two what he gets done by his assistants, followers or team. The first relates to his personal efficiency and the second to his capacity to mobilise his team and get the maximum out of it for the organisation. Virtually, right from the beginning, we all have to work with a group of people and as we go along our career, we start leading a section, or a wing or a department or an organisation. Apart from your personal efficiency your success now depends largely on the extent to which you are able to develop leadership qualities. You have to develop professional ability, the art of taking decisions, the capacity to motivate and inspire your team for higher levels of performance. A host of other qualities necessary for administrative leadership have to be acquired and developed. I do not propose to discuss this second aspect relating to man management and leadership but I do want to discuss a little the first aspect of personal efficiency. Who is an efficient administrator? Different answers may be given to this question and different traits of personality may be emphasised to different degrees by different persons. I find there is a lot of confusion as well about the meaning of efficiency.

There are four simple basic requirements of efficiency: Who is an efficient administrator? Different answers may be given to this question and different traits of personality may be emphasised to different degrees by different persons. I find there is a lot of confusion as well about the meaning of efficiency. There are four simple basic requirements of efficiency: (a) First is the quality of work. The performance or the output of a worker must be of good quality. It must be free from mistakes, accurate and well considered. A worker must learn the technique of his job, he must be thorough and his superior must be able to rely on the quality of his output. When we say that the quality of work must be high, it presupposes certain other things. The worker must posses full knowledge about the facts, rules, and regulations applicable to them, he must be able to think of various alternatives and the pros and cons of the different alternatives, and must be able to arrive at a sound decision. Then only his output would be of good quality. (a) The second essential ingredient of efficiency is the speed at which the work is done. A ten-minute job must be finished in ten minutes and not in twenty. In other words, an efficient worker has a large output per unit of time. At this state, I may also make it clear that the speed in working is not acquired at the cost of quality but in addition to it. Quality, accuracy or excellence is an indispensable condition of good work and it should not be sacrificed to quickness of performance.

Herein lie the basic requisites of an efficient worker; he is both accurate in his work, quality of work is of a high order and at the same time he is also fast. His disposal is quick. I am telling you all this because I have observed that a large number of workers do not realise these two basic essentials of efficiency. A number of people work for long hours with little output. They have not understood the importance of speed of working. An efficient worker is both accurate and fast.

Delay, in fact, is a sure sign of inefficiency. (c) The third factor of efficiency is the use of minimum effort in doing one's work. This means that in the day-to-day work an efficient worker feels little or no fatigue. This implies that he is able to put in long hours of work without getting tired. Thus, a worker who has these three qualities can turn out more and more work of high standard with less and less fatigue. (d) And finally, the highest level of efficiency is originality in one's work. An efficient worker must not merely carry on the routine or continue to do what he was doing before but must be able to produce new ideas, to initiate new schemes, make improvements in systems of working, introduce time, labour or money-saving devices. He must simplify procedures. He must plan for the future development of his organisation. This is the real contribution one makes to one's work and organisation.

There are the four basic requirements of efficiency; quality, speed, expenditure of minimum effort and creativity which is the highest phase of efficiency. You will do well to remember this. One must strive to be personally efficient in whatever one does. Then only he would be equipped to assume higher leadership positions. At this stage of your career developing personal efficiency is of greatest importance.

From the very beginning of our career we are all concerned about our postings and rightly so. Where we are posted and what we do affects our career as well as our personal life. It is nature to be concerned about it. But we must realise that once we have joined a service all posts encadred in it are the possible posts where one can be posted. There is no need to be choosy about it. In fact, a trend now noticeable about civil servants trying to secure particular postings for themselves goes against the basic concept of civil service. All posts are equally important. No work is inferior or superior to other. In fact, for you the job currently assigned to you is the most important of all jobs and you must do your best at it. While working on a particular job casting covetous eyes on the job of another is rather demeaning. I am reminded of a sloka in the *Gita* which advises against forsaking duty assigned to an individual. "Better one's own duty though destitute or merit, than the duty of another well discharged. Better death in the discharge of one's duty, the duty of another is full of danger."

Of course, there can be no objection to doing things necessary for improving one's prospects in life. I also realise that at times it may be difficult to go to a particular place of posting due to personal problems like illness in the family or children's education or other reasons. There is no harm in explaining your personal problems to your seniors. But we must understand that approaching other persons, particularly political leaders, for this purpose is bound to compromise your position. No favour is bestowed without seeking a return. And the first thing which becomes a causualty is your own self-respect.

Significance

Civil Service in the modern government has been succinctly summed up by Ogg: "The work of the government would never be done if there were only the secretaries of state and other heads of departments, the presidents of boards, parliamentary under secretaries, junior lords, and civil lords, in other words, the ministers—to do it. These people cannot be expected to collect taxes, audit accounts, inspect factories, take censuses, to say nothing of keeping accounts, delivering mail, and carrying messages. Such manifold tasks fall, rather, to the body of officials and employees known as the permanent civil service...It is this great body of men and women that translates law into action from one end of the country to the other and brings the national government into its daily contacts with the rank and file in the country—less in the public eye than the ministry; this army of functionaries is not a whit less necessary to the realisation of the purposes for which the government exists."[14]

Meaning

The term "Civil Service" has come to signify non-combatant branches of the administrative service of the State. The term has been defined in Britain as "those servants of the Crown other than holders of political or judicial offices, who are employed in a civil capacity, and whose remuneration is paid wholly and directly out of monies voted by Parliament." An analysis of this definition shows that the term excludes persons in defence forces, persons holding political or judicial offices, and persons who work for government in an honorary capacity or are not paid out of public revenues. In brief, the Civil Service is a "professional body of officials, permanent, paid and skilled."—(Finer). Of late a new category has been added to the Civil Service, namely, industrial workers. As more and more enterprises—industrial and commercial—come under public sector, the number of such workers increases.

Herman Finer has classified the British Civil Service into three categories—Administrative, Technical and Manipulative. The administrative officers are occupied in the general task of helping in the formulation of policies and executing them. The technical officials lend the aid of specific scientific knowledge and training, like doctors and engineers. The officials belonging to manipulative category, execute orders handed down by the first two classes by common physical activity.

Functions

The duties of the Civil Service today are many and varied and include: advice to Ministers on all matters of policy; supervision of all aspects of the government scientific research; carrying out the social services; and numerous routine functions, like collecting taxes, keeping accounts and selling postage stamps. The public officials, today, perform various kinds of functions. Their first function is the implementation of government's policies. Secondly they have quasi-legislative (delegated legislation) and quasi-judicial (administrative adjudication) functions. Thirdly, at the higher level, they advise the political executive on policy matters. Fourthly, public relations has become an important part of official duties. In addition, the officials, in certain positions are expected to explain the government policy to the people and to win their co-operation in its implementation. All these functions of the public official are exercised in the context of parliamentary democracy in India, and he is accountable directly to the political executive and indirectly through him to Parliament and the people.

On every post you have a certain duty which you must discharge to the best of your ability. The only way to qualify for better jobs and senior assignments is to give full attention to one's present job and do it as well as possible. Please remember no jobs are good or bad. And how can you expect your another colleague to take up a job which you yourself are not prepared to do? You must approach a job with a feeling of not what it can give to you but what you can contribute while on it. It is not the job from which you derive your importance but it is you who lend prestige and glory to the chair you occupy.

That is the right approach. In a democratic setup, there are broadly two executive wings of the government. The first is the political leadership and the second is the civil service. It is extremely essential for a good government that the relationship between the two is smooth and harmonious. Any conflict results in a sharp decline in the quality of governance and jeopardises the very working of the government. It is, therefore, necessary that both work together and supplement each other for the common good of the people. One or two aspects of this relationship may be discussed. All civil servants whether at the junior level or at the top of the ladder, have to face politicians. While working on field assignments in the districts or other jobs. Political workers approach you with recommendations for transfers of petty officials and other small works.

All such works which fit in the norms and guidelines or rules and regulations may be done. It is obvious but I am saying this because I have seen some of my colleagues reacting sharply to any approach by politicians. Even if they would have done that work in the normal course, they would not do it only because a political worker has recommended it. This is to my mind not a right approach. But the problem arises when the recommendation made is about something which cannot be done being against the rules/regulations or against establishment procedures and guidelines. It is worse when the person approaching you comes from the ruling political party. Members of the ruling party tend to believe that they have a right to get things done the way they want it. This really creates problems for you. But I think in a situation like this also, the answer is obvious; one must learn to say no politely but firmly. Half the time people would understand if you explain to them why it is not possible to do a particular work. But sometimes they do not see reason and keep on pestering you. We then have to face it and withstand pressure. In this regard, the seniors have to support their juniors.

But the problem really arises when an impression is created

that an officer would do things if the request comes from a particular quarter and would not do similar things if the request comes from the opposite group. This impression of being partisan or being inclined favourably towards someone or being against someone immediately tarnishes one's reputation and leads to various other problems. This is one thing which all of us have to guard against. In fact, if one learns to say no and applies the same standards to all irrespective of their political affiliation, people generally come to appreciate such a virtue and respect the individual.

At the senior levels also one has to maintain his neutrality. The political government has its manifesto which it would like to implement. As civil servants, it would be our duty to assist the political leadership in implementing its policies but here again one has to be very careful in not aligning himself/herself with any political party or a political leader. Some time ago there was a lot of talk about a committed civil service. We should very clearly understand that we have to be committed to uphold the constitution and the rule of law and to implement the directions of the government of the day but it is not the same thing as being identified with a political party or a political leader.

Though the distinction is fine, we have to maintain it and the civil service must remain a non-political body. This was the basic tenet of civil service all along but it has assumed greater relevance in the present politically fluid situation. We see that the government at the Centre may be headed by one party at one point of time and another party or a group of parties at another point of time. In the States so many different parties are in power and the changes are so frequent that one tends to forget which State is being ruled by which party. In such a situation, you would appreciate the significance of the civil service remaining totally neutral and dedicated to the progress of the country. We must uphold this basic political independence of the civil service.

Freedom of Work

At the senior and policy making levels, civil servants have to interact directly with the political leadership comprising Ministers/ Chief Minister. They are involved in decisions having far-reaching consequences and policy implications. Even otherwise important decisions having financial angles may be required to be taken. As civil servants we must analyse the problem thoroughly and tender the best advice in the circumstances. We must not be afraid of likes or dislikes of our political masters. Whether the advice would be palatable or not, we must be frank in expressing our views, both orally and in writing. What I am saying is very obvious but the need of saying so has arisen because a different trend is now visible. Quite a few of us look to the political masters for ascertaining what they want and try to do their bidding. Before expressing their views or recording a note they would like to talk to the Minister and elicit his views and then tailor their own views to sit the political leadership. To my mind this is an incorrect approach. Sometimes, the Minister may call the officer for discussion and disclose his mind how he expects a particular matter to be handled. Yet it does not mean that one should follow all that a Minister says.

One must point out the pitfalls in his suggestions and advice him suitably. We must clearly understand the role of civil service *vis-a-vis* the political leadership. The final decision-making authority rests with the minister. But the bureaucracy has a grater role in advising the minister correctly. As I mentioned earlier, the pros and cons of various alternatives available in a given situation have to be brought out clearly, implications of a particular decision have to be anticipated and a well thoughtout line of action is to be suggested. Let the political leader then take a decision. He has the authority to overrule you and if you still think that a wrong decision is being taken it is your duty to point it out and submit it for reconsideration.

Only then you would have discharged your responsibility as a good civil servant. I think, for a civil servant, the right to express his views without any fear or favour is the right to be cherished most. Of course, the decision lies with the political leadership and one should not be afraid of being overruled but one should not surrender one of his basic rights to advise. One should have strength of his conviction to withstand political pressure irrespective of the consequences. And, I may assure you the consequence will not be anything more than a transfer which as I said earlier, should be of no significance to you. Any post is good enough for an upright officer.

There is no greater reward than the satisfaction of having done a right thing. Public services are the backbone of government. It is as necessary for them to be honest as to be efficient. And for administrative leadership, unimpeachable honesty is an essential qualification. No executive can command respect of his subordinates or fellow workers unless he is scrupulously honest in his words and deeds. He must set a high example for others to follow. He must be thoroughly upright in money matters. He should shun not only bribery and graft but also subtler forms of corruption such as awarding contracts to friends and relatives, circumventing rules for the sake of personal gain or in order to benefit someone else. In its wider connotation, integrity would include intellectual honesty, a free and frank expression of one's views, a scientific attitude of mind, a high degree of objectivity, and a high sense of justice.

All such things are necessary in an administrator. Unfortunately, an impression has gained ground and not without reason, that the bureaucracy is inefficient and corrupt. Some of the criticism may be justified but I think that the bulk of the civil service is still honest and it is only a small percentage of people which brings a bad name to the entire service. But this group however small is large enough to cause grave concern to all of us. We must give deep thought to this problem. Of course, there are no easy solutions but we cannot give up. The criticism of the bureaucracy being corrupt has to be looked at in a wider context of the general socio-economic climate in which we are living. The civil service is after all only a cross-section of society. In the matter of integrity, it cannot be expected to rise to a level much above that of the rest of intelligentsia. If the standard of integrity among public servants is to be raised it will have to be done in case of other professions as well such as lawyers, doctors, businessmen, industrialists, publicmen and politicians. In fact, the need today is to raise the moral values of the society at large. A permanent and long-term solution to the problem of integrity in public service will therefore be inculcation of this virtue in the coming generations at the right impressionable age. Much more emphasis will have to be laid on moral values and character building and it has to start in the homes, in the families, schools and colleges. But precept alone will not do. There have to be men and women of sterling character who can serve as models and whom the coming generation may emulate.

It is a different has but a beginning has to be made. Another important fact to be remembered is that being personally honest is not enough. You are responsible for the conduct of your subordinates as well. You have to evolve measures which minimise the opportunity available to your subordinates to exploit people. One can think of organisational arrangements and close supervision over the work of the subordinates which make it difficult, if not impossible to indulge in malpractices. I would like to discuss some of such measures with you. As mentioned earlier, delays in work are a sign of inefficiency. They are also symptoms of corruption. Orders passed on files are not communicated for days together. Delays in sanctioning licences or in issuing them, delays in payments – all such delays are warning signals. A host of other instances of delay in transaction of government business may just arise from unavoidable causes or sheer slackness or may be intentionally created to cause harassment in order to extract a benefit. It should be remembered that delays, whether intentional or due to inefficiency, equally provide opportunity to unscrupulous people to extort illegal gratification. If we want to stamp out corruption from our office we must first eradicate delays on which it thrives.

We must go into the causes of delays and try to remove them. The second danger signal of possible existence of corruption is the frequent change of orders. Penalties are first imposed on contractors and suppliers and later on cancelled or reduced; transfer orders are issued but subsequently revised; objections are first raised on bills but afterwards withdrawn and payments made someone is arrested but later released for want of evidence. Such changes in order readily lend themselves to corruption. To avoid such a situation one should take great care that the decisions one takes are sound and firm and one should be slow in changing them. Revising decisions readily on receipt of recommendations or pressure exposes the organisation to corrupt practices at the hands of unscrupulous. Please be on the guard against such practices. Another factor which helps in curbing malpractices is your accessibility to complainants. If your subordinates know that the harassment they cause will come to your notice and you may pull them up, they will desist from it. You should, therefore, make yourself easily approachable. A time for receiving visitors daily may be fixed and as far as possible no other engagements should be fixed during such visiting hours. Free accessibility does help not only in checking malpractices but also in remedying other complaints of various types. A word of caution must also be said about asking people to meet at the residence. For official business one should see you in your office and not at your residence.

There is no reason why representatives of staff, contractors or public should be received at the house and not in the office. Emergency apart, it is a sound practice to meet people in office only for official work. For a public servant it is not enough to be honest; he must also be known to be honest. In other words, he must have a reputation for integrity. A man's reputation travels far ahead of him and anyone who has established a reputation for honesty, is seldom if ever approached by tempters. Acquisitions of a good reputation is therefore also essential for a drive against corruption. No doubt reputation is an intangible thing and depends on what others think and talk about a person. A question may be raised how does a man create a reputation for himself if it largely depends on others' perception. Well, friends, there are certain measures which do help in building up a reputation.

As already mentioned, delays and frequent changes in orders are possible areas for corruption to flourish. These two factors mar the reputation of an administrator. One has to check these two things. As the old saying goes, "a man is known by the company he keeps." Being seen with or keeping company of persons of a doubtful reputation is liable to besmirch your own reputation. There is also the danger of such persons exploiting your relationship with them. There is need to exercise utmost caution in accepting recommendations of such persons. For the same reason, it is dangerous to have any favourites among your subordinates. Some of them may trade on your obvious kindness to them injuring your reputation. Though not many people realize, great harm is done to one's reputation by backing wrong or under serving persons. Extending protection to wrong persons when they are in trouble or supporting them for promotion, posting or preferment of any other kinds damags your reputation also. One must desist from it. In the end, I would like to say that we have to prepare ourselves for the challenges ahead. We have to be thoroughly professional in our jobs and have to maintain highest standard of efficiency and integrity. We must continue to learn and acquire new knowledge and skills. Only then we may be upto the mark and also able to face the assaults on the civil service. The turmoil at the political level and new alignments emphasis the need for impartiality and neutrality of civil service. There are certain other new developments which have a bearing on the functioning of the civil service which cannot be ignored. The media has emerged as a powerful segment trying to mould the functioning of both the political set up as well as the bureaucratic. We are all aware of how on the basis of reports in the media several actions are initiated or a new dimension is added. There is yet another group of the NGO's and activists taking up issues of public importance particularly in the field of social justice. Human rights activists, women's organisations and the like are trying to influence the working of the government. We have to take into account all these groups and their close interaction today with the government.

6

Local Governments and Economic Reforms

A new kind of nexus has developed between the bureaucrats acting at the behest of the politicians and the barons of Indian industry that track-two diplomacy has come to occupy its own place in the making of our foreign policy and its implementation. This is a new term that suggests the role of non-governemntal agencies in exercising pressure either by themselve sor through other multinatinal and international organisaiotn on the decision-makers of a country in orderto have favourable results. Several non-governmental agencies controlled by the business magnates are playing their own part in refining and strengthening their relatons with their counterparts in other countries of the world and thereby influencing the bureaucrats, the ministers and the diplomats of the concerned countries. The evolution of a subtle synergy may be noticed in the fact that now there is a much greater degree of openness in government and deeper appreciation of the need for mutual reliance between business and government in the following directions.

The focus in this chapter is on raising issues in the context of impact of recent developments on local government institutions in India. By now a lot has been written about Constitution (73rd and 74th) Amendment Acts of 1992, applauding them as landmarks in the history of development of local governments in India. Time has come that we subject them to a dispassionate and cool analysis and see how far the changes envisaged would accomplish the objectives behind the amendments and identify the direction of local government reforms in future. It is also necessary to look at the recent developments in the wider context of major transformations, basic in nature and substantially large in scope, which are taking place in the role of state and the philosophy of its governance.

Changes that are sweeping across all the nations have far-reaching effects on the institutional structure of political and administrative system of governance of the state, and the relationship of their constituents with the society at large. It appears that local governments, particularly in developing countries, are likely to present serious dilemmas in the design of the institutional framework for nation-building and development. The collapse of the bi-polar, competitive and mutually deterrent power-centres with their distinct ideological pursuits has deprived many countries of their options, and the breathing time for consolidation necessary for developing into nations.

The new ideological format of advancing national interests requires enormous internal strength—political, social and economic – to be effective for survival as a distinct entity in the comity of nations. Concern for human rights and environment, democratisation of highly fragmented and feudal societies, empowerment of micro-segments (be they castes, tribes, minorities, or distinct clans or ethnic and linguistic groups) of national population, reforms for global economic integration, easy, direct and intimate exposure to different and often socially destabilising ways of life, traditions and beliefs through satellite invasion via open skies, and finally the substantial changes in the quality of population and its consumption pattern have altered the conditions and created the stress on the institutions of governance of the state never experienced before.

Most western societies had developed the stability and the capacity to absorb these changes for them to pose any threat to their survival and national identity by ensuring a minimum level of requirements becoming part of the subconsciousness of their population, directing their thoughts and actions. It is easier for them to internalise these developments which otherwise have serious consequences for those struggling to develop nationhood out of disparate groups with strong local and ethnic loyalties with intense claim over extremely scarce resources. Decentralisation assumes different meanings and produces different results in these two different contexts.

Theoretical Basis and Scope for Local Governments

Strong advocacy of decentralisation in development has produced a powerful indoctrination in favour of local government. The discipline of public administration has accepted this indoctrination in India without questioning. Confined to being used as rhetoric, it has not been seriously taken for operationalisation and implementation. On the contrary, it has impaired our capacity to conceive decentralisation in the wider context of its application, and relating to the changing role of government at various levels. It has not enabled us to critically examine and review the distribution of functions at various levels of government in accordance with the stages of development. In short, it has virtually frozen institutional evolution and has created major distortions in our politico-administrative system of governance of the country. It is due to historical reasons? If so, what has been the contribution of the discipline of public administration in changing our dependency on historical legacy?

Teaching and research in public administration do not seem to have promoted inquiry for theoretical formulation of decentralisation for nation-building and development and for designing public services delivery systems in the country. We continue to teach descriptive aspects of structure, functions, powers, resources, etc., of local governments—urban and rural-occasionally injecting doctrinaire contents and selective recommendations of commissions and committees in support of it. Syllabi and prescribed textbooks even for the post-graduate courses rely promote a debate and reveal the level of intellectual inquiry necessary for the growth of knowledge, and the development of the discipline of public administration.

During the colonial rule and subsequent to their independence, the developing countries evolved centralised, bureaucratic and hierarchical structures for the machinery of government. Active state in a passive society virtually pursued the concentration of powers and resources, and used a variety of government organisations as conveyer belts for transmitting the authority of the state and lending supremacy to it. Strengthening of the state in highly fragmented societies was considered a prerequisite for development. The development assistance during 1950s and 60s reinforced the need for a strong state for efficient and effective use of scarce resources. Welfare state and socialistic policies further enlarged the size of government machinery built on centralised, bureaucratic and hierarchical structures, till dysfunctionalities of the system became increasingly apparent. James S. Wunsch reviews the literature and summarises these dysfunctionalities thus: . . . the centralist hierarchical—bureaucratic organisationl modality has been found generally to make administrative coordination among different organisations difficult; shift vast resources to the center from the field; increase coordination and managerial costs; design projects and programmes which poorly fit local wants, needs and conditions; reduce flexibility, adaptability, creativity and speed in field services; discourage learning and innovation; continue and even worsen systems of patron clientele and severe asymmetries in power, wealth and status between centre and periphery, and rich and poor; perpetuate the weakness of local governmental units; discourage local dwellers from raising resources to finance public services; at times destroy existing, effective locally based and managed infrastructure and service systems; perpetuate top-down authoritarian approaches to problems requiring a genuine partnership between urban-technical and poor and rural people; and, in general, to discourage participation in development process by poor and rural dwellers.

It is there inadequacies of and distortion caused by the centralisation which provide theoretical foundations for decentralisation. From early 1970s the emphasis shifted in its favour. Most of the internationally funded development programmes and projects began to provide for strengthening institutional framework at local levels and to insist on local governments' active participation for their success. A wide range of experimentations in decentralisation has by now provided the data for testing the basic hypotheses. Reviewing the literature further Wunsch concluded that "With all these diverse efforts in diverse countries, and good theoretical reasons to expect improved performance through decentralisation, it is discouraging and more than a little perplexing that the results so far have been rather dismal." Dennis Rondinelli and G. Shabbir Cheema, strong proponents of decentralisation in 1970s, observe with a note of disappointment that "Despite its vast scope, decentralisation has seldom, if even, lived up to expectations." Why is it so? Wunsch's thesis is that decentralisation as a concept has been very narrowly operationalised restricting its scope to identifying remedial measures through organisational level analysis.

The centralisation or decentralisation are not issues of restructuring the government organisation alone; there are a wide range of other factors, which have a decisive influence on their success or failure. Effective decentralisation requires a diversity of organisational forms, and fairly well dispersed powers, resources, and functions and opportunities in the society. This will perhaps approximate to Riggs's identification of many functionally specific rather than a few fused organisational structures within society. If decentralisation did not work during earlier period of post-Independence in India, it is because the conditions then were very different than today. No longer the state controls the commanding heights of the economy, nor does it seek to do so now. Political, economic, social powers and human resources (skills and abilities) are no longer concentrated in government or its machinery or in any one small segment of population. They are fairly well scattered within the society which is no longer passive. Decentralisation has a fair chance to succeed now than ever in the past provided we know what to expect from local governments and what we should not. Even if we clearly and carefully formulate our expectations; there would still be a lot to be done to create and foster conditions for their successful functioning.

Economic Reforms

During last over four decades, the central and state governments in India expanded their powers, functions, resources and bureaucracy. Lower level of governments became dependent on their successive higher level for transfer of resources for not only development work but also for their recurring expenditure. The manner in which the state functioned promoted dependency syndrome all around-among the different levels of government, public sector undertakings and citizens at large. Reluctance of the people to pay for the services they consume became epidemic. Private initiative in provision of services declined with state becoming more assertive. The government became the provider of employment rather than generating and expanding employment opportunities within the society. Over-extended bureaucracies of the centre, state and public sector organisations became the major consumer of government revenues. A very high-cost, heavy and complex organisation infrastructure of public administration has been erected to provide even for functions and services essentially local in character.

Flow of resources from above (higher levels of government) created upward looking accountability structures and reporting procedures. Performance in terms of expenditures and control, and not the impact of resources used, became the concern and the key to the profile of administration and the work-culture at all levels. Local governments became the worst victims. They began to be used as agents of central and state governments for implementing their financed and sponsored schemes. Their role in development process as institution of public participation, resource mobilisation and local accountability diminished. In fact, in many states, suffering from supersession, they were reduced to exist in laws and on records only. Faltering performance or politico-bureaucratic nexus of the state machinery ensured prolonged period of frequent supersession of local governments. Basic services increasingly became dependent on subsidisation in the absence of or due to poor local cost-recovery. With resource allocation from above and poor local resource mobilisation, the deterioration in the availability of these services has aggravated. How does the New Economic Policy (NEP) affect this scenario? The answer lies in the reasons necessitating the economic reforms.

Resource crunch and indebtedness of the central and state government building up from early 1980s have left very little scope for sustaining the continuation of this scenario of preponderance of dependency syndrome and subsidisation from above. In quite a few states, not necessarily poor or economically backward, the revenue expenditure in more than the revenue income. The government is thus under compulsion of its circumstances to reorient its role, redefine its functions and priorities and redesign its service delivery system with a view to making them more cost-effective and efficient. It does not mean lowering of responsiveness and less of people's participation in democratic institutions. On the contrary, it means more of responsible governance through these institutions. There is a silver lining for the local governments.

The success of the NEP depends upon the capacity of government at various levels to attract rather than direct and control private investment. Those cities which are better managed will in turn attract more investment than those which are not. The key to better management will be in the provision of a cost-effective and efficient system of providing physical infrastructure and urban basic services. Cities have the sources, and so also the rural areas of most parts of the country. What is lacking is the institutional capacity and political and administrative will to tap them. Scope for innovation and experimentation in resource mobilisation is enormous at the local level provided there is a will to do so, and the will cannot be injected from above without inviting the adverse consequences as noticed during the past few decades. State intervention will have to be highly selective, limited and purposeful in promoting the capacity of the local governments to provide local services. The State Finance Commissions envisaged under the Constitution

Amendments (73rd and 74th) will have a very positive role to play in this regard. But the primary task of local development and administration, urban or rural, will be of the local government; and it is they who have to make private investment in their areas attractive through better management, if they do not wish to remain behind in development under the economic reforms.

One of the key components of the New Economic Policy is that the government will provide safety net measures to ensure that those whom the market economy does not provide the benefits of development because of their disadvantaged position-such as poor, socially disadvantaged and physically handicapped—are not left behind. Most safety-net measures are in fact welfare services of state which are most appropriately and effectively provided either by the NGOs and CBOs (community based-organisations) or by the local governments. It is not without reasons, therefore, that under the Constitutional (65th) Amendment Bill in 1989 and later the Eleventh and Twelfth Schedule of the 73rd and 74th Amendment Act respectively incorporated these services as the responsibility of the local governments. Except for a few urban local governments and in a few states, by and large the local governments have neither the experience, nor tradition nor the capacity to provide these services. The alternative of providing them through the state field-level machinery, as discussed earlier, has proved to be very costly, ineffective and unresponsive. Therefore, one would envisage that the local governments will not be able to escape this responsibility for too long if the economic pressures continue on higher levels of government to devise more cost-effective, responsive and efficient system of delivery of services.

Defining Functional Responsibilities

Clarity in the definition of role and rational distribution of functional responsibilities between different tiers of government are prerequisites for allocation of powers and resources, in designing appropriate institutional framework and instrumen-talities for opening inter-and intra-governmental relations and public accountability structures. Most developing countries face difficulties in defining the role of local governments *vis-à-vis* higher levels of government.

Democratically elected local governments emerged during the British period on the Indian scene much earlier than the central (Union) and state (provincial) governments. In fact, they were known as local self-governments precisely because of the foreign rule. Promoting the concept of self-government at local level when there is already now self-government at the central and state levels is to continue the British legacy which has lost relevance. On the contrary, it tends to freeze the mind-set it had created, and which has not helped us to explore and evolve an appropriate institutional framework for local governance and administration in response to the growth in size of settlement and in the complexity of citizen's needs. We continue to expect, for instance, that the municipal government as designed during the late 19th century to manage urban areas, the population of which did not exceed 0.3 million, to be appropriate for mega cities with population exceeding five million. There are 10 states, each of which having a population of less than Bombay, Calcutta and Delhi, Compare the population size (in million) of states: J and K 7.7, H.P. 5.11, Tripura 1.21, Manipur 1.82, Meghalaya 1.76, Nagaland 1.21, Goa 1.16, Arunachal Pradesh 0.85, Mizoram 0.68, Sikkim 0.40, with Bombay 12.57, Calcutta 10.91, Madras 5.36, Hyderabad 4.28, Bangalore 4.08 in 1991. There are eight states with a population of less than three million but requiring a full-fledged state-level government. On the other hand there are 23 cities with a population of over one million but are considered fit to be managed by a government with no more than traditional municipal powers and functions. Finding them unfit to the task of managing the larger cities, the local governments have been ignored and bypassed rather than being enabled to evolve their role, powers, structure and functions appropriate to the requirements of good local governance and administration. It is not suggested that the mega-cities be given the status of a state. But what is required is to reshape and develop a more viable institutional framework for local governments and administration beyond the realm of limited municipal or maintenance functions. Since it would involve recasting functional responsibilities of the two tiers, the existing state-local government relations will undergo major transformation. Whether this recasting of functional responsibilities should be done through constitutional amendment or through amendment of the state legislation would require careful consideration of their implications.

The Constitution of India ensured decentralised system of governance of the country by adopting a federal structure and laying down a clear demarcation of functions, powers and resources between the Union and the states. The Founding Fathers after a considerable debate and discussion laid down specific provisions (Articles) dealing with various aspects of Union-state relations. Local governments did not fit in the constitutional scheme of division of responsibilities in the governance of the country, even though it was recognised that state policy should endeavour to promote them. As a subject, local government appears as item No. 5 of the State List of the Seventh Schedule. It has thus been left to the state governments to define their role and give shape to their structure, powers and functions. While during the earlier stages of our planned development, the role of central and state governments was crucial, we are now almost at a stage where further progress will critically depend upon the role and performance of local governments.

So long as local government appears in the State List, it would mean that the primary responsibility for performing local functions and providing local services constitutionally vests with the state governments, and the local governments essentially perform agency functions, *i.e.,* discharging this responsibility of state governments as their agent. Thus, state governments would continue to make their budgetary allocations and be accountable to the state legislature in respect of local governments who are otherwise sought to be made accountable to local people. It is thus accountability—one of the state's to its legislature in respect of local governments and the other of the local governments to its electorate—which shape the state-local government relations. Since an Indian state is the constitutionally recognised unit of sovereignty, its accountability to legislature would always override the accountability of local governments to their electorate as established through its statute. However, the states can develop healthy traditions of restraint on themselves for promoting greater autonomy in the functioning of local governments, and for ensuring their accountability to local people. By and large the trends in the state-local government relations do not appear to be developing these healthy traditions. To a lesser degree in Gujarat, Maharashtra and West Bengal but to a greater extent in other states, state supervision and controls over local governments have become more vigorous and extensive with a vast machinery (organisation) and bureaucracy exercising these functions. Greater dependency of local governments on state transfers than on local resources mobilisation has been one of the major reasons responsible for this trend. Since the compulsion on the local governments to mobilize local resources will inevitably grow under the economic reforms. The entire basic of state-local government relations will undergo substantial change. Unless there is a clear-cut national policy of allocating elastic sources of revenue and greater autonomy given to local governments in mobilising local resources, the tensions in state-local government relations are bound to build up. Moreover, after having given a power of taxation to local government, the state governments shall have to exercise restraint in depriving it (local government) of its yield. For instance, after having given them the power to impose property tax, the rent control legislation adversely affecting its yield would not be defendable. Nor will the exemption from property tax given by the state be justifiable. Similarly the traditional local taxes, such as entertainment tax, vehicle tax, etc., should revert to the local government. As the responsibilities of local government grow, one would have to think of giving them access to newer areas of taxation including local income-tax. Since the restraint on the part of the state governments is not encroaching upon the field of local taxation has been less evident, a stage will come in the state-local government relations when it would be considered most appropriate to seek clear delineation of powers and functions of local government under the Constitution itself. In that case, local governments as a subject in the State List may have to disappear, and then our entire approach to state-local government relations will have to be recast to meet the challenges of the future.

For over four decades, decentralisation and local governments (panchayati raj institutions) have been the theme of various commissions, committees and task forces set up by government –central and state—and they all have been recommending decentralisation below the level of state as vital necessity for development, and local governments a key to the scheme of decentralisation. And yet, the trend has been in the reverse direction. Partly the problem lies in the lack of consensus on what should be local government's functional responsibilities. The prescription depended upon their orientation, *i.e.,* whether it was political (participatory), planning or administrative. Each of these orientations, however, was well-articulated in terms of achieving development goals. In the process, it has not been possible to clearly delineate functional responsibilities appropriate to local government—rural and urban. Thus, the higher levels of governments in India are too often found to perform functions and provide services which are essentially local in character. On the other extreme, there is also a strong tendency to articulate and propagate the role of local governments which is incompatible with its level, and thus ill-suited to the functions and powers they are formally allocated.

How do we conceive the role of local government? It we define its role to be the provider of local services which include planning, programming of services, design of projects and their execution and developing an efficient and effective local services delivery system, we will begin to identify what attributes it should have in being most effective. To be effective, it must be responsive to local needs and priorities. To be responsive, its institutional structure has to be such that it ensures local accountability, which in turn would require local people to pay for its functions and services. "No taxation with representation" would require the institutional design to be democratically elected and representative character. Its development potential is incidental and is linked to its being a democratic and thus, a participatory institution designed to meet those needs of citizens which they individually cannot provide for themselves or which, if unmet, would endanger public health, safety and well-being. The scope of empowerment does not go beyond considering local people as collectivity and not as fragments, in deciding the health of service delivery system including its financing. All citizens living in a local government area are at par without any discrimination in the provision of services and in the participatory processes in decision-making and in financing of the institution which delivers them. For disadvantaged groups, it is the provision of social welfare services which get targeted on to their specific needs. That is how a system of local government has evolved primarily around its role, functions and tasks of providing local services in developed countries. Transplanted elsewhere, local governments have been loaded with multifarious national and development goals for some of which they can never acquire institutional capacity, instrumentalities and resources. On the contrary, the pursuit of these goals through local government often becomes dysfunctional to their basic tasks and create serious strains in inter-governmental relations, often leading to the reversal of decentralisation policies.

Empowerment

Consider such propagated virtues of local government reforms as "power to the people", development through empowerment of disadvantaged groups for their social, economic and cultural advancement," and finally "local government as a means of satisfying local aspirations and identities.' Democracy itself ensures empowerment of people, and empowerment of various groups/ segments of society takes place through the political processes which enable democratic institutions to function. How far are these rhetoric used in diverting attention from the basic institutional and administrative reforms at higher levels of government which have more significant functions, powers and resources? If at these levels, democratically elected and representative form of government does not ensure empowerment of people, local governments are least likely to do so despite strong rhetorical persuasion of people to believe in its possibility. In highly fragmented societies the use of such rhetoric arouses, at the local levels, feelings and prejudices against better judgment to act for the common good of all the citizens. In a recent article, C.P. Bhambhri observed that even though Harold J. Laski and Herbert Morrison in their classics on parliamentary government in England clearly maintained that role of elections and parliament was primarily to have a government and also an opposition to overview governance in the country, and even though 'p'olitics in society is expected to perform the role of promoting public good by even curbing and crushing some sectional demands which are not for the development of the whole society,' the electoral politics in India has created a different scenario.

He feels that sectionalised social constituencies will accelerate social conflicts when those who depend on their support govern on the basis of sectional interests. The consequences of existing electoral politics are observed thus: . . . Politics-related conflicts in rural India have increased because political power has assumed greater significance... Rural India becomes extremely volatile during elections and power assertions are witnessed in the form of rigging of elections, capturing booths and terrorising of the voters and even physical liquidation of aggressive political opponents.

Empowerment processes at higher levels of government being remote and distant have lesser potential to cause disruptions in economic and social life, and to foster separatism and inflict damage to the national identity and integration. But if our existing approaches to empowerment lead to political parochialism and particularistic orientation in decision-making and produce such consequences as Bhambhri observes, extension of the same approach to local governments will be devastating. They work in closed proximity and in full view of local citizens, and as such, empowerment would lead to paralysis of their functioning. Local governments are least equipped to control social and political tensions, and manage conflicts among disparate identities and bring them to the mainstream of national life.

Moreover, success of empowerment depends upon the enlargement of the scope and opportunities of social and economic development and sharp targeting on a small segment, and not on the majority of population broken into various small segments for coverage. Even at the state level, the policies of affirmative actions have severely restricted employment and educational opportunities to their sons of soil and belonging to their own lists of caste, ethnic or linguistic configurations. They have directly or indirectly curtailed the freedom to work and settle down anywhere in India without let or hindrance. Recently, the government of Himachal Pradesh by law has sought to debar citizens of India from buying any land/ property, even for a dwelling unit, in rural or urban areas of the entire state, and yet it wants to attract investment for economic development. Such policies which restrict population mobility not only obstruct national integration but also in the long run limit expansion of development and employment opportunities, which in turn breeds unemployment, and canalisation of frustration and alienation into separatism. Trends in India are visible for reflection. Today, the nation is spending far more on forces (armed, para-military and a variety of police outfits) for political system maintenance. Most gallantry awards to armed forces during last couple of years have been given for the heroic acts against their own citizens gone astray. Similar policies and prescriptions of empowerment at the local government levels can further atomise the society, unless, of course, we give no powers to local governments to follow affirmative action policies and no scope for fostering particularistic political aspirations. In that case, empowerment means nothing more than ensuring that the local governments operate as democratically elected institutions for performing functions and providing services local in character mainly with local resources.

Jurisdictional Viability

Rational allocation of functional responsibilities and quantum of autonomy to local governments also depend upon the character and size of their jurisdiction. In a few developing countries, a large number of functions have been devolved on local governments with the district as their basic unit, and rural and urban areas being their decentralised sub-units. In India rural-urban dichotomy has been retained with limited range of functions to local governments and providing a rationale for district administration as an extension of state machinery in providing many of the local services. There is also an apparent conflict between the needed jurisdiction for effective participation and for effective planning. Its objective is to seek greater participation of people in development programmes and services, larger devolution of functions and powers should take in favour of the lowest (in hierarchy, nearest to the people) unit of local government. But that is not the level at which planning organisational, technical and professional inputs become viable; they require a larger jurisdiction to be effective. It is, therefore, not without reason that planning—district (rural) or urban –has remained largely insulated from local political institutions and processes. Including socio-economic and spatial planning as a local government function is a recent development which has produced a lot of uncertainty among the town planners and officials of district administration. If sincerely, vigorously and successfully pursued, this development alone has the potential to shaking the entire Indian administrative system which rests on the district administration as its foundation. A strong district administration as the field machinery of state government cannot coexist with a system of strong local governments.

A variety of reasons can be held responsible for resorting to the Constitutional (73rd and 74th) Amendment Acts of 1992 according recognition to the role and responsibilities of local government in the governance and development of the country. While the objectives of these constitutional reforms were articulated in a broad context of diverse and strong needs, it may be mentioned that their actual scope and contents have limited relationship with the objectives. Some of the important reasons are evident from the discussion on the need for decentralisation, economic reforms, redistribution of functional responsibilities among the different tiers of government in the context of the changing social, economic and political scenario. The main focus here will be to examine whether these constitutional reforms are being used as a via media for the most needed administrative reforms or to what extent have they the potential to inject a powerful political force to demand, at a later stage, basic administrative reforms in the country.

During the post-independence era, the state had to assume a very active role in the development process, and the only well-organised institution within the society which could be used for development tasks was the bureaucracy. The pursuit of planned development and access to international development aid made the central government very powerful. But since the implementation of development policies and programmes lay within the functional jurisdiction of the states (being matters in the State List), they could not escape from the impact. Almost every centrally sponsored scheme required an agency to be set up at the state or local level for its implementation. Not only the central but also the state administrative machinery went through an era of massive expansion. The large well-organised bureaucracy became powerful to protect and promote its own carrier interests. Any political party will find it difficult to come to power with an agenda of administrative reforms. The fate of the recommendations of the Administrative Reforms Commission and that of the state governments which followed the policy of "no work, no pay" for the strike period of the government employees is well known. Despite recommendations of the ARC to the contrary, promotion has been demanded as an employee's right, and has more or less been recognised by the government. Its impact on the administrative machinery has been massive. It came to be recognised during the early 1980s that the growth of bureaucracy has become virtually independent of the expansion of the functions of the state. In many states, the administrative machinery has virtually exploded in size without having a positive impact on the performance of the state's functions or on delivery of services to the citizens. For one post of secretary to government in education responsible for policy formulation and other functions at the secretariat level, today one finds 5-6 secretaries—secretary (primary Education), secretary (secondary education), secretary (higher education), secretary (technical education), secretary (medical education), secretary (adult education), etc. There are ministers in-charge of portfolios as small as "savings", "building construction" separate from Public Works or Buildings and Roads. Even at the policy levels, excessive fragmentation of the administration has continued to occur in almost all the departments, more to provide for promotion avenues to the civil servants than in response to the expansion in the role of the government and quantum of work. Effects of these trends at the district levels have been devastating. Extended hierarchies and atomisation of a function or of highly inter-dependent functions each with organisationally demarcated boundaries, resources and patronage not only have made coordination more difficult but also, with top heavy superstructure and weak supervision and control, they have caused virtual collapse of the field administration in many states. Local governments were bypassed, and they had only notional existence.

In rural areas, the executive machinery of local government belonged to district administration. In urban areas, instead of evolving viable local institutions for urban development and management, the state government, mostly induced by centrally-sponsored schemes, resorted to setting up special purpose or functional bodies or powerful city development authorities. High cost, extremely complex, heavily bureaucratised system of development administration so evolved at the cutting-edge level could be least responsive and sensitive to local people's needs and priorities.

One may vividly recall Rajiv Gandhi's government initiating a series of district-level seminars on responsive administration. Increasingly it was being recognized through these diagnostic exercises that low level of performance and achievement-orientation was on account of poor system of accountability at various levels, but more so at local levels. Technology missions were set up as alternative to introducing basic administrative reforms, and even these were strongly resisted in their working by the departmental bureaucracies. It was under these circumstances that the government of Rajiv Gandhi came up with Constitution (64th & 65th) Amendment Bills of 1989 which sought to substantially alter the system of governance and administration at the district level and below. It allocated all functions and services local in character to local governments.

The sweeping ambit of the 64th and 65th Amendment Bills becomes apparent when one looks at their Eleventh and Twelfth

Schedules respectively. They expanded powers, functions and services of local governments to cover those responsibilities many of which had remained with the state governments and which account for a substantial proportion of state government employment and political influence. The Twelfth Schedule included a wide range of responsibilities as is evident from Annexure 1. Preparation of plans for economic and social development, town planning, social welfare services, women and child development, urban housing, city transport, education (primary, secondary, technical and vocational), hospitals and primary health centres, public distribution system, prevention of food adulteration, promotion of industrial and commercial estates, urban poverty alleviation in addition to the traditional municipal obligatory functions were included in the Schedule. The Bill could not be passed by Parliament. Reasons were obvious. Such vast devolution of functions and services in favour of local government implied that those performing them would have to be shifted to and made an integral part of local governments or come under their control. Moreover, the decentralization envisaged under the Bill was incompatible with strong district administration, particularly when power or supersession was made virtually ineffective. These changes were seen as weakening the state-level political leadership and bureaucracy.

Constitutional Amendments

It is not intended here to give the details of the Constitution (73rd and 74th) amendment Acts of 1992. Only those aspects which are significant and require critical scrutiny for understanding the immediate impact on and the long-term consequences for the development of local governments will be discussed. A comparative analysis of the range and type of functions allocated to rural and urban local governments is given to reveal the severe constraints on operationalising decentralisation within the framework of existing state political and administrative machinery.

The most significant contribution of these Constitutional Amendments (CAs) is that they make it mandatory to have democratically elected local governments, restrict the powers of supersession and ensure their security of tenure for five years. President's rule can be imposed on a state without giving a reasonable opportunity of being heard before such imposition. But not in the case of urban local governments. State governments are under constitutional duty (Art. 243 V) to give such an opportunity before dissolution of an urban local government. A new dimension has thus been incorporated in the Constitution for shaping inter-governmental relations in future. Strangely there is no similar constitutional obligation to be observed in case of dissolution of rural local governments. It is perhaps due to the assumption that they would continue to be totally dependent on state governments for financial resources and executive administration, and as such, they would be under the vigorous state supervision and control.

Moreover, no longer will it be possible for the state politicians or government officials—state or local—to wash away the role of elected representative working at the local level. The entire administrative ethos and managerial skills cultivated and fostered by an upward-looking accountability will become irrelevant for success in managing the local services and affairs. Over a period of time, the field administration of the state government will have to undergo radical transformation.

Making it mandatory for each state to have Finance Commission and Election Commission would ensure that the political and financial health of the local bodies is not left to be decided in an ad-hoc, arbitrary and whimsical manner. One would expect that the Finance Commission while assessing the requirements of the local bodies will have little choice but to adopt scientific basis in determining norms and standards of services, cost per unit of providing the services, etc. In the process, they would inject considerable degree of financial discipline, cost consciousness and a compulsion for more transparency and resource mobilisation at the local levels. Scope for research in local government would significantly expand and would in fact be used, if found relevant.

By requiring the states to set up panchayats at the village, intermediate and district levels for rural areas, and *nagar panchayats*, municipalities and municipal corporations, a certain level of uniformity at the level of third tier of government is being sought by the CAs. However, each type of urban local government has exclusive jurisdiction even though the range of functions as listed in the Twelfth Schedule is the same for each. But in case of rural areas, there is overlapping of jurisdiction with each level assigned the same type of responsibilities as mentioned in the Eleventh Schedule. In other words, while no distinction in functional responsibilities is maintained between the panchayat at gram sabha, or intermediate or district levels, a village itself has three distinct types of local government responsible for providing the same type of services since each one of them has the same set of responsibilities. There is no attempt either in the CAs or in the amendments to the local government legislation to give effect to the CAs, to differentiate the level of responsibilities according to organisational and financial viability which would vary very substantially among the three levels of panchayats. Since each panchayat level technically is independent of the other in terms of electorate constituents and functional responsibilities, the linkage will have to be provided by their dependency on the state and its field administration. It is therefore the state government which will determine administratively the hierarchy of functions and their activities, and allocate them to the different levels. Without the fear of being superseded, when the elected representatives will become more assertive, the inter-governmental relations and relationship among the three different tiers of panchayati raj institutions will experience greater tensions. Moreover, the major problems will emerge in determining the basis of distribution of resources by the State Finance Commission in favour of each level of panchayats.

There has never been any constitutional basis of the planning as a function or as an organisational machinery of government at the centre or state levels despite the fact that Five Year Plans have been formulated and implemented ever since 1951. It has always been considered as a function of the executive. The CAs create a planning machinery for the first time, and that too not at the centre or state level, but at the district level. The local governments are required to prepare plans for economic development and social justice (whatever it may mean). It is mandatory for each state to establish District Planning Committee in every district to consolidate the plan prepared by panchayats and municipalities, and to prepare a draft development plan for the district as a whole. In metropolitan areas a Metropolitan Planning Committee is to perform this task. Spatial planning has been included as one of the responsibilities of the urban local government. So far there has never been any linkage between urban planning, which was essentially physical planning, and the district planning, which was mostly the aggregation of different sectoral allocations/estimates. The sectoral planning ensured the linkage between the resources and the activities necessary for planning and execution of development programmes and projects. Since the resources were not local but that of the state government, the planning priorities and sectoral allocations of the state had the decisive force. If the same pattern of resource distribution continues, the draft development plans will have only symbolic value. If, on the other hand, the State Finance Commissions do succeed in transferring adequate resources to local governments for them to become active in local planning, and execution of development programmes and projects, the requirement from the District Planning Committees to submit their draft development plans to the state government would become illogical.

It is assumed that a District Planning Committee being a non-elected body, unlike the panchayats or municipal governments within a district, who would submit to it their draft plans for consolidation, will act as a specialist organisation like the Planning Commission at the national level in the preparation of the draft district development plan. Key decision-making in local planning thus will continue to be with a non-representative and non-participatory body.

A lot of confusion regarding the role and functions of the state town and country planning department has emerged after having allocated planning to local governments and the District or Metropolitan Planning Committee under the CAs. It is being asked as to why should there be a town planning department or a city development authority or an improvement trust, if the CA envisage under the Twelfth Schedule socio-economic as well as town planning to be the responsibility of urban local governments. The confusion exists primarily because of two reasons: (a) historical context of insulating local planning from the political processes and representative institutions of people's participation, *i.e.,* the local governments; (b) failure to maintain the distinction between planning as a process and as a function. As a function, it is technical and therefore it requires expertise and an organisation to perform it. This is what the city development authorities or state town and country planning department have been doing in the shape of preparation of master plans. But being devoid of local participatory processes which could create legitimacy and acceptance by the local people, their implementation suffered. What the CAs do is not to take away the function of planning from the state's department of town and country planning or from the city development authority, but to inject a process by which these plans should be adopted by local governments and reflect the support of the local people. The state technical department can still prepare plans, but on behalf of the local government rather than of their own accord or on behalf of the state government. If local planning is to be linked with local resource mobilisation, this is a step in the right direction. Once this distinction between the two, *i.e.,* planning process and the function, is understood and appropriately operationalised, status and effectiveness of local planning will improve.

Provisions relating to empowerment, however, are quite controversial. As discussed, local government, if ensured of being democratically elected, would no doubt "empower" the local people in deciding the services they need and their distributional aspects. But sectional empowerment assumes that the government machinery must be used for advancing particularistic interests, and public service ethics of impartiality and objectivity in the conduct of administration are less relevant. If so, administrative system is less likely to survive the disintegrative impact of particularistic empowerment at the local level.

The CAs make it mandatory that seats to be filled by direct

elections to every local government should be reserved for candidates belonging to SCs/STs in proportion to their population within their respective jurisdiction, and not less than one-third seats should be reserved for women. While the 73rd CA lays down the reservation for SCs/STs for the office of chairman of panchayats at different levels, their number being in proportion to the total number of such offices in panchayats, and in case of women, not less than one-third of offices to be reserved for them, there is no similar requirement under the 74th CA. The CA further lays down that the reserved offices are to be allotted by rotation to different panchayats at each level. Tamil Nadu has gone ahead with the similar reservations of offices in case of *nagar panchayats* and municipalities. In many places, a situation has arisen where the political party having even two-thirds majority in the council could not have its representative as the chairman, the office being council could not have its representative as the chairman, the office being reserved for a specified category. This has occurred when their candidates belonging to these categories lose election despite overwhelming majority in the council. This provision dealing with reservation of offices has been challenged in the court on the ground that in situations like the above, reservation amounts to the denial of popular mandate, and therefore is contrary to the democratic system of governance in the country, and as such it alters the basic structure of the Constitution.

One interesting aspect which has escaped the attention of the constitutional experts is that for the first time, women have been given reservation without any time limit. While the reservation for SCs/STs/OBCs is time-bound and will cease within local governments on the expiry of the period specified in Art. 334, there is no such limitation on reservation of one-third of total number of seats for women (Art. 243T (3). One wonders whether it is really necessary to tamper with the Constitution to accommodate political agenda and manifesto for electoral consideration of today and which may not be relevant after a few years to become a permanent feature of the Constitution. Moreover could not the same objective, if the political parties were indeed serious about it, be achieved by amending the party constitutions to provide for 30 or 50 per cent of tickets for women as candidates for elections. Sweden has more than 50 per cent of elected representatives as women at various levels of governance, but no provision of reservation under the Constitution.

Socio-economic upliftment of women and other disadvantaged sections of population is no doubt the most necessary and an urgent requirement of development. But five decades of our experience of securing it through passing legislation reveals the limited success of this approach. On the contrary the cosmetic actions of the state have impaired the society's operational capacity to initiate reform movement for which India has a long history and strong tradition. The rhetoric of empowerment provides another alibi to the political masters and prevents the emergence of leadership for social reform movements. If mushroom growth of legislation has made India a "highly regulated" but "least governed" society, the particularistic empowerment in financially, administratively and functionally weak government, particularly at the local levels, is likely to create hostile fragmentations rather than harmonious integration.

As mentioned earlier, the types of functions which have been included in the Eleventh and Twelfth Schedules of 73rd and 74th Amendment Acts respectively reveal the extent of acceptability of decentralisation in favour of local government. A comparative picture of the functions and responsibilities entrusted to the rural and urban local governments along with the list of the functions which the CA Bill of 1989 had envisaged for urban local government is given in Annexure I. It will be seen that while rural local governments have been entrusted with a wide range of responsibilities which include the provision of primary, secondary and even technical, vocational, adult and non-formal education; health including hospitals, health centers, dispensaries; women and child development and family welfare; housing; public distribution system; electricity distribution; promotion of small-scale industries, etc., these functions, though included under the 65th amendment Bill for urban local governments, have been excluded from the Twelfth Schedule of 74th Amendment Act. Why is it so? Are rural local governments jurisdictionally, demogra-phically, financially, organisationally or administratively more viable to provide these services than urban local governments? The answer is no. They depend entirely on the state's bureaucracy, resources and administrative machinery at field level to carry out these functions where as the urban local governments are, in these matters, fairly autonomous and can tap the local resources for supporting these services. To preserve the state's hold on these services which are basically local in character, they are excluded from the responsibilities of the urban local governments under the Twelfth Schedule, but included for rural local government under the Eleventh Schedule of the 73rd Amendment Act. Apparently, so long as the state government provides financial resources and controls administrative machinery and personnel to carry out these functions, the decentralisation in favour of local government will remain a myth.

There is another dimension which has not yet attracted much attention and analytical review. Even though it is obligatory, the provision that MPs and MLAs may be given representation in a municipality (Art. 243 R (2)) defies the logic of differentiation in the functions of different levels of government and constituency accountability. MPs or MLAs are not elected for local services and affairs. There will be considerable diffusion in the demarcation of accountability. Coupled with the recent trend of the central government to allocate to each MP to spend Rs. 1 crore in his constituency, mostly on works which are the responsibility of local government, and the state governments' similar scheme for MLAs, and further, making ministers incharge of specific districts, the impact of such provisions on the development of local government could hardly be in alignment with the objectives of reforms introduced under the Constitutional Amendments. If the central government has the resources for allocating Rs. 700-900 crores under the MPs Constituency Fund and state governments for their MLAs for spending on essentially local government works, the best test of their commitment to local governments would lie in transferring these to the financially starved local government bodies.

Decentralisation has been pursued more as an ideology of development than as a theory which examines and relates itself to conditions of its success and failure. The theory of decentralisation needs to develop beyond the narrow parameters of organisational-level analysis. Local government represents one level and type of institution in operationalising decentralisation. In the development process, a variety of institutions are necessary for effective dispersal of powers within society. Creation or addition of statutory authorities at various levels under the direct or indirect control of government do not necessarily create the conditions of success for decentralisation, nor do they cause dispersal of power in society. The Constitutional Amendments of 1992 in favour of local governments *ipso facto* would not ensure their effectiveness.

In recent years, "empowerment" has become a password for political, social and intellectual acceptability. Yet, very little is known about how far, it, as a concept and as an approach, can capture the realities and achieve the objectives for which it is used. Rhetorics have the tendency of numbing our sensitivity, spirit of inquiry and intellectual vigour necessary for searching better and alternative ways of accomplishing the objectives. Empowerment of people and "empowerment" of the disadvantaged sections are the acclaimed advantages of the Constitutional Amendments (73rd and 74th) of 1992. We have not yet begun to capture and document the effects and limitation of empowerment by using the government machinery for social engineering. Constitutional amendments may further freeze our spirit of inquiry and intellectual capacity for years to critically examine the existing approach and search for more effective, harmonious and sustainable methods of "empowerment" or upliftment of socially and economically disadvantaged groups. Paradoxically, these reforms came less by choice but more through compulsions arising out of the declining availability of resources at the centre and state government levels and their growing indebtedness. Local areas have the resources but local governments rarely tap them, dependent as they have been made on transfers from higher level of governments.

Economic reforms will make it necessary to redefine the role of the state and to rationalise the distribution of responsibilities between state and local governments. Services and functions essentially local in character are best performed by the local government. Huge bureaucratic machinery which the state governments have created to perform these functions or extend these services to citizens have proved to be inefficient, unresponsive and extremely costly. This machinery and local government can hardly coexist in the field; one of them shall have to wither away. If our service delivery system is to become more accountable and local resource-based, the chances are that local governments, after the CAs, will assert and demand major structural changes in the field of administration (district administration particularly). Own would also expect that during the next 20-25 years of working of local governments under the CAs of 1992, it will generate strong momentum in favour of a review of distribution of functions between Centre, state and local governments. Thus, recent developments in local government institutions in India are likely to have far-reaching effects on the governance of the country.

In spite of being rice in terms of natural resources and manpower, India is ranked among the economically backward countries of the world. The reason for this should be traced in her political subjugation and economic exploitation by the British colonial power. Apart from this, it should also be noted that their natural resources have not yet been fully exploited and that her economy is still predominantly agricultural. About half of this country's national income is derived from agriculture and some allied activities which absorb nearly three-fourth of this working force. But the matter of satisfaction is that the natural resources of the country are capable of greater utilisation and, more important than this, since independence the aim has been to diversify the economy of the country by accelerating the pace of industrial development, increase agricultural productivity, and achieve all-round progress through the machinery of planning.

India has adopted the pattern of mixed economy. The people have the right to private property. But the enjoyment and exercise of this right may be restricted or regulated by the state in the public interests. As such, we have a 'private sector' of economy that is in the hands of the individuals. On the other hand, there is the public sector that may be designated as the 'state sector.'

Article 39 of the directive Principle of State policy enjoins that 'the ownership and control of the material resources of the community are so distributed as best to subserve the common good and that the operation of the economic system does not result in the concentration of wealth and means of production to the common determinant." The Indian leaders well realised that a developing country like ours had no alternative to entering the field of industrial and commercial enterprise if it wished to increase its productivity and the general standard of living. Thus, the vast expansion of the public sector has not come out fortuitously, it is the result of planned development and the adaptation of the particular social and economic philosophy. This economic argument "aims at the achievement of a rapid growth of the economic infrastructure which, at the same time, would under private sector in its development.

NOTES AND REFERENCES

1. R.B. Jain: *Contemporary Issues in Indian Administration,* p. 210

2. James S. Wunch, "Institutional Analysis and Decentralisation: Developing an Analytical Framework for Effective Third World Administrative Reforms," *Public Administration and Development*, Vol. II, pp. 431-32.

3. Chrles Bettelheim: *India Independent,* p. 156.

4. Dennis A. Rondinelli and G. Shabbir Cheema, *Decentralisation in Developing Countries: A Review of Recent Experience* (Washington D.C.: The World Banks, 1984), p. 27.

5. C.P. Bhambhri, "Dangers of Polarisation", *The Hindustan Times*, July 16, 1995, p. 13.

6. Sukhomoy Chakravarty: "Policy Making in Mixed Economy—the Indian Case" in P.R. Brahmanand and V.R. Panchmukhi (ed.): *The Development Process of the Indian Economy*, p. 733.

7

Constitutional Developments in Indian Administration

Indian civilisation is very old. In most ancient times Indians could make marvellous researches in the fields of science, mathematics, astrology, astronomy, literature, philosophy, architecture, engineering, fine arts, medicine etc. The rishis (seers) produced the Vedas and the Upanishadas. Different schools of philosophy like Nyaya, Samkhya and Vaisheshek came into being. We may refer to the immortal contributions of Gautama, Kapila, Kanada, Gemini, Aryabhata, bhaskara, Panini, Charaka, Dganvantri, Vamiki, Vyas, etc. in this connection. The great seers wanted to discover and explain the secrets behind all the wonders; they kept on searching and inquiring till they felt that they had arrived at the truth. In occurs of time, different functions created a caste system having four main folds—the Brahimns or the worshippers, the Kshattriyas or the warrirors (defenders), the Vaishyas or the traders, and the Sudras or the social servants. This division was based on the *guna* (quality) and *karma* (action) which automatically implied the principle of merit and specialisation. In course of time, the caste system became very rigid and its membership flowed from the fact of birth in a particular caste.

Growth of the British Empire in India, which ultimately extended from the Himalayas to Cape Comorin and from the Hindukush to

Burma, the development of the Empire's manifold administrative systems was also a gradual process. The genesis of some of the systems can be traced back to the earliest days of British contact with India, when the concept of an Indian empire was not even a remote dream. Englishmen, coming to India for trade and commerce, were required to conduct their affairs under a system of law. With that as the starting-point, the evolution of an imperial administration was a long and complicated affair. The Charter of Privileges which a number of Englishmen received from the British Crown on that memorable day of 31st December 1600 marked the origin of a power for a particular purpose.

The purpose was trade, but the power was to be enjoyed in a far away country of which little was known to the Crown or its ministers. The Charter gave the traders legal recognition as well as an opportunity to organise themselves into a body-politic. They styled themselves 'The Governor and Company of Merchants of London, trading to the East Indies.' The organisation, so legitimised, was small and simple, but had the scope to evolve in its own methods to meet the needs of changing times and situations. The Company of Merchants later became famous as the East India Company. Even within Indian horizons, their adventures opened up vast prospects. The earliest English settlements in India were small 'factories', as the settlers were mere traders. In a strictly legal sense, the factories were in the territory of the Mughal Emperor and hence the latter was the *de jure* master of the foreigners. It was thus, under Indian authority, that the factory at Surat was established in 1613, that at Fort St. George (Madras) in 1640, and that at Fort William in Bengal in 1698, and began their activities. It was only the island of Bombay which became an outright British possession. Charles II of England had been given the island by the King of Portugal in 1661 as part of the dowry of the Princess Infanta Catherine and in 1669 Charles transferred the island to the Company. However, whatever the external control over the factories or possessions, each place where Englishmen settled to conduct their business assumed the nature of a 'settlement.' Such centres required internal administration; and a President and a Board generally constituted the internal authority in each settlement.

The small factories were modest beginnings indeed, but their potentiality for growth already lay in contemporary historical conditions. Smaller factories grew up at near and far places under the control of the main factories. The populations of the main factories also began to grow. It was in the process of such developments that the term 'Presidency Town' was applied to the main factories for the simple reason that at these centres lived the Presidents who from there managed the affairs of the territories under their respective jurisdictions. The meaning of the word Presidency was ultimately stretched to cover British territory or the territorial demarcation or even the general power. But that apart, from the beginning the real significance of the word lay in its application to the three main centres of the British in India, namely, Bengal, Bombay and Madras. When the Company assumed its vigorous political role and entered upon a career of conquest, the Presidencies of Bengal, Bombay and Madras began to expand in size with newly acquired territories placed within their respective spheres. In fact, it was from the presidency centres that conquests and annexations were planned and executed. Simultaneously with the expansion of the presidency centres into huge political territories, there evolved and developed an administrative machinery to cope with the problems of government. Before these administrative experiments and innovations are discussed, it is necessary to refer to the growth of the main territorial divisions which ultimately constituted the British Indian Empire.

Early Political Divisions

Throughout the seventeenth century, the British in India confined themselves mainly to commercial activities. Rivalry with other European traders was limited to diplomatic intrigues and frantic efforts to gain the favour of Indian rulers. It was only by the middle of the eighteenth century that commercial ambitions began to yield place to political adventures. The Mughal Empire was disintegrating. India, after the death of Aurangzeb in 1707, did not possess an effective central government. On the ruins of the Mughal Empire, a number of independent principalities sprang up. The Marathas, Sikhs, Rajputs, Rohillas, Jats, Bundelas, as well as the ambitious viceroys of the shadowy Mughal emperors, began to carve out territories for themselves. The Marathas, being the most powerful, could have established a Hindu empire had not internal dissension ruined their prospects right at the beginning. Added to this, the havoc which their armies created all over the country alienated even Hindus from the Maratha ambition. The dissensions and lack of foresight among the other powers were no less than among the Marathas. Their military systems were antiquated. In an atmosphere of decay and degeneration, they competed among themselves to hasten their own annihilation, exhausting their power in internal feuds completely blind to the growing power of the foreigners.

India's misfortune was Europe's opportunity. The French, followed by the English, were quick to understand the real condition of India. Duplexin's dream of a French empire in India was a logical result of India's political condition. He could have succeeded had there been no Englishmen to challenge his ambition. The English, envious of other Europeans, became alert against French political designs. The sequence of events, therefore, brought about the inevitable contests—the Anglo-French Wars. At the end of the struggle, with the French defeated, the British turned to defeat the Indian powers. The making of the British Empire began.

Through conquest and acquisition the British began to add extensive territories to their presidency centres and the main territorial divisions developed into the Presidencies of Bengal, Madras and Bombay. The Battle of Plassey which marks the beginning of the British Empire in India was fought in Bengal in 1757. No less significant was the grant to the British of the Diwani by the titular Mughal Emperor in 1765, which brought Bengal, Bihar and part of Orissa under British rule. The Madras Presidency began to grow with conquests from Haidar Ali and Tipu Sultan's kingdom of Mysore, and with territories conquered from the Nawab of the Carnatic. Similarly, the Bombay Presidency began to grow at the cost of the Maratha powers. For a number of years the situation was so fluid that the precise boundaries of the three presidencies could not be demarcated. Conquest followed conquest and annexations continued in successive phases. Throughout the nineteenth century the presidencies as well as other political divisions of British India continued to take shape. Additions and alterations continued almost till the end of the British rule. A brief account of the growth of the main territorial divisions of British India is given below.

Main Territorial Divisions

The Presidency of Bengal. The Battle of Plassey in 1757 marks the beginning of the real occupation of Bengal. The grant of the Diwani in 1765 legalised the conquest and extended its area under the name of Bengal, Bihar and Orissa (though the Orissa of the Diwani was only a small part of Orissa proper beyond the river Subarnarekha towards Bengal). In 1775, Benares was added. By 1801-3, territories then described as the North-west, surrendered by the Nawab of Oudh, were further added. They included Allahabad, Fatehpur, Kanpur, portions of Azamgarh, Gorakhpur, Bareilly, Moradabad, Bijnor, Badaon and Shahjahanpur. From the Marathas, in the 'north-west' area, the British conquered Etawa, Mainpuri, Aligarh, Bulandshahr, Meerut, Muzaffarnagar, Saharanpur, Agra, Mathura, Delhi, and a few more places. While the Presidency thus extended beyond Delhi, and a few more places. While the Presidency thus extended beyond Delhi, it also began to expand on the coastal belt. In 1805, the territories of coastal Orissa, namely, Balasore, Cuttack and Puri, were conquered from the Marathas. Finally, in the First Burmese War in 1824, Assam, Arakan and Tenasserim were annexed.

This wide expanse of territory was too large to be administered as a single unit. It was decided, therefore, to divide the Presidency into two parts, (1) the Presidency of Fort William in Bengal and (2) the Presidency of Agra. With changes, there finally emerged in place of the proposed Agra Presidency the so-called North-West Provinces. By 1834-36, the new province was separated from the Bengal Presidency.

The North-western Provinces and Oudh. Separated from the Bengal Presidency, the area of the North-western Provinces was still very large. In 1856, Lord Dalhousie, whose imperialism was responsible for many new acquisitions, annexed Oudh to the British Empire. For about twenty years it was kept under a separate administration, but finally it was amalgamated with the North-western Provinces.

The Presidency of Madras. The Presidency of Madras, which was also known as the Presidency of Fort St. George, started with the presidency town acquired from the Nawab of the Carnatic between 1750 and 1760. The Northern Sirkars, that is, the Ganjam, Vizagapatam, Godavari and the Krishna territories, were seized from the decadent Mughals and their Deccan Viceroy, the Nizam, by 1765. North Arcot, South Arcot, Tanjore, Trichinopoly, Madura, Tinnevelly, Coimbatore, the Nilgiris and the Salem areas were taken during the last decade of the eighteenth century. In subsequent years, Cuddapah and Nellore were acquired. The growth of the Madras Presidency was within a compact area and did not create administrative difficulties like the growth of the Bengal Presidency.

The Presidency of Bombay. The island of Bombay provided the nucleus for the growth of a great Presidency. The Marathas, who destroyed the Mughal Empire but failed to create a lasting empire of their own, had to surrender territory after territory that they had acquired under Shivaji and Baji Rao. The Nizam, another power of the south, who could have suffered the fate of the Marathas, escaped extinction by acknowledging the supremacy of the British and remaining faithful to the Subsidiary Alliance which deprived him of his freedom but gave him protection.

Between 1800 and 1805, the British from Bombay seized Surat, Broach and Kaira from the Nawab of Surat and the Gaikwad of Baroda. The latter was also forced to surrender Ahmedabad soon after. The Maratha Wars in successive phases increased the size of the Presidency and, by 1818, the vanquished Marathas had lost most of their possessions. The Peshwa alone surrendered Thana, Khandesh, Nasik, part of Ahmednagar, Poona, Sholapur, Kolaba, Ratnagiri and a few other places, including a part of Belgaum. In 1827, the rest of Belgaum was annexed from the Raja of Kolhapur and, in 1848, Satara was captured.

In the evolution of the Presidency of Bombay, frontier adjustments with the Nizam, Sindhia and the Madras Government became essential. Like Madras, however, the Bombay Presidency did not expand beyond manageable proportions. In 1843, Sind was conquered by the British and attached to the Bombay Presidency.

The Punjab. Long before the Punjab proper was conquered by Lord Dalhousie, territories to the right bank of the river Jumna had been acquired by the British in 1803 from the Marathas. They included the districts of Gurgaon, Rohtak, Karnal, Hissar and a part of Ferozepore. All these acquisitions were, for a number of years, attached to the North-West Provinces.

The rise of Ranjit Singh alarmed the British, but statesmanship on both sides kept relations peaceful. Soon after the death of the Sikh ruler, his army became uncontrollable. The British too became aggressive. This resulted in the First Sikh War of 1845-1846 which ended with the victory of the British and the conquest of the districts of Ferozepore, Ludhiana, and parts of Ambala, Jullundur, Hoshiarpur and Kangra. Finally, in 1849, the Second Sikh War was fought and Lord Dalhousie annexed the whole of the Punjab to the British Empire. The territories added included Peshawar, Kohat, Hazara, Bannu, Dera Ismail Khan, Dera Ghazi Khan, Multan, Montgomery, Lahore, Amritsar, Gurdaspur, Gujranwala, Gujarat, Sialkot, Shahpur, Rawalpindi and other places.

The Punjab was retained as a separate territorial unit. After the rising of 1857, during which the Punjab was en expectedly quiet, the authorities enlarged its extent by transferring from the North-West Provinces all those districts to the right of the Jumna which had been conquered from the Marathas in 1803.

The Central Provinces. It was from the Peshwa and the Bhonsla Raja of Nagpur at the end of the Maratha Wars in 1818 that the British acquired the greater part of the Sagar and Narbada territories. In course of time, extensive areas covering Nagpur, Raipur, Bilaspur and Sambalpur came under the British.

Burma. Burma was conquered part by part in the three Burmese Wars. The acquisitions of the First Burmese War, namely, Arakan and Tennasserim, were attached to Bengal in 1824. The Second Burmese War in 1852 added the district of Pegu. In 1885-86, the Third Burmese War acquired for the victorious British the territories of Upper Burma and the Shan states. Ultimately, the whole of Burma was made a separate administrative unit.

Other Divisions. Territories such as Ajmer and Marwar, the little hill state of Coorg on the Western Ghats, Berar, and the Andaman Islands retained their identity for one reason or another.

It is natural that the conquests and annexations of the British were carried out over a considerable length of time through the eighteenth and nineteenth centuries. The main territorial divisions of the empire (as briefly described above) developed in irregular ways. Administrative and constitutional developments, therefore, could not, in these initial stages, be uniform. They followed an irregular course and evolved through a process of trial and error, the initial experiments being tried out over limited areas. It was only later that Britain's Indian Empire came under a comprehensive, unified system of governmental organisation. The course of experimentation and evolution is briefly outlined below.

Evolution of the Powers of the Company

The name, East India Company, came into circulation only as late as 1833, but the word 'Company' was used from the earliest times briefly to identify the merchants of London trading with India and the East Indies under royal charter. The evolution of the powers of the Company may briefly be traced before the Company is studied as a political power.

To start with, the merchants engaged in the East India trade petitioned their home government for permission to form an association for trade and commerce, the exclusive right to send ships to Indian waters, and the authority to establish centres of trade in Indian territories with the permission of the local rulers. The British Crown conceded these requests and embodied them in a Royal Charter which also authorized the Company to govern itself and its servants. The privileges so granted were to be enjoyed for 15 years unless terminated by two years' notice, and could be renewed for another 15 years. In England, the Company elected annually a governor and twenty-four committees to look after its affairs. General meetings of all members of the Company were also called from time to time.

Among the powers granted to the Company the most significant was the power to 'make, ordain, and constitute such and so many reasonable laws, constitutions, orders, and ordinances, as...shall seem necessary and convenient for the good government of the said Company.' The officers and other employees of the Company on their voyages or elsewhere were subject to these laws and ordinances. For violation of the laws, the authorities had the right to inflict punishment, which was expected to be in accordance with the laws of England. Needless to say, both he powers of law-making and punishment were limited in scope.

The Charter granted to the Company by Queen Elizabeth I was the first in long series of Charters. Each successive Charter, as was to be expected, aimed at improving the existing position. James I, who succeeded Elizabeth, had to face difficulties arising out the establishment of the Company's footholds in India. English merchants on Indian soil were bound to obey the laws and commands of the Indian rulers. Disputes between Englishmen and Indians could also be settled under the verdict of local governments, but disputes among the Englishmen themselves were not usually the concern of the Indian rulers. Owing to jealousies arising out of economic factors, such disputes were frequent amongst the English merchants and other members of the settlements. It became necessary, therefore, to give the Company more power to control Englishmen in India. In 1623, James I empowered the Company to grant authority to its officers to punish any servant of the Company for offences in their new settlements. In case of capital offences, the system of trial by jury was authorised. Thus, the British had, in their tiny settlements in India, a system of government not long after actual trading activities had begun.

The growth of the Company's influence, both in England and India, was rapid. To cope with the new developments a significant step was taken by the British Crown in 1661. That year, Charles II issued a Charter which, in effect, permitted the Company to develop itself into a political power. The time had passed when the English required only factories for trade. Now they felt the need for erecting fortresses and citadels of military power. The Charter, therefore, granted power to the Company to despatch to India warships and ammunition, to erect fortifications and to garrison them with 'volunteers' from England. The Company could make peace or war with any non-Christian power to protect its trade interests. To rule over their fortresses and strongholds, the Company was authorised to appoint governors and officers. The governor and his council in each factory had the power 'to judge all persons belonging to the said governor and Company or that shall live under them, in all causes, whether civil or criminal, according to the laws of this Kingdom (England), and to execute judgment accordingly.'

It was during the rule of Charles II that the island of Bombay, which was under the sovereignty of the King Portugal, was transferred to the British Crown. King Charles made over the island to the Company in 1668, for an annual rent. Since the island had been under the full sovereignty of the King, the Company on acquiring it succeeded to the same absolute rights over the people of the island. Thus Bombay enjoyed a special status compared with other British settlements. The Company enjoyed the power to issue orders or ordinances, to make laws and to exercise full judicial authority. More important of all, to defend the island against any possible invaders, the Company was permitted to raise volunteers from among the King's soldiers. This was the beginning of the Company's European army—the so-called Bombay Fusiliers. Within the next few years (1676), the Company received a Charter to coin money at Bombay. The granting of the right of coinage was a definite assertion on the part of British Crown of its absolute sovereignty over Bombay. In contract, the Company at Madras could coin money only with the sanction of the Indian authorities.

The prospect of power encouraged some daring Englishmen at home to think of political adventure in India. It has been the usual historical hypothesis that it was the Fenchman, Dupleix, who first dreamt of an empire on Indian soil. But long before Dupleix, Sir Josiah Child (an active member of the Company) had been thinking of a political empire in India. It was under his influence that the British Crown granted to the Company in 1683 the power to declare was and make peace with any 'heathen' nation of Asia,

Africa and America. This was a very broad power with wider political implications. While the Company thus became a political force, the Crown retained for itself the right to exercise its supreme authority either in questions of war or peace or in any matter concerning English settlements abroad. When James II came to the throne after Charles II, he sought to extend the Company's power still further. Among a number of measures in that direction the most significant was the power to institute a municipal body at Madras for purposes of laying claim to territories and collecting revenues and taxes.

There were ups and downs in the Company's fortunes in England, but the main trend was always towards a promising future. Rivalry and competition from other English merchants were the greatest stumbling blocks. Eventually, however, wisdom prevailed, rivalry subsided and the merchants combined to exploit the prospects of a great future. Thus, a hundred years after the death of Queen Elizabeth, during the reign of yet another queen (Anne), the English traders strengthened themselves by agreeing (1702) to work together as 'The United Company of Merchants of England Trading to the East Indies.' This United Company was the 'East India Company' of future renown. From the opening of the eighteenth century, the Company at home became more and more stabilised with a definite constitutional system, and its affairs came to be conducted by that famous body called the Court of Directors. Simultaneously, the powers of the Company in India became more and more clearly defined. Whatever the first two Stuart Kings had authorired as powers and privileges of the Company were retained and upheld by succeeding monarchs—William III, Anne and the Hanoverians. Modifications of these powers and privileges, especially in judicial fields, were of course effected. In 1726, the Company received the power to establish the mayor's courts at Madras, Bombay and Calcutta. The system of the mayor's courts may be regarded as the foundation of the future system of British justice in India.

Such was the course of development during the first century of the Company's relations with India. The next phase opened with the struggle against the French in India, as well as with certain

Indian powers, which culminated in the emergence of the British as empire-builders. Of necessity, a new role awaited the empire-makers in the field of administration.

The British as Empire-makers

While the British were establishing themselves in India other European powers were working in their own ways to acquire similar privileges and power for themselves. A contest for supremacy became inevitable and in the final round it was the British and the French who fought to decide which of them should be the paramount power in India. During the first half of the eighteenth century the French East India Company had built itself up as a formidable rival to the English Company. From their main centre at Pondicherry, the French observed with acute jealousy the growing influence of the English in the south. Meanwhile conditions were ripe in Europe for the beginning of a relentless struggle between France and England for colonial supremacy. Finally, in 1744, a general European war, the War of the Austrian Succession, broke out and France and England were ranged on opposite sides. Sir Robert Walpole, the first Prime Minister of England, had fallen from power because of his policy of peace. The British people had global ambitions, and the East India Company in India reflected the general feelings of their countrymen. The French, too, had dreams of world conquest and their Company in India also looked ahead to a bright future. The outbreak of the European war was thus an opportunity for the rival Companies to try conclusions with each other. It was Joseph Dupleix, the French Governor at Pondicherry, who scored the initial successes. Madras fell to the French. But when the Peace of Aix-la-Chapelle was concluded in Europe in 1748, Madras was returned to the English. Dupleix, however, had proceeded to involve himself in the politics of the Deccan and the Carnatic. With spectacular courage, determination and strategy the achieved wonderful successes within a short time. By the middle of 1751 his puppet candidates were sitting on the thrones of the Deccan and the Carnatic. It was at that time that Robert Clive, an ordinary employee in the Company's civil service, rose to military fame and turned the tide in favour of the British. His siege of Arcot was the beginning of a series of military stratagems which finally resulted in the victory of the British and the collapse of the French. The French failure was not so much due to the Frenchmen in India as to their countrymen at home.

The government of Louis XV did not make available to Dupleix the military requirements which the latter's grand political designs demanded. Dupleix was recalled in 1754 and in his departure French diplomacy disappeared from the Indian political scene. Dupleix's downfall was Clive's good forture. The true political goal was rapidly taking shape and the means to be followed for the desired end depended on circumstance and situation. It was for a genius to exploit the circumstances and Clive, in the context of his time, proved himself more than able for the occasion. The Company's activities could not be confined only to the south, but, of necessity, covered Bengal. From an humble beginning in the three villages of Sutanati, Kalighat and Govindpur, English traders had developed their settlements into the thriving city of Calcutta, protected by a fort. From that stronghold, the English began to quarrel with the young successor of the sagacious Alivardi, Sriajuddaulah. Siraj had ascended the throne as the Nawab of Bengal, Bihar and Orissa in 1756. He was an imperious but inexperienced young man. He had enough political foresight to apprehend the political designs of the foreigners; but not the wisdom to halt the process of degeneration in the administration of his own state. Court intrigues and hostility to the young Nawab, together with evidence of general military weakness and administrative inefficiency, encouraged the English at Calcutta to openly defy the Nawab's authority. The success of the English in the south had inflamed their ambition, and they were ready to pick a quarrel on the slightest pretext. They pretended that the French of Chandernagore were preparing to attack them and that therefore they should fortify Calcultta. To the Nawab it seemed that this pretension was only the beginning of a grand political design. He, therefore, decided to strike before it was too late. There was also the temptation to acquire the wealth of the traders. In June 1756, Sirajuddaulah attacked Calcutta. The President, Drake, together with his Council, fled from the city. Holwell, a civilian, remained to defend it. On 20th June, Calcutta fell. The fall of Calcutta and the subsequent story of the 'Black Hole' tragedy prepared the way for a final showdown. 1756 saw the beginning of the Seven Years' War in Europe when England and France became engaged in their final struggle for supremacy in Europe, America and India.

Clive, who had by now become a colonel in the army, aimed his final blow at the French in India. He hastened to Bengal after the Calcutta tragedy, re-occupied Calcutta and entered upon a course of diplomacy and conspiracy backed by action, which, within a year enabled him to lay the foundation of the British Empire in Bengal. First, he patched up the quarrel with the Nawab; then he attacked and captured Chandernagore. With the defeat of the French, he felt free to turn on the Nawab. A conspiracy, in which Clive showed his skill as a superb manipulator, brought into his net Mir Jafar, a close relation of the Nawab and one of the chief commanders of his army. When everything was ready, war was declared. On 23rd June 1757, Clive's forces and those of Sirajuddaulah fought the decisive battle of Plassey. The Nawab lost the battle and fled. He was subsequently caught and killed. Mir Jafar was declared Nawab, but Clive was his virtual master. The foundation of the British Empire had been laid. No empire in history had its foundation laid at so negligible a cost—there were only 23 killed and 49 wounded on the British side. Plassey was the beginning. The subsequent British victories at Wandiwash (1760) in the South, and at Buxar (1764) in the North, opened for the victors wide political avenues for imperial expansion. In that venture, it was inevitable that in working out a system of administration, wisdom would only be found by the method of trial and error. The early administrators of British India from Clive onwards were indeed faced with stupendous problems. The Company's servants began their rule of Indian territory ignorant of India and her systems, inexperienced in politics and administration, and with strong personal inclinations to get rich quickly. Under such circumstances did the British administration of India begin.

Administrative Experiments

The Battle of Plassey (1757) was a landmark in British imperial history. Its significance and implications were promptly realised by the home authorities. The royal grants which were issued after Plassey clearly show how the British Government wanted to regularise the Company's conquests in far away India. The Charters of 1757 and 1758 granted the right to the Company to retain any booty taken in war, subject to a few conditions. The Charter of 1758 specifically sought to assert the British Crown's sovereignty over the territories acquired by conquest.

The crux of the problem, however, lay in matters concerning the internal administration of the acquired territories. After Plassey, Clive became the *de facto* master of Bengal, but what was his legal authority even among the English settlers themselves? For some time there was no answer to the question. Amid legal uncertainties, the Calcutta Council at last decided in June 1758 to request Clive to act as their Governor, and his appointment was regularised by an order from home.

Thus began the Government of Robert Clive. But the problem remained—what was the extent of his authority? The answer was far from clear. Clive was the *de jure* Governor of Calcutta, but in reality, he was much more than that. During that first tenure of office the adjustments he made were mainly political. The company recognised the Nawab as the ruler of Bengal. The Nawab, in turn, recognised the sovereignty of the English in Calcutta, and granted lands to the Company for the maintenance of a military force. The Company protected the Nawab, and the latter met the cost of the troops which protected him. The Company's agent stayed at the Nawab's durbar. The Nawab gave away the Twenty-four Parganas to the Company. All such political transactions were Clive's personal achievements, resting on the Company's military prestige. Three years after Plassey when he left for England in 1760, Clive could claim that his real success had been the establishment of the power of the Company in Bengal.

But his departure proved that the foundation of that power was still very shaky. The Company quarrelled with Mir Jafar and deposed him. Mir Qasim had been placed on the throne, but he wanted to be free from the clutches of the English. In the situation that followed, the Company was dragged into a conflict with powers outside Bengal. The sphere of the Company's political activities suddenly enlarged. Mir Qasim in his distress sought the help of the Nawab Wazir of Oudh, who was the nominal Prime Minister of the Mughal Empire, and of the Mughal Emperor himself, who, though titular, was yet the legal sovereign of India. Their combined forces were defeated at Buxar. The defeat of the Mughal Emperor, Shah Alam, at the hands of the Company was one of the greatest political events of Indian history, and Clive was needed to make the best of the new situation.

In May 1765 Clive returned. His deal with the defeated Emperor was a masterpiece of statesmanship. He did not want to lead the Company's army to Delhi to proclaim the conquest of India. This would have been too difficult and would have brought him into conflict with other powers. So he decided to legalise, through the generally accepted sovereign of India, his conquests of Bengal, Bihar and Orissa. The Emperor's power had shrunk severely, and he had no real authority over the territories in question. But it was not difficult on his part to grant them to the company. Thus the Mughal Emperor, Shah Alam, granted to the Company the Diwani of Bengal, Bihar and Orissa. Clive in return agreed to pay an amount of 26 lakhs annually. It was after the acquisition of the Diwani that Clive had to devise a form of government. Real power had now come to the company. Yet there was a Nawab with a shadow of authority. Clive considered his existence indispensable. He even thought it necessary to pay him every mark of distinction. His main object was to crush other foreign powers within the Nawab's jurisdiction, in the latter's name.

Thus, in an attempt to retain a Nawab as well as to enjoy real power by himself, Clive introduced a system of government famous as the Dual Government, or Dyarchy. Mir Jafar died in 1765. His son, a boy of eighteen, succeeded him on the *masnad*. The Company allotted to him a fixed payment so that he might maintain the dignity of his office. The actual tasks of criminal, civil and police administration were kept in the Nawab's hand, but the Company enjoyed the real authority. It was the Company's duty to defend the territory against external danger. But more important was the authority it assumed to collect the revenue.

Such a division of administration into two distinct spheres was destined to create acute problems. The Company had the power and the money, but no responsibility for the administration. The Nawab had the responsibility of conducting administration without resources and power. Such an anomaly clearly ran counter to the traditional form of government where authority and responsibility were vested in one and the same person. The new arrangement had the effect of concentrating powers in the Governor-in-Council and in making the Nawab a nonentity. The effective administration of the Nawab thus amounted to nothing.

Such was the character of Clive's Dual Government. The argument in his support that the Company's servants were ignorant of India, Indians, native customs and languages, and therefore could not have done justice to administrative responsibilities all of a sudden, is not entirely unsound. But to leave responsibility to a powerless Nawab with a demoralised staff, was no evidence of wisdom. Moreover, the administrative jurisdictions of the servants of the Governor-in-Council and of the staff of the Nawab were neither defined nor regulated. The former considered the plunder of Bengal their legitimate right by virtue of conquest. The latter remained the silent spectators of a general dissolution of the old order. Thus Dual Government became another name for misgovernment.

The author of the system left India early in 1767. His immediate successors, Verelst and Cartier, had no ability to improve the situation. Amid anarchy, corruption and plunder, there descended on Bengal a great famine in 1770 which took away more than three million lives.

The Era of Warren Hastings

The era of Clive was followed by that of Warren Hastings. The former had laid the foundation of an empire, the latter was destined to lay the foundation of an administration. Political developments in India had raised issues which required an early solution. While the statesmen in England began to ponder over the problem of the Crown's control over the East India Company and of Parliament's control over its affairs in India, Hastings set himself the task of giving to the conquered territories a sound administration. Perhaps he was the only Englishman at that time who possessed the wisdom and the will to give to the Indian people under the Company's control what was so necessary for their well-being, *i.e.,* good government.

Hastings assumed office in 1772. His immediate work was the abolition of the dual system. That called for the establishment of complete and direct control by the Company over the entire administration. During the days of the dyarchy, though the Diwani, that is the right to collect revenue, was granted to the Company, yet the latter retained the Indian agency for actual management and collection of the revenue. Hastings put an end to that dangerous arrangement. He established a Board of Revenue. A Collector was placed in charge of each district. He was assisted in the collection of revenue by Indian officers called *diwans*. Hastings shifted the treasury from the Nawab's capital at Murshidabad to the Company's capital at Calcutta. It was a symbolic gesture to signify that the seat of authority was where the English Governor resided.

Under the dual government, the ordinary concepts of law and justice had disappeared from Bengal. It was not in the capacity of the powerless Nawab to uphold the law and administer justice. Hastings paid his utmost consideration to this problem and organised a proper judicial system. In every district he established a civil court named *Diwani Adalat*. The Collector presided over it and was assisted by Indian officers. In every district there was also established a criminal court named *Faujdari Adalat*. An Indian *qazi* presided over it and was assisted by a *mufti* and two *maulvis*. The Collector supervised the work of the *qazi*. For appeals from the district *Diwani Adalats*, a *Sadar Diwani Adalat* was established at Calcutta. Similarly, for appeals from the district *Faujdari Adalats, a Sadar Nizamat Adalat* was established, also at Calcutta. These courts were respectively the superior civil and criminal courts of the country. The Governor and his council presided over the *Sadar*

Diwani Adalat; and the *Sadar Nizamat Adalat* was presided over by the *Daroga-i-Adalat* aided by the Chief *qazi,* the Chief mufti and three *maulvis*. The Governor-in-Council supervised the work of the *Sadar Nizamat Adalat*.

Hastings did not forget to respect the age-old Hindu and Muhammedan laws of the country. He left the need to codify these laws. While he was so concerned, the authorities in England were busy finding out how to regulate Indian affairs in the light of their sovereign rights.

The British Parliament and India: the Regulating Act of 1773

The East India Company had founded an empire yielding a revenue of four million pounds and possessing immense future potentialities. Yet the Company's affairs were far from being satisfactory. It was so much in need of immediate funds that in 1772 it applied to the British Government for a loan of one million pounds. The cause of the need was apparent. Many of the Company's servants had been exploiting the country, not for the benefit of the Company but for their own personal gain. Within ten years after Plassey, they had acquired in Bengal more than two million pounds as presents and a little less than four million pounds as compensation. Clive himself had been guilty in this respect and had even accepted a jagir. The servants of the Company were creating an empire far from their home and as they were not under the effective control of their government, they felt free to do what they pleased. To many in England it appeared absurd that the Company should be allowed so much liberty verging upon licence. The British Government had legislated in earlier days for smaller factories and settlements on foreign shores. But in India, after Plassey and Buxar, the traders ruled over territory larger in area than Great Britain itself. The Company in India enjoyed 'quasi-sovereignty.' In view of such developments, the British Government felt it necessary to evolve a new kind of relationship with the Government in India. The distance between England and India was too great for complete control of the Indian territories by the British Government. The authority of the Company, too, could not be satisfactorily curtailed. One school of thought held that the Company should be left to regulate its affairs without control or interference from home. But a more powerful opinion developed taking the opposite position. It claimed complete sovereign authority for the British Government over the Company's Indian territories.

Statesmen in England had to reconcile these opposite views and adopt a realistic attitude. A thorough investigation into the Company's Affairs was necessary. In April 1772, General Burgoyne, a prominent member of the House of Commons, demanded the appointment of a committee to enquire into the affairs of the Company. 'The most atrocious abuses that ever stained the name of civil government called for redress,' he said. The proposed committee was required to go into the 'promiscuous tumult and confusion' into which the Company had degenerated. Parliament, therefore, appointed a select committee of thirty-one members to thirteen was also appointed to go into the most confidential matters. Both the committees in their reports condemned the Company. Parliament became convinced of its right to intervene on the assumption that 'all acquisitions, made under the influence of a military force, or by treaty with foreign princes, do of right belong to the State.'

Lord North was the British Prime Minister. He prepared a Bill to regulate the affairs of the Company 'to the well-being, nay, to the existence of the Company' itself. The Directors of the Company complained and protested that Parliament wanted to transfer the Company's powers to the Crown in order to destroy the Company. The Government, however, proceeded with the Bill which was finally passed by Parliament.[3] It became famous as the Regulating Act of 1773.

The Act brought some changes in the constitution of the Company at home. The voting qualification in the Court of Proprietors of the Company was raised from £500 to £1000. This had the effect of bringing down the number of voters by the elimination of smaller proprietors. The directors of the Company were to be elected for four years, one-fourth of them retiring every year. The directors who constituted the Company's home authority were subjected to the control of Parliament. They were required to place before the Government all correspondence from India concerning the Company's revenues. All matters concerning civil and military administration in India were to be placed by the directors before a secretary of state. Thus the British Government sought to control the Government of India through the directors of the Company, for the Court of Directors in effect directed and controlled the Government of India.

Regarding the composition of the Government in India, the Regulating Act provided that at the head of the Indian administration there should be a Governor-General of Bengal assisted by four Councillors. Everything was to be decided by majority vote, the Governor-General enjoying merely a casting vote in case of an equal division. The Governor-General and the Council were given power over the other Presidencies with regard to questions of war and peace. The Regulating Act named Warren Hastings as the first Governor-General and Clavering, Monson, Barwell and Philip Francis as the first Councillors. Their term was for five years. Subsequent appointments were to be made by the Company. The Regulating Act also provided that the British Crown should establish by Charter a Supreme Court of Justice, consisting of a Chief Justice and three puisne judges.[4] Thus it came about that the Supreme Court, which enjoyed wide powers, and the judicial system in British India, took their origin directly from the British Crown.

The Regulating Act provided the first constitution emanating from the British Parliament for the governance of the British Indian possessions. The aim of Lord North was to place 'the affairs of the Company on a solid, clear and decisive establishment.' But with the best of intentions, the authors of the Act could not make it a perfect working system. No sooner was it put into operation, than the inherent defects of the Act became apparent. The control which Parliament sought to exercise over the Company was neither adequate nor effective. Because the Company's servants worked far away from the Cabinet's supervision, their conduct could not be properly regulated. The Court of Directors was not in any real sense responsible to the Cabinet. The relation between the East India Company and the British Parliament thus remained vague. In India, the Act created confusion in a number of ways. A Governor-General had been created without the required power in his hand to govern. Whether the Governor-General was superior to his Council or vice versa became the cause of quarrels between Hastings and the members of his Council. The famous Hastings-Francis quarrel culminating in the Nanda Kumar affair, with its implication that Hastings had accepted bribes, was a disgraceful outcome of these quarrels, made possible by the shortcomings of the Act. Similarly, the extent of control which the central government in India was to exercise over the presidency governments was ill-defined. This created many problems in the external affairs of the Company. Finally, the relation between the Governor-General-in-Council and the Supreme Court was left vague. The spheres of their jurisdictions overlapped and therefore conflicts followed. Even the law which the Supreme Court was to follow in India was not properly defined, leading to serious complications.

Such being its defects, the Regulating Act invited grave criticism followed by the demand for a new Act. It was destined to survive only for eleven years with only one Governor-General, Warren Hastings, to operate it. Of all persons, Hastings suffered the most from the defects in the Act, even though the Act had raised him from the position of a Governor to that of Governor General.

Pitt's India Act, 1784. While the Regulating Act was being worked in India, far-reaching political developments were taking place elsewhere. Across the Atlantic, the thirteen American colonies of England revolted, fought and became independent. The loss of the American colonies was a serious blow to the prestige of Britain and it had the effect of making the British Parliament more cautious about the governing of its Indian possessions. So, while the American War was being waged, Parliament was debating Indian affairs in a search for a more effective control through a new Act.

Thus, in 1781, Parliament appointed a select committee and a secret committee of enquiry. Once again, many defects in the Indian administration were exposed. There was no doubt that the Regulating Act had failed. To bring matters to a head, the Company, yet again in financial difficulties, applied for assistance in 1783. If the Company deserved any such relief, as Edmund Burke demanded, 'the relief and reformation of the Company must go together.' In

April 1783, Henry Dundas introduced a Bill to enhance the power of the home government over the Governor-General, and to increase the power of the Governor-General over his Council as well as the subordinate Presidencies. The Bill was good, but Dundas, as a member of the Opposition, could not carry it through and therefore his proposals came to nothing. In November of the same year, Charles James Fox introduced a Bill suggesting sweeping changes. He condemned the Indian administration as 'a system of despotism unmatched in all the histories of the world', and condemned Warren Hastings as 'a man who, by disobeying the orders of his employers, had made himself so great as to be now able to mix in every question of State, and make every measure of government a personal point in which he had a share.' Burke supported Fox, describing the Company's administration as one of the most corrupt and destructive tyrannies that had probably ever existed in the world. His noble suggestion was: 'Our Indian Government is in it best state a grievance. It is necessary that the correctives should be uncommonly vigorous; and the work of men sanguine, warm, and even impassioned in the cause.' Fox's Bill aimed to have a powerful government at home to control the government in India. The Bill was worthy of consideration. But the political blunders of Fox, which led him to join hands with Lord North in forming a coalition ministry, made him so unpopular that his Bill was doomed to failure. The fall of the coalition sealed the fate of Fox's Bill.

It was thus left for Pitt the Younger to introduce his famous India Bill in January 1784, after assuming power as Prime Minister. The discussions on the previous Bills had made him wiser. The dissolution of Parliament and Pitt's return with a solid majority strengthened his hands. He introduced his Bill again and got it passed in August 1784.

According to Pitt's India Act, for the better control of Indian affairs a Board of Control was established in England. As James Mill described it: 'The Board of Control was composed of six Members of the Privy Council, chosen by the King, of whom the Chancellor of the Exchequer, and one of the principal secretaries of state were to be two; in the absence of whom, the senior of the remaining four was to preside. In point of fact, the whole business has rested with that senior; the other commissioners being seldom called to deliberate, or even for forms' sake to assemble. The senior is known by the name of the President of the Board of Control, and is essentially a new Secretary of State; a secretary for the Indian department.' The President of the Board was given considerable power to superintend and control all revenue and civil matters as well as the military forces of the Company in the East. The Court of Directors was retained, but was subjected to the authority of the Board of Control. The former was required to submit to the Board copies of all communications received from India, and all their resolutions, orders, minutes and despatches to India. The Board could modify, change or prepare despatches to be sent to India. Secret and urgent orders were to be sent to India through a secret committee of the Court of Directors. Thus the Board of Control became the real ruling authority over the Indian territories. The Company's Court of Directors lost much of its former power, though it was allowed to retain its powers to appoint all servants of the Company. The Court of Proprietors of the East India Company also lost much of its power. It could not annul or suspend any resolution of the Court of Directors approved by the Board of Control. Thus the political authority of the Company in relation to their Indian possessions was much reduced. Its commercial privileges, however, remained as before.

Regarding the administration of India, Pitt's India Act aimed to be precise and practical in pin-pointing where actual power should lie. The Governor-General and a Council of three constituted the central government. The Governor-General was given more effective power over the Council. The central government, located in Bengal, was given definite authority over the subordinate Presidencies in matters of revenue, war, peace and diplomacy. The Presidency governments were required to send their papers to and seek directions from the centre.

To endow him with an appropriate and more dignified status in his position, the Governor-General was to be appointed by the Court of Directors with the approval of the Crown, the latter being given power to recall him. The powers of the Indian Government were to be moderated at home, particularly in matters of war. The Governor-General and Council could not declare war without permission from the home authorities.

In the Presidencies, the administration was vested in the hands of a Governor and a Council of three. They were to be appointed by the Court of Directors, but the Crown had the power to recall or remove the Governor of a Presidency.

After years of irresponsible and reckless administration, Pitt's India Act came as a measure to rationalise the governmental machinery and make the government responsible to a system. The underlying principle which the establishment of the Board of Control introduced was that two responsible ministers of the British Government came to be directly associated with the administration of the Company's territories in India. They had power to see all papers and to approve all orders and despatches. The Company's authority remained untouched in matters of commerce. Its Court of Directors continued to enjoy the power of patronage to appoint its servants to conduct its affairs. The Act was, thus, a compromise in the dispute between Parliament and the Company, with weightage in favour of the former. Pitt made it clear that the administration of India 'could not, with safety or propriety, be placed in any other hands than those of the genuine and legitimate executive power of the Constitution,' meaning thereby the British Cabinet. The emergence of a Secretary of State working as the President of the Board of Control was the beginning of a process by which the British Government ultimately proceeded to rule India. Pitt had outlined the image of the future so-called 'White Mughal'.

Within the framework of Pitt's Constitution, the development of Indian administration began to take shape, phase by phase, under successive Indian governments.

Administrative Developments after Pitt's India Act

With Pitt's India Act the administration of Warren Hastings came to an end. He left India early in 1785. A series of charges were being drawn up against him by his enemies in England leading to his impeachment and trial, which continued for seven years.[5]

Cornwallis, who succeeded Hastings, reached Calcutta in September 1786. He was not in the Company's service and therefore was independent of Company influences. He was selected for the high office by the British Cabinet, though he was appointed by the Company. He accepted responsibility on his own terms. A military man, he wanted to work both as Governor-General and Commander-in-Chief. Aware of the unfortunate relations of Hastings with his Council, Cornwallis claimed superiority over his Council. With such advantages, he assumed office determined to tone up the administration, even though he did not have any experience of India himself. But he had the good sense to avail of the judicious advice of such men as John Shore, James, Grant, Jonathan Duncan, Charles Grant and William Jones.

Cornwallis wanted to reform the civil and military services by eradicating the evils of corrupt practices. The British servants of the Company had, in the days of Clive and Hastings, performed their public services with motives of plunder, exploitation, extortion and bribery. They did not cavil at their small salaries, as their indirect incomes were profuse. An administration resting on such an immoral foundation could not enhance its prestige. Cornwallis wanted to remove the root of the evil. He prescribed higher salaries for the officers, while denying them the liberty to make money by other means. Merit was recognised as the passport to appointment and promotion, and not recommendation, favour or patronage. Efficiency and honesty were reward-sed, whereas dishonesty was punished. Although he improved the standard of British Indian administration, Cornwallis did a great injustice to Indians by not taking them into confidence for higher responsibilities. All higher posts in public service were reserved for Englishmen.

The most outstanding work of Cornwallis was the consolidation of the Indian districts into definite administrative units. Each district was placed under a magistrate and a Collector. The magistrate represented the executive, presided over the civil court as a judge, and finally supervised the police force in his district. Thus the magistrate, working as the district judge as well as the head of the police, combined in his person both judiciary and executive powers.

The Collector, on the other hand, remained in charge of the revenue administration of the district. The judicial and executive powers which he had previously enjoyed were taken away from him. For effective police administration, each district was divided into a number of police circles, or *thanas*. Each such circle was placed under an Indian *daroga* who was responsible for peace, and for the prevention and detection of crime in his area.

In the judicial field, Cornwallis aimed at establishing a comprehensive system of justice. In matters of civil justice, smaller courts such as the munsifs' and amins' courts and registrars' courts were established in the bigger towns of each district. Above these courts was the district court in each district, on which a British magistrate presided as judge. He was assisted by a Muslim *qazi* and a Hindu Pandit who knew their respective laws. Next, there were the Provincial Courts, or Courts of Appeal, established at four places, Calcutta, Patna, Dacca and Murshidabad. In each such court there worked three judges, a registrar, a *qasi,* a *mufti,* and a Pandit. Above them was the Supreme Court at Calcutta known as the *Sadar Diwani Adalat.* The Governor-General, his Council, a registrar, a *qazi*, two *muftis*, and two pandits constituted the Supreme Court. Finally, at the top there was the Privy Council in England to which appeal could be carried from the *Sadar Diwani Adalat.* From the lowest court to the highest, appeals could be taken according to the value of the case.[6]

Criminal justice was vested in the hands of the four provincial courts. These courts conducted the administration of justice by circuit and hence were called Circuit Courts. At the bottom of the ladder were the Justices of the Peace in each district including such officers as the amins, registrars and district judges to try small cases. At the top was the Supreme Criminal Court or *Sadar Nizamat Adalat* to hear appeals from the Circuit Courts. The Governor-General and his Council, assisted by a *qazi* and two *muftis*, constituted the *Sadar Nizamat Adalat.*

The most famous work of Cornwallis in India was the Permanent Settlement (to be discussed in a subsequent chapter). On the whole, his administration served the purpose of consolidating the British hold upon India. Among the notable defects of his administration was his inability to give India a modern code of law. Warren Hastings had felt the need for such a code. Sir William Jones was making serious researches into the laws of the country. But yet a definite code remained only a *desideratum*. Consequently, the judicial machinery of Cornwallis remained imperfect. Similarly, Cornwallis, who was so much concerned with raising the standard of Cornwallis remained imperfect. Similarly, Cornwallis, who was so much concerned with raising the standard of administration to a high level and had increased the salaries of English officers, did scant justice to the low paid Indians in the lowest services. The *darogas*, registrars, amins and *muftis* received such poor remuneration that they could only live in miserable conditions. Not unnaturally, therefore, Indian policemen in the British days were not above suspicion. Above all, exclusion of Indians from the higher services gave the administration a foreign colour. The judges, magistrates and collectors, all white men, remained far from the people, their needs and problems. It was the conviction of Cornwallis that 'without a large and well-regulated body of Europeans, our hold on these valuable dominions must be very in secure' and hence the feeling that the Europeanisation of the Indian administration was a necessity.

With its merits and demerits the Cornwallis system continued to exist. It was also introduced in other parts of India besides Bengal. Following the French Revolution of 1789 and the rise of Napoleon to power in 1799, European developments engaged the attention of England. The system of Government in India was allowed to mature. For Lord Wellesley, the able successor of Cornwallis, the real problem was to remove defects from the administration, but to convert the British Empire in India to the British Empire of India. His theory of Subsidiary Alliance, coupled with imperialist wars, extended the British territories far and wide. The course of aggressive campaigns continued under the Marquis of Hastings who completed the work begun by Wellesley. Most of India became part of the British Empire.

Of course, during such periods of expansion, the administration was at times modified according to needs. Among such minor changes, the office of Superintendent of Police was instituted in each district for more efficient functioning of the police system. This innovation completed the police structure of the districts. The *thanas* with *darogas* became a universal phenomenon in India. In a broader sense, the system was inexpensive considering the services it rendered. In many places it proved both efficient and vigorous.

It was the judicial system which created a perpetual problem. People did not know the laws of the rulers. The rulers did not know the laws of the land. The language in the courts was unknown to most of the litigants. To most judges, the language of the people was foreign. In such circumstances mere establishment of courts did not necessarily bring justice to the people. Delay became synonymous with court procedures. Once one was involved in a case, his fortune was exhausted in its pursuit. Such difficulties drove the weak to the arms of professional lawyers who began to thrive in the mass of legal complications.

Various measures were adopted to improve conditions. To reduce the number of suits, a fee was imposed on them. Appeals from lower courts to higher were made more difficult. To avoid delay at the highest court, Wellesley thought it desirable that the Governor-General and his Council should not act as judges, since they were busy men. So, independent judges were appointed for the *Sadar* court. Further, the number of judges was increased at the district level. The magistrates were given greater power in matter of small criminal cases. In spite of such measures, the legal system remained difficult and defective.

Thirty-five years after Cornwallis' innovations, Lord William Bentinck assumed office as Governor-General and inaugurated an era of reforms. His social and educational reforms, which produced far-reaching results, will be described in subsequent chapters. In administrative and judicial fields his achievements were also remarkable.

Bentinck was shocked to see that the provincial courts of appeal had become 'resting places for those members of the service who were deemed unfit for higher responsibilities.' The standard of those courts had gone down greatly and they deserved abolition.

A thorough reorganisation became necessary, with the civil judges being given sessions duties. The future district judges were to evolve out of the system. The district judges of Cornwallis' creation had to surrender their magisterial powers to the district collectors. Thus there emerged the district officer who was the district magistrate, the collector of revenue and the head of the police force—all combined in one and the same person. Side by side, each district had a sessions judge with criminal and civil jurisdiction. The district magistrate of Bentinck's time continued till the end of British administration. He performed many functions and enjoyed wide powers. Bentinck broke down the barrier erected by Cornwallis against Indians in the administrative machinery and convinced the home authorities to accept the principle of giving Indians higher positions.

In the mid-nineteenth century, when Lord Dalhousie ruled India (1848-56), the British Empire extended from the Hindukush to Burma and from the Himalayas to Cape Comorin. With the completion of the empire, the administrative features became common over the whole subcontinent, except for the native states. By that time, the nature and scope of administration had also considerably changed. Dalhousie pursued a policy of relentless imperialism in his conquests and annexations. But he also represented modernism in his administration. Through the Doctrine of Lapse he extinguished a number of small States. The intention was to bring the whole of India, as far as possible, under a uniform system of government.

Dalhousie's fame rests on his introduction of railways, the electric telegraph and the introduction of a modern postal system. These innovations benefited the administrative machinery as much as the people. To meet the needs of growing public works, Dalhousie established the Public Works Department. Division of governmental functions into well-defined departments was yet another of his reforms.

Dalhousie left India in 1856. In 1857 India witnessed the Great Rising against the British, described by the latter as the Sepoy Mutiny or Sepoy War. With the end of that rising the rule of the East India Company also came to an end. The British considered their success as the reconquest of India. The British Crown took over power from the Company which had ruled from 1757 to 1857. Thus ended the first half of the period of British rule and the second half began. Before we survey the constitutional developments under the Crown, it is necessary to take into account the various Charter Acts passed by Parliament during the period from Pitt's India Act to the transfer of power from Company to Crown.

The British Parliament and the Charter Acts

Once the principle of parliamentary sovereignty over the East India Company's territorial acquisitions and administrative and commercial functions was established on a sound basis, periodical parliamentary regulation of the Company's affairs became imperative. In the year of the Regulating Act of 1773, Parliament granted to the Company the monopoly of trade for a period of twenty years only. In 1793 this term expired and a new lease of rights became necessary. From 1793, the Company's Charter was renewed at the end of each twenty year period. These Charter Acts dealt with the Company's external and internal affairs and brought about any necessary changes. In the evolution of the British Indian administration, the Charter Acts therefore had great significance. A brief outline of the Acts is given below.

The Charter Act of 1793 was passed when Pitt the Younger was Prime Minister, Henry Dundas, President of the Board of Control, and Cornwallis, Governor-General. There were many enemies of the Company in England who wanted its trade monopoly to go. But the Company had its supporters in the Government, including Dundas, who created an impression that all was well in India and that the Company deserved appreciation. Parliament obliged Pitt and Dundas and passed the Charter Act of 1793. It gave the Company its trade monopoly for another twenty years. Side by side, private traders in England were given permission to trade in the East, but to a very limited extent, *i.e.,* upto three thousand tones of shipping only.

In the structure of the government, the Act did not effect any big change. Yet, some of the changes were noteworthy. The salaries of the members of the Board of Control and its staff were to be henceforward a change on the Indian revenues. The expenses of the Crown forces in India were to be paid by the Company. The Crown was given power to divert revenues from India towards the defence of India, if and when necessary. Like the Governor-General, the Governors of the Indian Presidencies were given power to override the decisions of their Councils in certain circumstances. A significant provision of the Act was the enhancement of the powers of the Governor-General over the Presidency Governments in matters relating to foreign policy. He was also empowered to supersede the local Governor whenever he visited a Presidency.

Thus two trends were taking shape. First, Indian revenues were to be spent for officers and establishments in England; secondly, centralisation of power in India was considered a matter of necessity. The Act declared in the name of the nation that the conquest of territories was not the intention of the British. But, in fact, the era of aggressive imperialism was soon to follow.

Within the next twenty years, through political turmoils and wars, England emerged as the greatest imperial power of modern history. Through the opening decade of the nineteenth century she was fighting a life and death struggle against Napoleon's France. At the end of that decade Napoleon's empire was beginning to sink beneath the Continental System, the Peninsular War and the Russian expedition. In India, the era of Wellesley had ended with the British supremacy established over a greater part of the subcontinent. It was in this moment of glory that the time came for the renewal of the Company's Charter in 1813.

The economic crisis arising out of the Napoleonic wars, the Continental System, and the first effects of the industrial revolution, demanded a new economic outlook in the greater interest of the British nation. The monopoly of the Company over trade in the eastern hemisphere was a stupendous barrier in the path of other English merchants who, inspired by he *laissez-faire* doctrine, wanted economic freedom and the abolition of monopoly business. This movement proved a serious threat to the Company's commercial position. Internally, the Company's financial crisis revealed a source of weakness. The wars in India cost the Company dearly, and it was running a debt of many millions of pounds. It had no other alternative but to appeal to Parliament for aid. In such circumstances the Parliament discussed the renewal of the Charter and finally passed the Charter Act of 1813.

In several ways the Act of 1813 marked the beginning of the decline of the Company, even though it had many more years to run and many more areas to conquer. Its monopoly of trade and commerce with India was abolished. The Indian trade was thrown open to other English merchants. The Company, however, was allowed to enjoy its monopoly of trade with China for another twenty years. In political and administrative matters, the Act of 1813 did not initiate any major change. The Company was permitted to enjoy, as before, its power over the Indian territories and revenues for another term of twenty years, under the sovereignty of the Crown. The power of the Board of Control was further enlarged. The Act gave it the authority to control the civil and military training of the Company's servants. In matters of popular interest, the Act of 1813 is remembered for its initiation of an educational policy. It directed the Company to set apart one lakh of rupees annually for 'the revival and improvement of literature and encouragement of the learned natives of India and for the introduction and promotion of knowledge of the sciences among the inhabitants of the British territories in India.' The Act contained yet another novelty. Christian missionaries who wanted to come to India for religious or other 'lawful' purposes were to be given licences for the said purpose by the Court of Directors, or on their objection, by the Board of Control. Thus, the Charter Act of 1813 emphasised the Crown's sovereignty, enhanced the power of the Board of Control, reduced the commercial privileges of the Company, opened India to all English merchants for the greater economic benefit of the home country and permitted missionaries to come to India for religious activities.

The period from 1813 to 1833 saw further extension of the Company's territories. Towards the close of the period hectic warfare for conquests had come to an end and a period of peace dawned in Indian political life. The time synchronised with the movement for reforms in England. It was a natural phenomenon in the history of

Indo-British relations that the character of the different epochs of British history was more or less reflected in the corresponding epochs of Indian history. The movement for political liberalism and parliamentary reform in England culminated in the passing of the first Reform Act in 1832. In India the new spirit was symbolised in the person of the Governor-General, Lord William Bentinck, who arrived there in July 1828. Working on the principle that the well-being of the governed is the duty of the government, Bentinck launched upon an extensive programme of economic, administrative social and educational reforms. He had governed India for five years when the time came for the renewal of the Company's Charter in 1833.

By that time opinion in England in regard to the East India Company was sharply divided. According to open school of thought, the Company had outlived its usefulness. It was an anomaly that a company of traders should continue as the sovereign masters of one of the biggest empires of all times. Another school strongly held the view that the Company's Government still had a most useful purpose to serve in the interests of both India and England. Bentinck's reform measures were a clear testimony to the Company's usefulness to the Indian people. On behalf of the view that the Company had a right to rule in the context of British interests, a vital question was raised—if not the Company, who else should rule India? Was Parliament in a position to take over the Indian administration? The Company found in Lord Macaulay a powerful advocate of its cause. He advanced his famous argument that the House of Commons had neither the necessary time, nor the necessary knowledge, nor had it the motive to acquire that knowledge, to settle Indian matters. His still greater argument was that while the British Parliament was divided into political parties quarrelling over political issues, the Company was 'neither Whig nor Tory', and that it had maintained strict neutrality in party affiliations.

Amid such opinions, Parliament passed the Charter Act of 1833. The champions of the Company's cause carried the day, though of course its opponents had to be satisfied as far as possible. Thus, the Charter was renewed for another twenty years. The Company retained the power to govern India in trust for His Majesty, his heirs and successors. But the Company's functions as a trading concern were put to an end. That is, the Company continued as the rulers of India, but not as traders in India. It also lost its monopoly of the China trade which was thrown open to all merchants.

Noteworthy changes were effected in the constitution of India with a view to making the Indian administration more centralised. So far, the Governor-General was called 'the Governor-General of Bengal', even though he had power over other Presidencies. The Act of 1833 introduced a new designation for him. He was hereafter to be styled as 'the Governor-General of India.' Thus, in a strictly legal sense, Lord William Bentinck may be regarded as the first Governor-General of India.[7] The Act of 1833 also provided the Governor-General with wider powers in administrative, legislative and financial matters. In administration, his authority became supreme over the Presidencies of Bengal, Bombay and Madras in all matters. In legislation, formerly there had been five categories of law, such as, the Acts of the British Parliament, the various Charter Acts, regulations passed by the Governor-General-in-Council, orders given by the Supreme Court, and the orders of the Presidency Governments. The Act of 1833 put an end to such as variety of laws for the country, for all places and purposes and persons, and on all subjects. These laws were to be enforced by all the courts of India. Of course, the Governor-General had no power to encroach upon the prerogative of the Crown and the powers of parliament, but otherwise he became the supreme law-giver in the country. To lend support to his law-making functions, the Act of 1833 added a new member to his Executive Council, called the Law Member. Macaulay came to India as the first Law Member. The genesis of the future legislative wing of the British government in India may be traced to the institution of the office. The central government took over from the Presidency governments all their previous powers concerning taxation and expenditure. The revenues of the entire British India were controlled and managed by the central government from its headquarters. Every item of expenditure, big or small, required the sanction of the Government of India.

The Act thus converted the East India Company into a purely political organisation and reorganised the Indian administration into a strong centralised system with the Governor-General as its pivot. True to the liberal spirit of the time, the Act contained the famous clause: 'Be it enacted that no native of said territories shall by reason only of his religion, place of birth, descent, colour, or any of them, be disabled from holding any place, office, or employment in the said company.' In a general way, the doors were now opened to Indians to occupy modest administrative positions, such as deputy collectors and deputy magistrates.

The twenty years following the Bentinck era saw the last phase of the Company's Indian career. The last great conquests, including those of Sind and the Punjab, were effected. The centralised system, too, proved effective. In 1853, when the question of the renewal of the Charter came up again, India was being ruled by Lord Dalhousie who, in his conquests and administration, combined the qualities of Wellesley and Bentinck. But his aims and achievements were the outcome of his uncommon personality rather than of the Company's vitality. On the other hand, the Company as an organisation, had become out-dated. The proprietors were still there as in the good old days. Some 1800 of them, each possessing a minimum stock of one thousand pounds, had the right to vote and elect the Court of Directors. In fact, they were interested only in receiving their dividends. The Directors had the power. But controlled by the Board of Control since the days of Pitt's India Act, they had gradually lost genuine interest. The decline of the Court had led to a corresponding increase in the power of the Board. The President of the Board was a member of the British Cabinet, with the power of secret communication with the Government of India. 'Thus,' writes Dalhousie's biographer, William Lee-Warner, 'the Court of Directors was tied hand and foot by the Board, which signified the President, while he in turn signified the Government or Crown.' It was evident that the Company was hastening towards a natural demise as far as its political authority was concerned.

Yet, the Company wanted to continue as long as it could. Its opponents claimed that the Court of Directors should go since it served no valuable purpose. Moreover, what was the use in having a type of double government at home with a Court and a Board sharing power or duplicating the same functions? Even in the face of such criticism Parliament decided upon the renewal of the Charter and the Charter Act of 1853 was passed. Significantly enough, the Company's powers were not extended for another term of 20 years, but for such time as parliament should otherwise provide. It was an ominous signal regarding the future of the Company. The status of the Board of Control was raised further with the salary of the President being made equal to that of any other principal Secretary of state in the British Cabinet. On the other hand, the status of the Court of Directors was further curtailed with the number of its members being reduced from 24 to 18. Six of such members were again to be nominated by the Crown. The most useful privilege which the Court of Directors had enjoyed was the power of appointment of the Company's servants. The Act took away this power of patronage and provided for appointment to the Indian services through open competitive examinations.

Regarding the Government of India, the Act of 1853 brought about a significant change in the field of legislation. The former Law Member of the Governor-General's Council was given the right to sit and vote in the executive meetings, a power he had not previously possessed. The Executive Council of the Governor-General was enlarged with six new members for the purpose of legislation. Those new, or additional, members were called the legislative members. Thus the legislative function of the Government was recognised as separate from the executive function. The Governor-General, the Commander-in Chief, the four members of the Council and the six new legislative members together formed the Legislative Council. Among the six legislative members there were the Chief Justice and a Puisne Judge of the Calcutta Supreme Court, and four officials representing the four provincial governments of Madras, Bombay, Bengal and the North-western Provinces. A rudimentary type of local representation in legislative affairs is traceable in the above composition of the Legislative Council.

The Charter Act of 1853 was the last of the Charters enjoyed by the East India Company. In 1857, the great Indian Rising against British rule took place. That called for an assessment of the strength and weakness of the British administration in India. The Parliament and the people of England spent anxious moments till the rising was suppressed. At the end of the rising, the Company's rule was terminated and its power was transferred to the British Crown. So 1857 stands as a dividing line in British Indian history.

The Transfer of Power and the Rule of the British Crown

During the rising, the local administration in unaffected areas functioned without dislocation. In the affected areas, the administration was restored as soon as the rising subsided. Thus, the administrative machinery of the previous regime was not destroyed at its base. The transfer of power affected the higher branches of government, both with regard to policy matters and practical administration.

After the rising of 1857, the assumption of the Government by the Crown was signified by the Government of India Act, 1858 and in the Queen's Proclamation of the same year. Lord Palmerston, the Prime Minister of England at the time of the rising, first moved his Bill in February 1858 for the transfer of Government. He began by praising the Company: 'I believe the East India Company has donw many good things in India. I believe that its administration has been attended with great advantage to the population under its rule.' But next he proceeded to argue against the Company's continuance by criticising the system of 'double government'. And finally he concluded by saying: 'I cannot bring myself to think that Parliament is less capable of wisely administering the great affairs of State in connection with India than the Court of Directors in Leadenhall Street. I am not afraid to trust parliament with an insight into Indian affairs...Therefore, so far from being alarmed at the consequences which may arrive from bringing Indian affairs under the cognisance of Parliament, I believe that a great benefit to India, and through India to the British nation, will result therefrom,' Palmerston's ministry fell before the Bill had become an Act. The succeeding Government of Lord Derby took up the issue and the President of the Board of Control, Lord Stanley, brought in a Bill which, when passed, became the Act of 1858.

According to the Act: 'India shall be governed by and in the name of Her majesty.' One of Her Majesty's principal Secretaries of State was to perform all the powers and duties relating to the Government or revenues of India as formerly enjoyed by the Court of Directors and the Board of Control. For this purpose a fifth principal Secretary of State was to be appointed. He and his staff were to be paid out of the revenues of India. There was to be a Council of fifteen members, styled as the Council of India, to aid the Secretary of State. The latter was to act as the President of the Council. The Council, under direction of the Secretary of State, was required to transact business concerning India. The Secretary of State could overrule the Council. The salaries of the Council members were to be paid out of the revenues of India.

Regarding the Indian Government, the Act of 1858 made the Governor-General of India the direct representative of the British Crown. The Act vested in the Governor-General in the power of superintendence, direction and control of the civil and military administration of India. It was for the Crown to appoint the Governor-General and the Governors of the Presidencies. The Lieutenant-Governors were to be appointed by the Governor-General with the approval of the Crown. The Secretary of State-in-Council appointed members of the various councils of India.

The Secretary of State being a member of the Cabinet, the Cabinet being responsible to Parliament, and Parliament to the British people, it became obvious that by virtue of his position he became supreme. It was for him to lay before Parliament the annual statement of the Indian accounts and to report on the progress of the country. The absolute position of the Secretary of State at home *vis-à-vis* the authority of the Governor-General ruling over the Indian Empire far from Britain, raised the problem regarding the real jurisdictions of the man in Parliament and the man on the spot. The theory that 'the Government of India must be, on the whole, carried out in India' was sound. Yet the power of the Secretary of State was almost invincible. Naturally, conflicts between the stronger personalities in their respective positions were bound to occur.

The Act of 1858 was quickly followed by the Queen's

Proclamation. In a grand durbar held at Allahabad, Lord Canning read it out on 1st November 1858. The Proclamation designated Canning as the Queen's first Viceroy and Governor-General in and over the Indian territories. It confirmed the appointment of all persons in the service of the East India Company. It announced to the Indian princes that 'all Treaties and Engagements made with them by or under the authority of the Honourable East India Company are by Us accepted, and will be scrupulously maintained... We shall respect the Rights, Dignity, and Honour of the Native Princes as Our own.' To the people of India the Proclamation said: 'And it is Our further will that, so far as may be, Our Subjects, of whatever Race or Creed, be freely and impartially admitted to offices in Our Services, the Duties of which they may be qualified, by their education, ability, and integrity, duly to discharge.'

The Crown's assumption of power did not put an end to the process of administrative evolution in India. Rather, in necessitated further developments in the light of changing times.

Developments in Executive, Legislative and Judicial Branches

The pattern of government which evolved under the East India Company was modified by the Government of India Act, 1858, but the Act did not give a final shape to things. Further modifications were imperative and through such changes the executive, legislative and judicial branches began to assume a more and more modern shape.

To begin with the executive branch: the first Viceroy, Lord Canning, though very powerful, wanted to be still more powerful. He could not feel free in system of collective work with his Executive Council. He wanted therefore to reduce his Councillors to mere secretaries and to concentrate all executive functions in himself. His wishes, however, could not be fulfilled. Instead, he brought in the portfolio system, by which the Executive Council as a whole discussed broad policy matters and large problems of general interest. Individual members of the Council were given the charge of minor departmental matters. Thus each had a portfolio. Canning's innovation was legalised by the Indian Council's Act of 1861, which the British Parliament passed in order 'to make better provision for the Constitution of the Council of the Governor-General of India, and for the Local Government of the several Presidencies and Provinces of India.....'

Under the Act of 1861, the Governor-General's Executive Council contained five members of whom two were civil servants, one was a soldier described as the military member, one was a financial expert and one a legal expert. The Commander-in-Chief attended the meetings of the Executive Council as an extra-ordinary member. The five ordinary members remained in charge of the different departments. The Governor-General could overrule his Council.

The Indian Councils Act of 1874 created a sixth member to be in charge of Public Works Department. But the need for such a department was doubted and it was later abolished. Instead, the Department of Commerce and Industry was established. After some time, the military member was substituted by a military supply member and in 1909 the latter post was abolished. In 1910, the education and health portfolios were placed in charge of a separate member. It was in the year 1909, under the famous Morley-Minto Reforms, that for the first time an Indian entered into the Viceroy's Executive Council as the Law Member. He was S.P. Sinha. The entry of an Indian Member did not increase the number of members. Thus by 1914, the Home Member, Finance Member, Law Member, Commerce and Industry Member, and the Education Member constituted the Executive Council as the five ordinary members, and the Commander-in-Chief continued as the one extraordinary member. The Foreign portfolio remained in the hands of the Governor-General himself and included relations with India's neighbours as well as with the Indian princely states. Ultimately, the number of departments increased to nine. They were, Foreign, Home, Legislative, Finance, Revenue and Agriculture, Public Works, Commerce and Industry, Education, and the Army. But the size of the Central Executive remained as before, namely, the Governor-General and six members of Council. They distributed all the departments among themselves.

Whatever might be the power of the Executive Council, the Governor-General's authority was above dispute. Both by law and convention his absolutism was accepted as inevitable. Moreover, the bureaucratic machinery of an imperial government helped enhance the powers of the Governor-General at the cost of his Council. The permanent secretaries in different departments advised the Governor-General on all vital issues and carried on administration subject to his direction and order. Till the last days of British rule, the executive power of the Governor-General to govern Indian remained a reality.

It was on the evolution of the Central Legislature that much of the Parliamentary and, in future, popular attention centred. In earlier days when Parliament began to look into Indian affairs, it thought of giving India an appropriate executive, but did not think of the necessity of providing a Legislature. Therefore, in 1773, the Governor-General-in-Council was given the power to make regulations for the purpose of administration. Lord Cornwallis collected these regulations into a Code in 1793. Subsequently, similar regulations were applied to Madras, Bombay and the North-West Provinces. All these territories came to be known as Regulation Provinces. When new territories were conquered, the old regulations could not be applied to most of them. The new areas were administered by officers of the government who applied the laws and regulations framed either by the Governor-General-in-Council, or by the Lieutenant-Governors or by the Commissioners and approved by the Governor-General. Those areas came to be known as the non-regulation provinces.

The law-making power was thus purely a monopoly of the executive body. The first significant step in a modern direction was taken in 1833, when the famous Charter Act of that year added to the Council of the Governor-General a new member known as the Law Member whose presence was necessary for passing all legislative measures. Simultaneously, the whole legislative power was centralised in the Governor-General-in-Council.

The legislative experiment within the next twenty years showed up one great defect in the system, namely, that the law-making authorities at Calcutta did not understand the problems of other distant Presidencies. Moreover, the Executive Council of the Governor-General, with the assistance of only a single legislative member, proved itself incapable of performing the increasing duties of a great empire. So, in 1853, the next big step was taken to improve matters. To the Council of the Governor-General were added four members, one each from the different Provinces of India, together with the Chief Justice and one Judge of the Supreme Court of Bengal for making laws and regulations. The intention was to give a recognisable size to the legislative body and to make available to the Executive Council their special knowledge of local problems.

Within a few years, and shortly after the transfer of power from the Company to the Crown, radical changes in the system of legislation became necessary. Three main issues captured attention. The size of the Legislative Council required expansion along with the scope of functions confined to legislation. Decentralisation of legislative powers was necessary to give Presidency governments legislative authority. Furthermore, the rising of 1857 had led many people to believe that 'the minds of Natives of high rank' could be better understood by taking the native element into the legislative system. In the light of such needs, the Indian Councils Act of 1861 brought about certain noteworthy changes in the field of legislation.

Under the Act, not less than six and not more than twelve additional members were to be added to the Governor-General's Council for the purposes of legislation. They were to be nominated by the Governor-General and to hold office for two years. One half of such members were to be non-official. The powers and functions of the Legislative Council were defined and a measure passed by the Legislative Council required the assent of the Governor-General to become an Act. The Crown, acting through the secretary of State, could disallow any such Act. Though the legislative power of the Governor-General covered all of Her Majesty's Indian territories, yet legislative decentralisation was brought in. The Governments of Madras and Bombay were given legislative authority (powers which had been taken away from them under the Charter Act, 1833). The Councils of the Governors were increased in size for legislative purposes with the addition of the Advocate General and other nominated members. The laws passed by the provincial legislative councils could be vetoed by the Governor and the Governor-General. Moreover, there was nothing to distinguish provincial subjects from central subjects. Besides Bombay and Madras, legislative councils were also to be established in Bengal, the North-West Provinces and the Punjab where Lieutenant-Governors and some nominated members were to form the Councils. Thus legislative decentralisation was being introduced on a very small scale. Regarding the admission of Indians into legislative councils, the Act decided to remain silent, but implied thereby that there was no restriction against their entry. Any broader consideration for real Indian participation was out of the question. During the discussions on the Indian Councils Bill, 1861, Sir Charles Wood made it clear in the House of Commons that 'You cannot possibly assemble at any one place in India persons who shall be the real representatives of the various classes of the Native population of the empire...To talk of a Native representation is, therefore, to talk of that which is simply and utterly impossible.' However, he admitted that in the newly constituted legislative councils, the 'additional members may be either Europeans, persons of European extraction, or Natives.' Thus, after 1861, in the legislative councils of the centre and the provinces, a few non-official seats were available to select Indians.

During the last quarter of the nineteenth century, political consciousness in India was growing fast. The birth of the Indian National Congress in 1885 symbolised that consciousness. The need for Indian participation in legislative functions was felt by some enlightened Englishmen themselves. The benevolent Lord Ripon wanted to bring in elected Indians into the Legislative Councils. But that being difficult at the time, he gave India the benefit of local self-government. He wrote: 'What I want to secure by the extension of Local Self-Government is not a representation of the people of a European democratic type but the gradual training of the best, most intelligent, and most influential men in the community to take an interest and an active part in the management of their local affairs.' Ripon's resolution of 18th May 1882, paved the way for a country-wide experiment of giving the people of India the responsibility of managing their local affairs through rural boards and municipalities.

The Indian consciousness, however, aimed at higher responsibilities. By the end of the nineteenth century, the nominated Indian members in different legislative councils had proved their worth. By that time the legislative bodies created by the Act of 1861 were becoming outdated. They appeared too small, and their powers too limited. The rising generation of Indians demanded more real power in legislative spheres. Voices were heard in favour of elective principles. In the changing atmosphere, Parliament passed the Indian Councils Act, 1892, to satisfy Indian aspirations.

The Act satisfied certain logical needs. The Imperial and the Provincial Councils were enlarged in size with new additional members. The local bodies, such as the municipalities and district boards, were to elect some additional members. The scope of the legislative councils was also enlarged. They gained the power to discuss the financial statement prepared by the government, but without the power to vote on it. The right to put questions to the government was also granted to members of legislatures.

At the dawn of the nationalist era, the legislatures created by the Act of 1892 became the platform for some of the leading Indians of the time, like Gopal Krishna Gokhale, for voicing further demands and criticising the misdeeds of an alien government. Within the next few years the National Congress took a definitely anti-British stand. The autocratic rule of Curzon hastened the growth of nationalism. His partition of Bengal led to the beginning of the first phase of the nationalist struggle against the British. While the movement was gathering strength, the next big step towards constitutional development was taken by the British Parliament, by the Act of 1909.

In the meantime, the judicial system had been taking a new shape since the transfer of power in 1858. From the earliest days, the maintenance of law and justice had presented almost insurmountable difficulties. The Company had tried to do much, but its systems had proved to be far from being successful or satisfactory. In the three Presidencies, there were smaller law courts under the provincial courts. But over all was the Supreme Court with a totally different origin and with a different set of laws. Thus, the Supreme Court representing the British Crown, and the country courts representing the Company's administration made the entire legal system paradoxical. After the transfer of power it became essential to remove legal anomalies and bring the legal system of the Empire into one uniform pattern. So an Act was passed by the British Parliament in August 1861 for establishing High Courts of Judicature in India. Under that Act, it was lawful for Her Majesty, by Letters Patent under the Great Seal of the United Kingdom, to erect and establish High Courts of Judicature at Calcutta, Madras and Bombay. Upon the establishment of such High Courts, the existing Supreme Courts as well as the *Sadar Diwani* and *Sadar Nizamat Adalats* of those places were to be abolished. The High Courts thus to be established were to derive their original jurisdiction from the Supreme Courts, and their appellate jurisdiction from the *Sadar Adalats*. Thus there was an amalgamation of the two previous systems into one. Each High Court was given the power of superintendence over all courts under its appellate jurisdiction, power to direct the transfer of any suit or appeal from any such court to any other court of equal or superior jurisdiction, and power to make and issue general rules for regulating the practice and proceedings of such courts. The Act of 1861 finally provided that 'It shall be lawful for Her Majesty, if at any time hereafter her Majesty see fit so to do...to erect and establish a High Court of Judicature in and for any portion of the Territories within Her Majesty's Dominions in India, not included within the limits of the local Jurisdiction of another High Court.'

In accordance with the Act, the actual Charters to establish the High courts at Calcutta, Madras and Bombay were issued in 1865. Another High Court was established at Allahabad in 1866. Establishment of subsequent High Courts did not take place till many years later in the twentieth century.

The Act of 1909, or the Morley-Minto Reforms

The Secretary of State, John Morley, and the Viceroy, Lord Minto, bestowed careful thought on the drafting of the Act of

1909, and indeed some notable steps were taken by them within the framework of reform before the Act was passed. In 1907, Morley admitted two Indians to the Council of the Secretary of State at London. Subsequently it was decided to admit an Indian to the Executive Council of the Governor-General. There was considerable opposition to the latter proposal from the British administrators in India. But to the British Cabinet it seemed that such appointments to high offices would please the Indian people, and so was the decision taken. Some raised the question, what would happen should the decision taken. Some raised the question, what would happen should the Muslims object to the appointment of a Hindu to the Viceroy's Council? Against it Morley declared; "I want to say that reference to the Hindu Community or the Mahommedan Community, in respect to the position of the Viceroy's Executive, is entirely wide of the mark in the view... If...it may be my duty by-and-by to recommend to the Crown the name of an Indian member, it will not be solely for the sake of placing on the Viceroy's Executive Council an Indian member simply as either a Hindu or a Mahommedan." Though that was the official declaration, yet in truth communalism was being practised in making the highest appointments. Firstly, when two Indian members were taken into the Indian Council in London, of the two one was a Hindu, K.G. Gupta, and, the other was a Muslim, Sayyid Hussain Bilgrami. Secondly, when it was decided to take an Indian into the Governor-General's Executive Council, the appointment was first given to a Hindu, S.P. Sinha, in 1909.

But when Sinha decided to resign in 1910, the Secretary of State searched for a Muslim to succeed him. 'In my view', he said, 'we must have a Mahometan, or else the Mahometans...will raise a howl; in fact there have been already letters in our newspapers. I am pretty certain it will have to be Ali Imam, and I fancy he will feel bound to take it.' Thus, a most unfortunate policy of the British was taking shape through the Morely-Minto reforms—the policy to divide Hindus and Muslims in the politico-constitutional set-up. The Act of 1909 aimed to increase the representative elements in the Indian legislatures and to increase their powers. It was thought desirable that the official majority should be maintained in the

Central Legislature, whereas a non-official majority could be tried out in the provincial legislatures. The maximum strength of each Council was fixed by the Act. Excluding the head of the Government and the members of the Executive Councils, it varied from 60 for the Council of the Governor-General, to 30 for the Councils of the Punjab and Burma, the number for each of the other five Provincial Councils being 50.

The concesion of increased representation or non-official majority in the provinces was vitiated by the introduction of the principle of separate electorates. Special provision was made for the representation of the professional classes, the landholders, the Mohammedans, European commerce and Indian commerce. Similarly, though elective principles were introduced, elections were to be held not according to territorial constituencies, but according to classes and interests. For example, the following was the position in the case of the Central Legislature. Out of the total 67 members of the House, 35 were officials and 32 were non-officials. Of the 32 non-officials, 5 were nominated by the Governor-General, and the remaining 27 elected. Of the 27 elected members, 13 were to be elected from the General Electorate, made up of the non-official members of the provincial legislatures. Of the remaining 14 members, 12 came from the Class Electorates, such as 6 from the landholders' constituencies and 6 from separate Muslim constituencies.

The remaining 2 members came from the Special Electorates, such as Chambers of Commerce. For provincial legislatures, too, class and special electorates were introduced. The so-called non-official majority in the provincial legislatures was not really the majority of elected members; because, among the non-officials, there were some members nominated by the provincial governors who naturally supported the official group and this placed the elected members in a rather difficult position. The only redeeming feature of the Act was that the Legislative Councils received some more powers by way of extended rights to discuss the budget estimates, to put supplementary questions, and to move resolutions on general matters of public interest. But such rights were more nominal than real. The discussions or resolutions had no effective force against the Government's policies or decisions. The Government also had no right to disallow questions or resolutions. The legislatures also had no right to discuss many vital matters, such as the foreign policy of the Government or its policy towards the Indian princes. The elective principles were also based on restricted franchise. Discrimination on grounds of communal consideration made them still worse. There was no uniformity of any kind. Voting rights varied from community to community, class to class and within the same community from person to person. While the moneyed classes got the franchise, education was not a qualification for it.

The Act appeared ridiculous when, in fact, constituencies were created containing ten voters or less. Even the largest constituency could claim to possess only about 700 members. The non-official members of the provincial legislative councils who formed the General Electorate numbered only 200. They elected only 13 members to the Central Legislature. Such numbers show how inadequate was the concession given. The Act of 1909 was thus dangerous with its conception of separate electorates and ridiculous for its extremely limited franchise.

The evil effects of the Morley-Minto Reforms were soon realised. But few people in 1909 anticipated the far-reaching consequences of the introduction of communal principles into the constitutional system.

The Montagu-Chelmsford Reforms or the Act of 1919

No sooner was the Act of 1909 put into operation than the general dissatisfaction against its nature and scope became apparent. Within a few years, greater political developments began to take shape. The First World War broke out in 1940. Mohandas Karamchand Gandhi returned from South Africa in January 1915. With his return a new epoch began. He was, however, loyal to the Government during its worst trial of the war period. India gave all possible help to the British in men, money and material. But aspirations to gain constitutional concessions at the end of the war became a natural outcome of India's war efforts. To satisfy the Indian people, the new Secretary of State for India in the Cabinet of Lloyd George,

Edwin Montagu, made a historic declaration in the House of Commons on 20th August 1917 regarding the future of India, that 'The policy of His Majesty's Government, with which the Government of India are in complete accord, it that of the increasing association of Indians in every branch of the administration and the gradual development of self-governing institutions with a view to the progressive realisation of responsible government in India as an integral part of the British Empire.' In November of the same year, Montagu himself came to India to study the situation and assess the needs of the time. In consultation with the Viceroy, Lord Chelmsford, a programme of reforms was drawn up. Finally, the reforms were embodied in the government of India Bill which became an Act in December 1919. The Act is commonly named the Montagu-Chelmsford, or Montford Reforms, or the Government of India Act, 1919. The Act was born at a critical time. The war had ended at the end of 1918. Forgetting India's loyal help, but anticipating nationalist agitation at the end of the war, the Government decided to impose repressive and restrictive measures on India. The Rowlatt Bills were framed for this purpose. They roused Gandhi's conscience against the British. He started peaceful agitation against the Rowlatt Bills but the Government resorted to oppressive measures. Such confrontation culminated in the Jallianwallah Bagh tragedy[10] where the Government massacred an unarmed crowd—which included old people, women and children—who had gathered together in a peaceful meeting. The Act of 1919 saw the light of day under the shadow of a gloomy political atmosphere, pointing to a much more serious struggle in the future against foreign rule.

The Act of 1919 provided for a distribution of powers between the Centre and the Provinces. The central subjects included such matters as Defence, Foreign Relations, Relations with Native States, Railways, Post and Telegraph, Currency and Coinage, All-India Services, Civil and Criminal Law and Procedure, Imperial Revenue, Public Debt, and Ecclesiastical Administration. The provincial subjects included such items as Local Self-Government, Education, Sanitation and Public Health, Public Works, Agriculture, Excise, Fisheries and Cooperative Societies, Famine Relief, Land Revenue Administration, Irrigation, Forests, Administration of Justice, Police,

Prisons, etc. The subjects which were not given to the Provinces,
Prisons, etc. The subjects which were not given to the Provinces belonged to the Centre. As the powers were divided, so also were the sources of revenue. The main sources of income for the Centre were income tax, customs, railways, post and telegraph, opium and salt. The Provinces derived income from land revenue, excise, irrigation, forests, stamps and registration fees.

This division of powers and revenues did not make India a federation. The powers of the Centre were so formidable that its decisions were final and always binding on the Provinces, irrespective of whether such decisions related to central or provincial subjects.

The Act of 1919 provided for a bicameral legislature at the Centre. The Lower House was called the Legislative Assembly, and the Upper House the Council of State. The strength of the Council of State was 60 members, with 33 elected and 27 nominated members. The Legislative Assembly contained 145 members of whom 103 were elected and the rest nominated. Among the nominated members, 25 were officials and the rest non-officials. Among the 103 elected members, there were 51 from general constituencies, 30 from Muhammedan constituencies, 2 from Sikh constituencies, and 20 from special constituencies, such as, Europeans, Landholders and Indian commerce. The duration of the Lower House was for 3 years and of the Upper House 5 years. The elections were direct, but the franchise was restricted. In 1920, voters for the Council of State numbered a little over 17 thousand only, and for the Legislative Assembly a little over 9 lakhs.

Though the Central Legislature was given much legislative powers, yet the extensive powers vested in the Governor-General made him supreme in legislative matters. In the name of 'the safety or transquillity of British India, or any part thereof' he could do a great deal. In certain subjects his permission was necessary to introduce a bill. In the name of safety and tranquillity he could stop the course of a bill at any stage. He had himself the power to Legislature failed to enact what he wanted. To face an emergency he could issue ordinances which were as good as law for six months. His assent was necessary for any measure passed by the Legislature.

He could give his assent, could return the bill for reconsideration, or reserve it for His Majesty's consideration. Finally, the Act of 1919 vested the ultimate authority in the Crown to reject any act of the Governor-General or the Legislature.

In view of such executive domination, the Legislature remained powerless. The Legislative Assembly was given the power to pass the budget. But in that matter, too, the executive ruled supreme. The Assembly had no right either to discuss or to vote on certain items. The Governor-General had the power to restore in the budget what the Assembly thought necessary to withdraw. In an emergency, he could sanction expenditure, irrespective of the Assembly's wishes. Thus, the Act of 1919, while giving extended power to the Central Legislature in theory, imposed on it too many restrictions in practice. Internally, the Assembly enjoyed an elected majority, but the elected members were divided into communal groups, a system which perverted all principles of parliamentary life.

In the provincial sphere, the Act of 1919 brought about the novel system of administration known as Dyarchy. The objective was to transfer to Indian hands a limited amount of responsibility at the provincial level. There were eight full-fledged provinces—Bengal, Bombay, Madras, the United Provinces, Bihar and Orissa, Punjab, the Central Provinces, and Assam. Each of these provinces were placed under a Governor. The provincial subjects were divided into two groups—reserved and transferred. The reserved subjects were kept in the hands of the Governor—in—Council. The transferred subjects were to be administered by the Governor, acting with his Ministers. The reserved list contained such powers as Finance, Land Revenue, Justice, Police, Prisons, Famine Relief, Irrigation and Waterways, Control of Newspapers, Printing Presses and Books, Inspection of Factories and Mines, Labour Welfare and Industrial Disputes, Public Services, Excluded Areas, Agency Functions, etc. The transferred subjects included, Local Self-Government, Education, Medical Administration, Public Health and Sanitation, Agriculture, Excise, Public Works, Development of Industries, the Veterinary Department, Fisheries, and Cooperative Societies.

The system of Dyarchy rested on a principle. In the

administration of reserved powers, the Governor, through the Governor-General, the Secretary of State and the British Parliament, remained responsible to the people of Great Britain. In the administration of the transferred powers, the Governor with his Ministers remained responsible to the voters of the provinces through the elected Legislative Councils. The control of the British Government over the provincial ministers was reduced while the latter worked in their transferred jurisdiction. The system introduced the experiment of giving to Indian hands some amount of responsibility.

The Ministers were to belong to the provincial legislatures. The Act provided for a Legislative Council in every Governor's Province, consisting of the members of the Executive Council, the Governor's nominated members, and elected members. At least 70 percent of the members were to be elected. The life of the Legislative Council was three years unless it was dissolved earlier. The size of the Legislative Councils differed from province to province. The Act increased the size of the legislatures, but did not provide for a second chamber. In theory the legislatures were given adequate powers, but in reality most of those powers could be contradicted by other factors. The legislatures had no power to control the executive in the usual parliamentary sense. The Ministers were appointed by the Governor and held office during his pleasure.

It was the Governor who was supreme in provincial administration and legislation. The budget was to be presented to the legislatures but if it refused to accept any demand regarding any of the reserved subjects, the Governor could sanction such expenditure. He could also sanction any expenditure on the pretext of emergency. The Act of 1919 gave the Governor powers to give assent to any bill passed by the Legislative Council, to withhold his assent, to return the bill for reconsideration, or to reserve it for the consideration of the Governor-General. In regard to the reserved subjects, the Governor could himself recommend a bill. If the legislature refused to pass it, the Governor could certify that it had been passed. All bills passed by the provincial legislatures required the assent of the Governor and the Governor-General.

In his relations with the Ministers, the Governor could accept their advice regarding the transferred subjects. But he had the power to reject that advice and act on his own. Thus, the provincial legislatures as well as the provincial ministers enjoyed only limited power because of the overriding powers vested in the Governor in all matters.

The Act of 1919 provided for direct elections to the provincial legislatures. But the number of voters to elect the members was small. High property qualifications were necessary to get the voting right. Besides, communal and class electorates were created to divided the people on unhealthy lines. People voted as Muhammedans, Europeans, Anglo-Indians, Indian Christians, Sikhs and even as non-Brahmins (for example in Madras).

The system of Dyarchy revealed grave defects as a constitutional machinery of government. The division of provincial powers into reserved and transferred subjects created complications and broke down the unity of administration. To maintain a semblance of unity the Governor assumed extra precautions which eventually made him more supreme. The Governor and his Council on the one hand, and the Governor and his Ministers on the other, jurisdiction were demarcated, yet they overlapped. Disputes, therefore, became inevitable. The bureaucracy showed greater loyalty to the English members in the Executive Council than to the Indian Ministers in the legislature. The Ministers were placed in an unenviable position by constitutional circumstances. There was no organised party to which all of them were supposed to belong in a parliamentary way. There was no harmony and co-ordination among them in matters of policy. There was no collective responsibility. They faced criticism in the legislature for actions of the Governor and his Government. Furthermore, the Governor did not extend his unqualified support to his Ministers. Ministries felt helpless to carry on their programmes since Finance was in the reserved list and it often proved difficult to obtain the funds necessary to carry out ministerial policies. The permanent secretaries, if and when they differed with the Ministers, had the protection of the Governor. In such difficult circumstances, the Ministers felt powerless to shoulder the responsibilities given to them by the Constitution. The legislatures, too, were in a delicate position. They had the parliamentary privilege of freedom of speech. They put questions, moved resolutions, brought adjournment motions, and criticised the conduct of the Ministers, but they could not remove a Minister. The latter could not be removed by a no-confidence motion in the Legislature. He stayed as long as the Governor wanted him to stay.

Nevertheless, with all its defects and demerits, the Act of 1919 was yet another step in the constitutional development of India, and the system of government it introduced endured till a better system was brought about in 1935.

Political Developments from 1919 to 1935

There was an interval of fifteen years between the Act of 1919 and the next Government of India Act of 1935. That period saw the beginning of the Gandhian revolution and its growth and logical conclusion. As soon as the Act of 1919 was passed, the National Congress declared it as 'inadequate, unsatisfactory and disappointing.' The Congress was prepared for responsive cooperation, but everything depended on political developments. In 1920, the Indian Muslims launched a countrywide agitation against the British, known as the Khilafat agitation. While giving it all support, Gandhi initiated his Non-cooperation movement with the declaration that the attitude of the Government 'made it impossible for him to continue cooperation with a Government that had acted so unscrupulously and for whom he could retain neither respect nor affection.' By December 1921, nearly forty thousand men had been put in jail as a result of the movement. That was the state of affairs at the end of the year in the early months of which the Act of 1919 had been put into operation.

Early in 1922 Gandhi suspended his movement on account of an incident of violence at Chauri Chaura in the United Provinces where a mob had killed 22 policemen. He wanted his revolution to be absolutely non-violent and his followers highly disciplined. From 1922 Gandhi devoted his energy to rousing the conscience of the people against various socio-economic maladies, while making them conscious also of their ultimate purpose. The Congress movement and ideologies spread to every corner of the land and inspired the masses.

The next stage of unrest opened in 1928 when the British Government appointed a Commission under Sir John Simon to enquire into the working of the 1919 Constitution and to suggest further action. Though Indians had been clamouring for radical reforms for so long, no Indian was given a place in the Simon Commission. If the purpose of the Commission was to observe the working of a constitution and to prepare a better one, the exclusion of Indians form such a body was taken as a grave injustice to India. The countrywide boycott of the Simon Commission began in right earnest and proved successful. Everywhere Simon went in India, he heard the slogan, 'Simon, go back.'

In the meantime the Congress was developing on radical lines and Gandhi was preparing for his next move. In December 1929 the Congress met at Lahore under the presidentship of Jawaharlal Nehru and passed a resolution on independence, directing that 'all Congressmen will henceforth devote their exclusive attention to the attainment of complete Independence for India.' It was decided to launch a programme of Civil Disobedience.

Gandhi began the movement by his historic march in March-April 1930 from Sabarmati Ashram to a place named Dandi on the seashore of Gujarat to manufacture salt in violation of the government salt laws. Within months sixth thousand people had entered the British Indian prisons for disobedience of the law.

While India was thus in the grip of virtual revolution, the Simon Commission completed its work in June 1930 and submitted recommendations for a new federal constitution for India with autonomy to the provinces under the control of the Governors. In November 1930, the King Emperor inaugurated the First Round Table Conference in London which began to consider a future constitution for India. Prime Minister Ramsay MacDonald presided, with 57 representatives from British India, 16 from Indian States, and 16 from the British Parties attending the Conference. But without the participation of the National Congress, the decisions of the

Conference became meaningless. Consequently, attempts were made to come to an agreement with Gandhi and bring him to London. Finally Gandhi attended the Second Round Table Conference in September 1931. But differences on fundamental issues were wide. While to Gandhi the prime objective was to frame a constitution, to the British the first consideration was the communal problem. Gandhi returned to India in December 1931 and resumed the Civil Disobedience movement. The Government retaliated with strong repressive measures. Winston Churchill and his Conservative colleagues appreciated such measures as the most convincing show of firmness since the Mutiny.

To make matters worse, in August 1932 Ramsay MacDonald announced his infamous Communal Award. While providing that the Muhammedan, European and Sikh voters would elect candidates by voting in separate communal electorates, the Award aimed to separate the Depressed Classes from the rest of the Hindus by declaring that 'a number of special seats...will be filled by election from special constituencies in which only members of the "Depressed Classes" electorally qualified will be entitled to vote.' To counteract such a move Gandhi commenced a fast unto death, unless a common electorate was restored. The fast was broken with the signing of the Poona Pact (25 September) which retained in principle a common electorate for all Hindus, while keeping for the Depressed Classes a sufficient number of reserved seats.

Soon after, in November 1932, the Third Round Table Conference was held in London, without, of course, the participation of the Congress. The resulting decisions were issued in a White Paper in March 1933. A Joint Committee of both Houses of the British Parliament considered the proposals contained therein. On the basis of the White Paper, a Bill was prepared and introduced in Parliament in December 1934 and was finally passed as the Government of India Act on 2nd August 1935. In the meantime, the Civil Disobedience movement had run its course.

The Government of India Act, 1935

The Government of India Act of 1935 was the last of the

constitutional measures prepared by the British Parliament for India. Though it proclaimed again the supreme authority of the Crown over India, yet it relaxed its autocratic control in certain spheres in favour of more popular government. The unpopular India Council in London was abolished, but the Secretary of State remained in overall control though with a new body of advisers in place of the old council. In theory, the Secretary of State was required to relax his hold on local matters in view of the provincial autonomy, but in reality he could continue to exercise it, if he so desired. Till the end of the British rule he was destined to enjoy the supremacy of the so-called White Mughal, as in former days, though circumstances forced him now to appear less powerful than before. Such contradictions were a characteristic feature of the Constitution of 1935.

The most conspicuous feature of the Constitution was the concept of an All-India Federation. It was to contain the Governors' Provinces, the Chief Commissioners' Provinces, and those of the Native States which would join it. With the separation of Burma from India and the creation of Orissa and Sind as two new provinces, the number of Governor's Provinces became eleven. They were Assam, Bengal, Bihar, Bombay, the Central Provinces, Madras, the North-west Frontier Province, Orissa, Punjab, Sind, and the United Provinces. The six Chief Commissioners' Provinces were Ajmere-Marwara, the Andaman and Nicobar Islands, British Baluchistan, Coorg, Delhi, and Panth-Piploda. For the above named provinces it was compulsory to join the proposed federation. But for the third group—the Indian States—it was voluntary. It was not unnatural that the autocratic princes would be reluctant to federate with the democratically conscious Indian provinces. They, therefore, did not join and the hoped-for All-India Federation was never formed. A good-portion of the Constitution thus remained self-contradicting. The only redeeming feature of such a paradoxical situation was that even though the federation could not be formed, some federal features were nevertheless in evidence. These features were manifested in a written constitution, in the division of powers into federal, provincial and concurrent lists, and in the supremacy of a Federal Court, which was established under the Act. The federal part of the Constitution carried provisions for a federal executive and a federal legislature with a dyarchic form of government at the centre. The authors of the 1935 Act knew that dyarchy, as a system and as established in the provinces by the Act of 1919, had been a sad failure. Yet they wanted to experiment with the same idea at the centre by breaking the federal powers into reserved and transferred subjects and by creating two types of executives, namely, the Governor-General with his Councillors and the Governor-General with his Ministers. It is unnecessary to discuss these provisions of the Act as they never worked. At the centre, the old system continued.

The real significance of the Act of 1935 lay in the changes it brought about in the provincial sphere. As the provincial part of the Constitution became operative, the changes it introduced were worked out in the British Indian Provinces. The existing dyarchical system with the division of powers into reserved and transferred subjects was abolished. Instead, all subjects of the provincial administration were placed in the hands of the Ministers, who belonged to the elected legislature and were responsible to it. This transfer of provincial powers into the hands of elected Indian Ministers, and the element of responsibility attendant on such a transfer, brought to the provinces some element of distinct individuality. The system of government it inaugurated has come to be known in history as 'Provincial Autonomy.' The presence of a Governor with tremendous powers made each ministry not wholly effective. Yet, the system was an experiment in giving power to Indians. Moreover, till the Act of 1935, the provinces were controlled by the Centre in every respect as part of a unitary machine. But under the new system, each province became an entity by itself and derived its legal powers, like the Centre, from a common Constitution.

The chief executive authority of the province was vested in the governor. He could exercise powers 'in his discretion,' when he was not required to consult his Ministers. He exercised powers in his 'individual judgment' when Ministers were consulted but their advice was not binding. Finally, he exercised powers in his 'individual judgment' when Ministers were consulted but their advice was not binding. Finally, he exercised powers on the 'advice of the

Ministers'. These three categories of powers made the Governor absolute. His discretionary powers were wide and varied, including prohibition of discussion on a bill and assumption of all powers if and when the constitutional machinery broke down. Acting in his individual judgment the Governor discharged such special responsibilities, as safeguarding the interests of the minorities, of civil servants, of British subjects, and the princes, etc.

While giving such executive powers to the Governor, and also such legislative powers, as summoning or proroguing the legislature or dissolving the Assembly or passing the Governor's Act and issuing Ordinances, etc., the Act of 1935 created a Council of Ministers to aid and advise the Governor. The Ministers were members of the Legislature. The Governor appointed them and they held office during his pleasure. But as the Ministers belonged to the elected Legislature and were responsible to it, the Legislature could remove them by passing a vote of no-confidence. In appointing the Ministers, the Governor consulted the leader of the party which commanded a majority in the Legislature. The Ministers were required to develop the principle of collective responsibility in the exercise of their office. The real merit of provincial autonomy lay in the powers vested in the elected Ministers. But the Act of 1935 contained in that field the usual self-contradiction. The Governor was vested with so much authority that the powers of the responsible Ministers appeared unreal. The value of autonomy and the system for responsibility depended on the real scope to be given to the Ministers in actual administration, without interference by the Governor.

The Act of 1935 enlarged the legislatures in the provinces. Assam, Bengal, Bihar, Bombay, Madras and the United Provinces were given two Houses, each namely, the Legislative Council and the Legislative Assembly. The rest of the provinces had only one House, namely, the Legislative Assembly. The size of the Legislative Assemblies varied from province to province, such as, the United Provinces with 288 members, Bengal 250, Madras 215, Bombay 175, Punjab 175, Bihar 152, Central Provinces 112, Orissa 60, Sind 60, and North-west Frontier Province 50. There were to be no official members in the Assemblies. All members were required to be directly elected. The Assembly was to be elected for five years, though it could be dissolved by the Governor before the completion of its term.

The right to vote mainly rested on property qualifications. For the Legislative Assembly the level of property was kept low. Consequently the number of voters increased considerably. Educational qualifications were also introduced. While such measures were an advance towards democracy, the Constitution extended communal representation to the extreme limit. The value of elected legislatures, direct elections, popular ministries, majority rule, and responsible government were considerably reduced by undemocratic communal and class elections. This was yet another self-contradiction in the Act of 1935.

The Act was received without enthusiasm. Prolonged consideration followed whether to accept it or not. Finally it was agreed to accept it.

From 1935 to the Independence of India

Provincial autonomy, as embodied in the Act of 1935, was finally brought into operation on 1st April 1937. The Congress fought the elections, not so much to accept and work out the Constitution as to demonstrate through elections its effective hold over the people. After an overwhelming success at the polls the next problem for the Congress was whether to accept or not to accept office. Gandhi wanted a commitment from the Governor-General that the Governors would not exercise their overriding powers, and should act on the advice of the Ministers. A vague assurance was ultimately given to that effect and the Congress agreed to take up office. In eight out of eleven provinces, Congress Ministries were formed.

But the nature of British absolutism, as well as the meaninglessness of the power given to Indians, was exposed all too soon. On 1st September 1939, the Nazi army invaded Poland and, on 3rd September, England declared war on Germany. The Second World War had begun. The Viceroy, Lord Linlithgow, without consulting the Ministries of the so-called autonomous provinces or any political party or person, committed India to enter the war against Germany. This was too much for the Congress to tolerate and, therefore, in October, the Congress governments resigned.

Events moved in rapid succession. Inside the Congress, Subhas Chandra Bose advocated more radical policies against the British. In their worst moments in history, Mahatma Gandhi had always wanted to extend his sympathies and moral support to the British people. But the country desired to know the exact mind of the British Government. In March 1940, the Muslim League met at Lahore and passed its resolution for the formation of Pakistan. The war-time Prime Minister of England, Winston Churchill, while mobilising the entire Indian administration to make the fullest possible use of India's resources in the war efforts, showed that he had no intention of paying any heed to Indian aspirations. The situation was getting beyond his control. By 1941, the war had entered its most critical phase. With the entry of Japan into the war, the political condition of the whole of South and South-east Asia became uncertain. The Japanese captured Singapore and advanced through Burma. War came to the very doors of India with the prospects of an imminent invasion. To Jawaharlal Nehru and others it was the need of the hour to fight the invaders, but they felt that Indians should fight not as slaves of the British but they felt that Indians should fight not as slaves of the British but as free citizens. The country became impatient. Gandhi could not wait indefinitely while Churchill maintained a sphinx-like attitude. Pressure on Churchill, too, for a compromise with India mounted from many quarters. At length he sent Sir Stafford Cripps to India in March 1942. But Cripps did not bring with him the promise of independence in the very near future. Instead, his proposals contained within them provisions which could divide India into hundreds of independent pieces if the Indian Princes and the Muslim League so desired it. The most fitting epitaph to the Cripps Mission naturally, therefore, came from Gandhi when he said to Sir Stafford: 'Why did you come if this is what you have to offer?' Cripps returned. Gandhi prepared for his last step. 'My firm opinion is that,' he said, 'the British should leave India now in an orderly manner and not run the risk that they did in Singapore and Malaya and Burma. The act would mean courage of a high order, confessions of human limitations, and right doing by India.'

From the failure of the Cripps Mission in April 1942, determination began to take shape in Gandhi's mind to ask the British to withdraw in two stern words—'Quit India'. On 14th July 1942, the Congress Working Committee adopted the 'Quit-India' resolution and on 8th August the All –India Congress Committee, meeting at Bombay, passed it. The resolution declared that 'the immediate ending of British Rule in India is an urgent necessity, both for the sake of India and for the success of the cause of the United Nations. A free India will assure this success by throwing all her great resources in the struggle for freedom and against the aggression of Nazism, Fascism and Imperialism.' The Congress authorized Gandhi to start a non-violent mass strugle on the widest possible scale. But within a few hours, early in the morning of the 9th, the Government carried Gandhi and others away to prison. It was an irony of history that Gandhi could not guide the course of his greatest and last battle against the British. But the movement continued. The discipline to which the country had been subjected for long had its result. The revolution was virtually without violence. On the other hand, the Government which made the movement leaderless, resorted to force to suppress it. According to Government estimates, more than a thousand persons were killed, more than three thousand wounded, and more than sixty thousand arrested.

The movement inside India subsided. In the meantime, Subhas Chandra Bose, who had escaped from India early in 1941, was organising the Indian National Army outside India. In 1944, his soldiers were seen advancing to the outskirts of Assam and in March of that year Kohima was conquered by them. On its mountain heights for the first time was hoisted the tricolour flag of India, as on independent soil.

The war ended in 1945. With the dropping of atom bombs on Hiroshima and Nagasaki, Japan surrendered. In one of those disastrous days of August 1945, Subhas Chandra Bose lost his life in an air crash, as reported by the Japanese. But stories of his patriotic deeds and the heroic achievements of the Indian National Army spread. The mood of the people in 1945 was highly optimistic. They awaited the final struggle. But a change was taking place in Britain which made further revolution in India unnecessary. At the end of the War the British electorate rejected Winston Churchill and voted the Labour Party to power with Clement Attlee as Prime Minister. For Attlee, it was neither the time to deny nor delay the question of Indian independence. In September 1945, the Governor-General, Lord Wavell, announced the intention of the Labour Government 'to convene as soon as possible a constitution-making body' and the Prime Minister appealed to the Indian leaders for a united effort to prepare a Constitution. But there was still a stumbling block on the path towards independence—the Muslim League, with its demand for Pakistan.

To make the Indians agree to a common solution of the problem, the British Government sent to India a Cabinet Mission with three Cabinet Ministers—Lord Pethick-Lawrence, the Secretary of State, Sir Stafford Cripps and A.V. Alexander. The Mission reached Delhi in March 1946. After serious discussions, it announced its proposals in May 1946. While ostensibly seeking to preserve the essential unity of India, the Cabinet Mission proposal retained in it the very essence of Pakistan and recommended the formation of a Constituent Assembly. As the situation developed in favour of a united India and steps were taken to summon a Constituent Assembly and form an Interim Government, the Muslim League became desperate and Muhammad Ali Jinnah observed 16th August 1946 as Direct Action Day. That day there began in Calcutta an unprecedented bloodbath, which in its turn became a signal for countrywide communal strife. Amid chaos, confusion and conflict, the Constituent Assembly met on 9th December 1946, to draft a Constitution for Free India. The League did not joint it. It became gradually apparent that with a hostile League to oppose every step towards independence, there could be no solution to India's problems unless the proposal for Pakistan was accepted. It was a grim realisation that the British would not, because they could not, withdraw without dividing India.

In February 1947, Attlee announced his final intention to transfer power into responsible Indian hands before June 1948.

Lord Louis Mountbatten was sent as Governor-General to finalise the transfer. He became convinced of the need for Partition and in turn tried to convince the Congress that for the sake of a strong and consolidated India it was desirable to sacrifice some parts of the country on either side. The plan which Mountbatten prepared was not to create the greater Pakistan as demanded by Jinnah, but to make a mutilated Pakistan by dividing the Punjab and Bengal. With most parts of India in the grip of communal frenzy, the Mountbatten Plan was accepted by the Congress and the League. With the inevitable having been agreed upon the British Parliament passed the Indian Independence Act in July 1947. It provided for the creation of two separate Dominions of India and Pakistan, and for the lapse of British Paramountcy over the Indian States, making them free to join either of the Dominions or to remain independent.

On 15th August 1947, India became independent. The Constituent Assembly continued with its great work of preparing the Constitution for independent India. It was adopted on 26th November 1949, and came into force from 26th January 1950.

The Constitution of Independent India

The Constitution of India declares India a Sovereign Democratic Republic. It rests on the democratic philosophy of justice, liberty, equality and fraternity. The following are the salient features of the Constitution.

The Constitution of India aims to make the people the supreme source of all power and authority. This purpose is served through universal adult suffrage and equal political opportunity to all men and women. The Constitution provides for a representative democracy, in which the people elect representatives who control the executive on their behalf and make laws in the interests of the nation. Thus, though the people do not themselves exercise direct power, the power of executive authority emanates from them.

Though the Indian Constitution is a written constitution, it is not a rigid constitution. In fact, it is more flexible than rigid, for many provisions of the Constitution can be altered by the Parliament by a simple majority. Even such important matters as the abolition of the Second Chamber of a State Legislature, and changing of the boundaries or areas or names of States, or their amalgamation or separation can be effected by the above simple process of a majority vote in Parliament. Many other provisions of the Constitution can be amended by a two-thirds majority in each House of the Parliament present and voting. Of course, members present and voting will not mean that only a few can enact an amendment. There must be a majority of the total membership of each House to support an amendment. By this process, such vital clauses in the Constitution as the Fundamental Rights can be amended. Only a few provisions of the Constitution have to be amended through a direct process, namely through ratification by the Legislatures of the States. But that again is not too difficult because ratification by half of the States only is enough to bring amendment. The Constitution has given enough scope to Parliament to meet the constitutional needs through parliamentary legislation. Thus, in essence, the Indian Constitution aims to keep pace with progress in accordance with the needs of the time. It is not a conservative constitution.

The Constitution declares India as a Union of States. The subcontinental dimensions of the land, with its various diversities, demanded of the Constitution a federal structure with autonomy for the component units. While accepting that obvious necessity, the Constitution nevertheless retained a strong unitary bias. This assimilation of federal and unitary Principles makes the Constitution unique. In normal circumstances, the federal system works, but whenever circumstances so demand, the Constitution can be used to convert India into a unitary state. There is greater emphasis on unity, much less on administrative separation.

The Constitution gives India a parliamentary form of government. In this respect it has derived considerable inspiration from the unwritten British Constitution. Many constitutional features implied in the British system are also inherent in the Indian system. Even though there is an elected President as the head of the nation, yet the Constitution binds him to act on the advice of the Ministers. It is thus the Ministry which really rules. But the Ministers are required to rule according to the parliamentary principle of ministerial responsibility. The essence of the parliamentary system is a responsible government. The Ministers forming the executive are responsible to the Legislature for everything they do. And, in turn, the Legislature is elected by the people to whom it gives an account of itself periodically.

A responsible executive is bound to be a flexible executive, not rigid. Ministers are required to account for their responsibility not at infrequent intervals, but almost on a day-to-day basis. In that process, the moment they lose the confidence of the House, they fall. Thus, though elected for a term, the completion of the term depends on the pleasure of the House.

The Constitution of India has created an independent judiciary. A written constitution needs its own custodian. Democracy needs a watch-dog to safeguard the democratic rights of citizens. A federal structure needs an impartial non-political body to look into the conflicts between the centre and the units or between unit and unit. Such necessities call for the supremacy of the judiciary. This is a prominent feature of the American Constitution. The makers of the Indian Constitution desired to give India the same benefits, as far as possible. When rights are infringed either by a law sought to be enacted by the Legislature, or by a decision of the executive, the individual can seek redressin the courts. The Supreme Court, or the High Court, can declare a law or an order void. Such is the power of the judiciary, especially with regard to the Fundamental Rights granted by the Constitution to the people of India.

But absolute power for the judiciary to invalidate the laws of the Legislature, which represents the people and passes laws for the benefit of the people, was considered somewhat unnatural. The Americans have adjusted themselves to the supremacy of the judiciary. The British feel happy under the supremacy of the Parliament. The Indian Constitution strikes a balance between the virtues of both the systems. Thus, while giving the judiciary its independence, rights were also given to Parliament to amend the Constitution in the light of the greater interest of the community. The judiciary is supreme in protecting the provisions of the Constitution while they are in force, but the provisions themselves can be changed by the Parliament if and when necessary. Similarly, the judiciary will protect the Fundamental Rights of the individuals, but such Fundamental

Rights as the right to property and liberty are subjected to the authority of Parliament so that the interests of an individual are not protected at the cost of the interests of the community. Thus the Constitution of India aims at balance and harmony in the respective interests of the individual citizen and the nation.

Regarding the main provisions of the Constitution, Part I deals with the Union and its territory, and part II with citizenship. Part III contains provisions regarding Fundamental Rights. The first among such Rights is the Right to Equality, which includes equality before law and equal protection under the laws, and equality of opportunities, etc., irrespective of religion, race, caste, sex or place of birth. The next is the Right to Freedom which includes freedom of speech and expression; freedom to assemble peaceably; to form associations; to move freely; to reside and settle in any part of India; to acquire, hold and dispose of property; and to carry on any profession, occupation, trade or business. Other rights are the Right against Exploitation, the Right to Freedom of Religion, Cultural and Educational Rights, the Right to Property and, finally, the Right to Constitutional Remedies. Part IV of the Constitution deals with Directive Principles of State Policy.

Part V of the Constitution deals with the Union Executive, the Union Parliament and the Union Judiciary. The chief executive power of the Union as well as the supreme command of the Defence Forces are vested in the President. But in discharge of his duties, he is required to work in accordance with the Constitution. The President is elected by the elected members of both Houses of Parliament and the elected members of the Legislative Assemblies of the States. It is, thus, an indirect election. Direct election of the President by the entire nation was considered unnecessary in the light of his constitutional position in a parliamentary system where the Prime Minister and his Cabinet possess the real power, the President being a nominal head. The President holds office for a term of five years. The Constitution provides that he may be removed from office by impeachment for violation of the Constitution. A resolution for impeachment can be moved by any one House of the Parliament and passed by that House by a majority of two-thirds of the total membership of the House. Thereafter, the other House shall investigate the charge and if, after investigation, it passes a resolution upholding the charge by a two-thirds majority of its total membership, the President shall be removed from his office.

The Constitution provides for the office of a Vice-President of India. He is the *ex-officio* Chairman of the Council of States. In the event of the death, resignation or removal of the President, the Vice-President acts as President until a new President is elected and enters office. The Vice-President is elected by the members of both Houses of Parliament assembled at a joint meeting. Both the President and the Vice-President should have reached the age of 35 to be eligible for election. The Vice-President holds office for a term of five years. He may be removed from office by a majority resolution of the Council of States, agreed to by the House of the People.

The Constitution provides for a Council of Ministers, with the Prime Minister at its head, to aid and advise the President in the exercise of his functions. The Prime Minister is appointed by the President, and the other Ministers are appointed by the President on the advice of the Prime Minister. Though the Constitution says that the Ministers shall hold office during the pleasure of the President, yet the very same article (Article 75) says subsequently that the Council of Ministers shall be collectively responsible to the House of the People. It is apparent that the pleasure of the President really means the pleasure of the Lower House.

Though all executive action is expressed in the name of the President, yet it is the Council of Ministers which holds the actual strings of administration. The Constitution requires of the Prime Minister to communicate to the President all decisions of the Council of Ministers relating to the administration of the affairs of the Union and proposals for legislation.

The Constitution does not elaborate the nature and scope of the powers of the Cabinet. But many things go by implication. The objectives of a parliamentary system and the rules through which a responsible government functions are settled and clear. Therefore, the few details in the Constitution are enough to signify the real nature of the Cabinet system.

The Constitution provides for a Parliament for the Union with two Houses—the Council of States and the House of the People. The Council of States consists of : (a) twelve members nominated by the President for achievements in literature, science, art and social service; and (*b*) not more than two hundred and thirty-eight representatives of the States, elected by the elected members of the Legislative Assemblies of the States. The House of the People is to consist of not more than five hundred members directly elected by the voters in the States. The States are divided into territorial constituencies for this purpose.

The Council of States is not subject to dissolution, but one-third of its members retire at the end of every second year. The House of the People, unless sooner dissolved, continues for five years. To be a member of the Council of States, a person shall be not less than thirty years of age, and for the House of the People not less than twenty-five years of age.

It is for the President to summon the Parliament, to prorogue both Houses or either House, and to dissolve the House of the People. He may address or sent messages to either House of Parliament. At the commencement of the first session of the House of the People, after each general election, and at the commencement of the first session of each year, the President addresses both Houses of Parliament assembled together. The Vice-President of India is the *ex-officio* Chairman of the Council of States, while the Council chooses on e of its own members as Deputy Chairman. The House of the People chooses two members of the House as Speaker and Deputy Speaker.

With the exception of Money Bills and Financial Bills, a Bill may originate in either House of Parliament. A Bill shall be deemed passed when both Houses agree to it either with or without amendments. In case of differences, the President may summon both Houses to meet in a joint sitting and if the Bill is passed by a majority of the total number of members present and voting, it shall be deemed to have been passed by both Houses. The Constitution does not permit a Money Bill to be introduced in the Council of

States. It is to be introduced and passed in the House of the People, and sent to the Upper House for its recommendations. It is to be returned by the Upper House within fourteen days with recommendations, if any. The Lower House may or may not accept such recommendations, yet the Bill is to be regarded as passed. Similarly, if the Upper House does not return the Money Bill within fourteen days, it shall be deemed to have been passed by both Houses at the end of that period. Whether a Bill is a Money Bill or not, the decision of the Speaker of the House of the People is final on the subject.

A Bill after being passed by the Parliament is presented to the President for his assent. The President may return the Bill, if it is not a Money Bill, with his recommendations for amendments. In that case, if the Bill is passed again by the Houses with or without amendment and presented to the President again for his assent, the President shall not withhold assent therefrom.

The powers and functions of the Indian Parliament have been established in the pattern of the parliamentary system and in the spirit of democratic rules. The Parliament controls the Executive, criticises its actions, approves or amends Executive decisions, and finally holds the power to bring about the fall of a government through a no-confidence motion. With such away over the Executive, Parliament is supreme in the sphere of legislation.

The Constitution provides for the Union Judiciary to be embodied in the Supreme Court of India, initially consisting of a Chief Justice and seven other judges, with power vested in Parliament to prescribe by law a larger number of judges. The President appoints the judges of the Supreme Court who hold office till the age of sixty five. But a judge can be removed from his office by the President after an address by each House of Parliament for such removal on the grounds of proved misbehaviour or incapacity. The Supreme Court possesses original jurisdiction in any dispute concerning legal rights (*a*) between the Government of India and one or more States; or (*b*) between the Government of India and any State or States on one side and one or more other States on the other; or (*c*) between two or more States. In respect of other powers, an appeal lies to the Supreme Court from any judgment of a High Court if the case involves a substantial question of law as to the interpretation of the Constitution. An appeal shall also lie to the Supreme Court from any judgment in a civil proceeding of a High Court if the value involved is above a specified sum. Similarly, an appeal shall live to the Supreme Court from any judgment in a criminal proceeding of a High Court if the case involved is a sentence of death. The Supreme Court has been given many other wide powers and Parliament has been authorised to confer by law further jurisdiction and powers on the Court as necessary. Among the Fundamental rights granted by the Constitution to the Citizens of India, there is the Right to Constitutional Remedies. This includes the right to move the Supreme Court by appropriate proceedings for the enforcement of the rights conferred by the Constitution. The Supreme Court has the power to issue directions or orders or writs, including writs in the nature of *habeas corpus, mandamus*, prohibition, *quo warranto* and *certiorari*, whichever may be appropriate for the enforcement of any of the rights conferred as Fundamental Rights. The Parliament may also by law confer on the Supreme Court similar powers for any purpose other than those mentioned above. To conclude, the law declared by the Supreme Court is binding on all courts of India. The President may obtain its opinion on any question of law or fact. And all authorities, civil and judicial, in the territory of India shall have to act in aid of the Supreme Court.

Part VI of the Constitution deals with the States. The executive power of the State is vested in the Governor. He is appointed by the President and holds office during the pleasure of the President. His term of office is for five years. Nominated by the Centre, the Governor is under the control of the Union authorities. Since the Constitution provides for a responsible system of government at the State level, a nominated Governor is bound to be a more or less nominal head of the State Executive in normal times. It is only when the constitutional machinery of the State breaks down that the Governor is required to shoulder the responsibility of administration on behalf of the Union Government.

In each State there is a Council of Ministers with a Chief Minister at its had to aid and advise the Governor in the exercise of his functions. The Chief Minister is appointed by the Governor, and other Ministers are appointed by the Governor on the advice of the Chief Minister. The Ministers hold office during the pleasure of the Governor. A subsequent clause, however, lays down that the Council of Ministers is collectively responsible to the Legislative assembly of the State. That explains the real position. The Ministers, as long as they command the confidence of the Legislature, work as the real executive of the State in accordance with the Constitution.

In the States of Bihar, Bombay, Madras (now Tamil Nadu), Punjab, Uttar Pradesh and West Bengal, the Constitution provided for two Houses of Legislature—namely, the Legislative Council and the Legislative Assembly. In other States, there was provision only for one House—the Legislative Assembly. The Upper House in a State Legislature is taken so lightly that Parliament can abolish it or create it if the Legislative Assembly of the State concerned passes a resolution to that effect. Thus the real legislative power in the State lies with the Legislative Assembly which is directly elected by the voters of the State. The State is divided into territorial constituencies on the basis of population on a scale of not more than one member for every seventy-five thousand of the population. According to the Constitution, the total number of members in the Legislative Assembly of a State shall in no case be more than five hundred or less than sixty. The Legislative Assembly, unless sooner dissolved, continues for five years. For a seat in the Assembly, a candidate should not be less than twenty-five years of age.

Like the President at the Centre, the Governor in the State summons, prorogues and dissolves the Assembly; addresses the House and sends messages, etc. Every Assembly chooses its Speaker and Deputy Speaker. In the spirit of parliamentary democracy, the Legislative Assembly controls the Ministers and legislates for the State within the scope afforded it by the Constitution.

The Constitution provides for a High Court for each State. Every High Court consists of the Chief Justice and such other judges as the President from time to time deems it necessary to appoint. The High Court has the power to issue to any person or authority, including the Government, directions, orders or writs, including writs in the nature of *habeas corpus, mandamus*, prohibition, *quo warranto* and *certiorari*, or any of them, for the enforcement of any of the rights conferred by Part III of the Constitution (Fundamental Rights), and for any other purpose. Every High Court shall have superintendence over all courts and tribunals throughout the territory in relation to which it exercises jurisdiction.

Part XVIII of the Constitution deals with the Emergency Provisions. Article 352 says that if the President is satisfied that a grave emergency exists whereby the security of India or of any part of the territory thereof is threatened, whether by war or external aggression or internal disturbance, he may, by Proclamation, make a declaration to that effect. He may revoke it subsequently. Such a proclamation shall be laid before Parliament. It shall cease to operate after two months unless Parliament. It shall cease to operate after two months unless Parliament approves it meanwhile. During the emergency, the executive power of the Union is extended to give directions to any State, and the power of Parliament is extended to make laws on subjects beyond the Union List. The Constitution prescribes it as a duty of the Union to protect every State against external aggression and internal disturbances. Article 356 says that if the President, on receipt of a report from the Governor or otherwise, is satisfied that a situation has arisen in which the government of the State cannot be carried on in accordance with the provisions of the Constitution, he may, by Proclamation, assume to himself the functions of the State Government and declare that the powers of the State Legislature shall be exercisable by or under the authority of Parliament. The President may also suspend any provisions of the Constitution relating to the State, except the provisions relating to High Courts. The most significant emergency measure in relation to the citizens is the restriction on Fundamental Rights. When a Proclamation of Emergency is in operation, the President may declare that the right to move any Court for the enforcement of Fundamental Rights shall remain suspended. Such an order may extend to the whole or any part of India. Finally, there is a third type of emergency. Article 360 says that if the President is satisfied that a situation has arisen whereby the financial stability or credit of India or any part of India is threatened, he may be a Proclamation make a declaration to that effect. During such an emergency the executive authority of the Union shall be extended to give directions to any State to observe necessary canons of financial propriety and other given directions.

Democracy in India

It began as the largest democracy on earth in consideration of the size of the demos. The democratic freedom which the people were given to enjoy had more potential than the freedom prescribed in many established democracies. The people quickly got accustomed to a democratic way of life and showed appreciation of the democratic apparatus. Universal adult suffrage, representative governments, decentralisation of power, respect for public opinion, and popular response to national needs became the important features of Indian democracy. During the decade after independence, democracy established deep roots, both as an ideology and as a system of government, and its success became assured on the Indian soil. But its real success depended on the constitutional machinery which democracy provided. The machinery was a Parliamentary system in a quasi-federal set up, with a Parliament for the Union and separate Legislatures for the States. The system presupposed majority rule, which implied the existence of more than one party indeed, but not the existence of numerous political groups. The growth of the multiple party system in India has affected the functional side of democracy adversely. The flexible Executives in the States gradually began to suffer instability when it became difficult for any single party to gain or retain a majority, and when coalition governments began to emerge as an inevitable outcome. The latter did not function as satisfactorily as was hoped because of various factors, including the sharp ideological differences among the partners in such coalitions. Defection has become yet another evil to add uncertainty to the duration of any government. The centre managed the States when the State coalition governments collapsed. But there was often political discontent among the people whenever the Centre imposed its sway over a State. In the case of the Centre itself, the decline of the Congress Party after the Nehru era of absolute majority, and the rise of many parties in Parliament, brought the Cabinet system close to instability for a time. The break up of the historic Congress Party in 1969added further to the decline of executive stability. Thus with the foundation of the Cabinet System of Government appearing somewhat shaky, voices were heard in favour of a fixed type of executive. But such voices have been stilled, perhaps, for a time, by the decisive result of the General Election of 1971. The future of Indian democracy depends on more vital issues than politico-constitutional problems. It is economic stability which democracy is expected to establish.

The political culture has now become an important part of a study of political system of a country in view of this realisation that "every political system is embedded in a particular pattern of orientation to political action. The political culture of a people refers to their beliefs, convictions, view and commitments in relation to political values and institutions. according to sidney verba, it "consists of the system of empirical beliefs, expressive symbols of values which define the situation in which political action takes place.

REFERENCES

1. G.A. Almond: "Comparative Political System" in Journal of Politics, Vol. 18, 1956 reprinted in Eulau and others: Political Behaviour, pp. 34-42.
2. Lucian w. Pye. "Introduction: Political Culture and Political Development", *Ibid.*, p. 7.
3. R.B. Jain: *Contemporary Issuesin Indian Administration*, p. 210.
4. Sukhomoy Chakravarty: "Policy Making in Mixed economy—the Indian Case" in P.R. Brahmanand and V.R. Panchmukhi (ed.): *The Development Process of the Indian Economy*, p. 733.

Glossary

Adjournment Motion It means a motion which seeks to suspend the work of the house so that some matters of urgent public importance can be discussed.

Amendment The term amendment means change or modification. Usually this term is used in connection with one or more changes made in the Constitution of a country.

Bureaucracy The literal meaning of this term is 'rule by the officer' or 'rule by officials'. Bureaucracy refers to the organisations. Officials and set procedures associated with any large administrative set up. It also refers to routine patterns, large volume of work and impartiality in big governmental offices.

Budget It is statement of estimated revenue and expenditure for the coming financial year. I includes the sources of income of the government and programmes and items on which the expenditure is to be incurred.

Coalition Government A government in which different political parties join together and form a government.

Coastal Plain A stretch of lowland adjoining the coast.

Cold War The period of rivalry between the USA-dominated west and the USSR-dominated East that began after the Second World War to the collapse of the USSR in 1991.

Democracy It is a form of government and a way of life. A democratic government is chosen by the people and can be changed by them.

Discretionary Powers The powers exercised by the Governor on the basis of his/her own judgement and without consulting the Council of Ministers.

Emergency It is an abnormal situation which calls for immediate action. A state of Emergency can be declared in the country by the Central Government, if country's national borders are attacked or there is internal disorder or if there is a financial crisis. Some Fundamental Rights of citizens are generally suspended during emergency.

Equality Equality means equal treatment to all citizens irrespective of caste, creed, colour, religion and sex.

Exploitation Using the labour and services of others for one's selfish purposes.

Globalisation Is the emergence of a complex web of inter-conjugateness that means that our lives are increasingly shaped by events that occur, and decisions that are made, at a great distance from us. It highlights the deepening as well as the broadening of the political process, in the sense that local, national and global events constantly interact.

Judiciary An organ of the Government which decides disputes and adjudicates on the meaning of the law.

Justice A legally justifiable apportionment of rewards on punishments, each person being given what he/she is 'due.'

No-confidence Motion It is a motion which is moved in the Lok Sabha or the Legislative Assembly to disapprove the policies and actions of the ruling party. If such a motion is passed by a majority of vote, it amounts to the lack of confidence in the ministry by the Legislature. As a result of this, the ministry has to resign.

Ordinance An order issued by the President or by the governor, generally when the Legislature is not in session. Such an order carries the effect of a law.

Panchayati Raj It is a three-tier system consisting of gram Panchayat at the village level, Panchayat Samiti at the block level and Zila Parishad at the district level.

Republic It is a country in which the Head of the State is an elected person. For example, India has an elected President. The United Kingdom is not a Republic because its Head of State is a Queen who is not elected.

Residuary Powers Our Constitution divides powers between the Central Government and the Constituent units. The Central Government and the Constituent Units can make laws only on those matters which are allotted to them by the Constitution. Matters which are not included in the division of powers, are known as residuary powers. In India, they are with the Central Government.

Secular State A state which does not favour any particular religion and treats all religion alike. India is a Secular State.

Socialist State A state in which the means of production such as land, mineral resources, mills and factories, and the means of distribution are in the hands of the Government.

Sovereign a state/community is sovereign when it is independent of legal/state control by another state/community and is legally free to determine the nature of its relations with all other states/communities.

Unicameral Legislature It means a legislature with only one house elected by the voters for specific terms.

Bibliography

Almond, G.A., "Comparative Political System" in Journal of Politics, Vol. 18, 1956 reprinted in Eulau and others: Political Behaviour.

Amal Ray and J. Kumpatla, "Zilla Parishad Presidents in Karnataka. Their Social Background and Implications for Development," *Economic and Political Weekly*, 17-24, October, 1987.

Anandaswarup Gupta and Venugopal Rao, "Administration of Law and Order: A Trend Report," I.C.S.S.R., *A Survey of Research in Public Administration*, Vol. II (Bombay: Allied, 1975).

Blachly, Fredrick F. & Oatman, Miriam E., Their joint contribution in the *Encyclopaedia of the Social Sciences*, Vol. III. (New York, Macmillan, 1954).

B.K. Patnaik, "Specialist and Generalist: The Red Tape Binds them All," *The Statesman*, 3 December 1987

Budhadev Ghosh, "Bhartiya Sanbidhana Sthaniya Sarkarer Bhumika" in *Panchayati Raj* (in Bengali) (Calcutta : Dept. of Panchayats, Government of West Bengal).

Dahl, Robert A., "The Science of Public Administration," in *Public Administration Review*, Vol. VII, 1947, No. 1.

Dimock, Marshall, E., Dimock, Gladys O., & Koeing, Louis W., *Public Administration*, New York, Rinehart & Co., Inc., 1959.

Dimock, Marshall E., *A Philosophy of Administration*, New York,

Harper & Bros., 1958, pp. vii-viii.

Dubhashi, P.R., "Man on the Spot: Failure of District Administration," *The Statesman*, 15 April 1963.

Eswar Anand was told so by several Collectors during his work on a research project on district administration in Orissa. See V. Eswar Anand, "Importance of Being the Collector," The Statesman (Calcutta), 8 November 1984.

Gladden, E.N., *An Introduction to Public Administration*, London, Staples Press, Second Edition.

Gorwala, A.D.: *Report on Public Administration*, Delhi, Planning Commission, 1951.

Government of Kerala, *Report of the Administrative Reorganisation and Economy Committee* (Trivandrum, 1967).

Gulick, Luther, *Science Values and Public Administration*, Luther Gulick & L. Urwick (Eds.), Papers on the Science of Public Administration, New York, Institute of Public Administration 1937.

His address at the inaugural meeting of the Indian Institute of Public Administration, New Delhi, in March 1954, Vide *The Indian Journal of Public Administration*, Vol. I.

Jackson, R.M., *Machinery of Justice in England* (Cambridge, Cambridge University Press, 1953).

K.S. Krishnaswami, "Karnataka's New State Backwards" *Economic and Political Weekly*, 1 May, 1993.

L.C. Jain, "Panchayat Act Clerical in Outlook" *Deccan Harald*, 2 August, 1993.

L.M. Singhvi Committee Report (1986) in *Kurukshetra*, February, 1986

Lucian W. Pye. "Introduction: Political Culture and Political Development", *Ibid.*

Marx, Fritz Morstein (Ed.), *Elements of Public Administration*, New Delhi, Prentice-Hall of India, 1964.

Minutes of Evidence, taken before the Committee on Administrative Tribunals and enquiries (London, H.M.N.S.O., 1956)

Nigro, Felix A., *Public Administration—Readings and Documents*, New York, Rinehart & Co., Inc..

Nirmal Mukarji, "Panchayat Governments" *Seminar*, August 1989.

N. Mukarji and D. Bandyopadhaya, "*New Horizons in West Bengal Panchayats—A Report for the Government of West Bengal* (Mimeo)

Pfiffner, John, M., & Presthus, R. Vance, *Public Administration*, New York, Ronald Press.

Pfiffner, John M., & Presthus, R. Vance, *Public Administration*. The Ronald Press Company New York, Third Edition.

Paul H., *Big Democracy*, New York, Alfred A. Knopf. 1945, p

Paul H. Appleby, *Public Administration in India: Report of a Survey* (New Delhi: Publication Division, Government of India

Quoted in L. Urwick's Foreword to Fayol's *General and Industrial Management*, London, Pitman, 1949.

Rajni Kothari, *Politics in India* (New Delhi: Orient Longman, 1970).

Report of the Team for the Study of Community Projects and National Extension Service, Vol. 1 (New Delhi: Committee on Plan Projects, 1957).

Report of the Committee on Reorganisation of the District Administration, Government of Punjab, 1954.

Report of the Indian Statutory Commission, vol. 1—Survey, London, H.M.S.O., 1930.

Report of the Royal Commission upon Decentralisation in India, Cmd. 4360, London, H.M.S.O., 1909.

Report of Committee on Panchayati Raj Institutions, New Delhi, Ministry of Agriculture and Irrigation, Government of India, 1978

Robson, W.A., *Justice and Administrative Law* (London, Stevens & Sons, 1951)

Simon, Smithburg & Thompson, *Public Administration*, New York, Alfred, A. Knopf, 1950.

Sukhomoy Chakravarty: "Policy Making in Mixed economy---the Indian Case" in P.R. Brahmanand and V.R. Panchmukhi (ed.): *The Development Process of the Indian Economy*

Tusharkanti Das (served as Collector and District Magistrate in West Bengal), "The District Ruler," *The Statesman*, 15 October 1983.

Urwick, L., "Executive Decentralisation with Functional Coordination," in *Public Administration*, 1935.

Waldo, Dwight, "Philosophy, Science and Art of Administration" in (Ed.), *Ideas and Issues in Public Administration*, New York, McGraw-Hill, 1953, pp. 76-77.

Warner, Richard A., *The Principles of Public Administration*, London, Isaac Pitman & Sons, 947, p. 133.

Willoughby, W.F., *Principles of Public Administration*, Washington, D.C., Brookings Institute, 1927.

Willoughby, W.F., *Principles of Public Administration*, Indian Edition, Allahabad, Central, Book Depot.